THE HIDDEN GOD

Indiana Series in the Philosophy of Religion

Merold Westphal, *editor*

THE HIDDEN GOD

LUTHER, PHILOSOPHY, AND POLITICAL THEOLOGY

MARIUS TIMMANN MJAALAND

Indiana University Press
Bloomington and Indianapolis

This book is a publication of

Indiana University Press
Office of Scholarly Publishing
Herman B Wells Library 350
1320 East 10th Street
Bloomington, Indiana 47405 USA

iupress.indiana.edu

♾ The paper used in this publication meets the minimum requirements of the American National Standard for Information Sciences—Permanence of Paper for Printed Library Materials, ANSI Z39.48–1992.

Manufactured in the United States of America

Library of Congress Cataloging-in-Publication Data

Mjaaland, Marius Timmann.
The hidden God : Luther, philosophy, and political theology / Marius Timmann Mjaaland.
pages cm. — (Indiana series in the philosophy of religion)
Includes bibliographical references and index.
ISBN 978-0-253-01816-8 (cloth : alk. paper) — ISBN 978-0-253-01820-5 (e-book) 1. Luther, Martin, 1483–1546. 2. Philosophy and religion. I. Title.
BR333.3.M55 2015
230′.41—dc23

2015035568

1 2 3 4 5 21 20 19 18 17 16

CONTENTS

PREFACE

Luther's distinction between the hidden and the revealed God is one of the most puzzling and controversial topics of his thought. For centuries it was mostly neglected within theology, whereas it played a crucial role in the development of modern philosophy. Pascal and Kant insisted on this distinction, whereas Hegel rejected it in favor of a total revelation of the Spirit. Even political imagination was affected, where it played a significant but secluded role, from apocalyptic visions to the hard currency of *oikonomia* and sovereignty. The modest ambition of the present volume is to examine the source of this development, namely, to trace an original difference between absolute hiddenness and the light of scripture, of reason, and of revelation in order to reconsider it as a topic of controversies in the twenty-first century.

Theologians in early modernity were reluctant to discuss the notion of the hidden God due to its threatening and monstrous gestalt in religious imagination. When Luther introduced the *distinction* between the hidden and the revealed God, however, the point was to avoid such speculations concerning the hidden God, and also to venture a *destruction* of Aristotelian metaphysics and thus raise a critical discussion on the rationality of philosophical and theological discourse—and the crucial *difference* between them. Hence, the history of perception has witnessed an ironic twist of fate: The theological discussions on the topic have ended with a rather confessional response, either pro or contra the hidden God, whereby the *status confessionis* in the early twenty-first century goes in favor of the latter, namely, an exclusion of the notion from theological discourse.

The history of modern philosophy, conversely, demonstrates a continued discussion on the distinction between hiddenness and revelation as a primary topos of thought, which concerns the ultimate conditions for philosophical discourse, linguistically, metaphysically, and epistemologically. From a somewhat different approach, namely, from the question of sovereignty, revolution, and political decisions in the most fateful historical states of exception, the *hidden* God has come to play a controversial role even for political philosophy and theology. Both trajectories will be submitted to further inquiry in a planned second volume on the hidden God in modernity, also including controversies in philosophy and political theology.

This volume goes back to the textual origins of this modern topos in the writings of Martin Luther. Already here we find that the traces of the hidden God proceed beyond the limits of theology, raising questions of metaphysics, of political philosophy, of phenomenology in a critical sense, questioning the entire tradition from medieval philosophy. This critical approach gradually becomes a virtue in philosophical reflection in modernity. Kant's transcendental critique of metaphysics is perhaps the most crucial example of modern philosophy, and he dedicates several chapters to the question of God's hiddenness in *The Critique of Pure Reason.* Pascal demonstrates the political interpretation of the hidden God in his *Pensées,* and Hegel is deeply concerned with this topos, insofar as he does a major effort at including theological patterns like the "death of God" within a philosophical system, admittedly emphasizing the *revelation* of divine truth rather than the opposite. The most crucial but also controversial example is Nietzsche, though, who proclaims the death of God to be a prophetic message of modernity and its *ends,* thereby adopting a topological approach to philosophy and its ultimate points of reference, and a genealogical approach to morality. My suspicion is that this "death of God" belongs to the genealogy of an ancient topos called *deus absconditus,* but that is a topic by far transgressing the limits of this preface. What Nietzsche has understood about the limitations of his own approach and his prophetic assertions is that knowledge and philosophy can never be good "in itself." Its apparent goodness is always deceptive, and the problem of drawing distinctions between truth and delusion remains a continuous task. This is an insight he shares with Martin Luther, who admits that he continuously distrusts his own reason and therefore has taken recourse to paradox as a way of seeking truth.

When scientists claim the discovery of a "god delusion," as Richard Dawkins does in a popular publication known by this audacious name, we may calmly expect that they have not even begun considering their own delusions. If someone made them aware of this disproportion, I would not be surprised if the response took the form of resentment and disturbance. In this respect the present volume will hopefully be disturbing, by making people aware of such disproportions in the commerce with illusions.

In some respects the notion of the hidden God seems to *produce* such images of the divine that generate questions and accusations. Rudolf Otto's definition of the Holy (numinous) in religion as *mysterium tremendum et fascinans*—a terrifying but fascinating mystery—is based on Luther's notion of the hidden God. We could think of endless fairy tales, myths, and horror films where the hidden God is presented in the most fantastic images. The conscientious theologian Gerhard Ebeling even warns us against the terror of the hidden God and gives us the friendly advice to flee "from God to God." Yet I am afraid I will have to disappoint every reader who had hoped for a juicy horror story. A core task of this book is to *ques-*

tion such myths and monstrosities of imagination, which tend to overrule more-rational inquiries on the conditions of thought. My concern is the opposite, namely, to analyze these notions carefully but critically in order to disillusion some illusions and make readers aware of disproportions. And if someone should claim, as Eberhard Jüngel does in a famous article, that this hidden God should be "no concern of ours," I will once more make the reader aware of this *difference:* Although a disturbing topos, it remains at the heart of the controversy.

In the writings of Martin Luther, this original difference is in one respect theological, but then again *pre*-theological, preceding every doctrine and *logos* of theology. It forces us to take into account the concealment of the divine, and the *conditions* for speaking or not speaking about God. The difference is at work whenever we offer critique or defense of religion, whenever we look for revelation, experience, or interpretation, whenever we discuss theism or atheism, the dead or the living God.

ACKNOWLEDGMENTS

If it takes ten months to write a book like this one, it takes ten years to think through it, and one may still wonder if all the key questions have been raised with the scrutiny they require. For such questioning, the discussions with colleagues, friends, and opponents are invaluable. Since this topic invites controversy, and has done so since time immemorial, let me begin with a word of thanks to my critics, enemies, and opponents: Your contribution to clarification and scrutiny has been most important, so keep up the good work!

For support and funding, I send warm thanks to the Research Council of Norway, to the Alexander von Humboldt Foundation, and to the five universities where I have worked and lived over the last ten years: The University of Oslo, the University of Tübingen, the University of Hamburg, the University of Rostock, and the University of Chicago. My deepest gratitude and respect go to colleagues and friends at these and other universities for reading drafts and papers, listening, discussing, and suggesting improvements, literature, and novel ideas. Far too many people have contributed that I would be able to mention them all, but let me at this place say particular thanks to Martin Wendte and Christoph Schwöbel in Tübingen; Philipp Stoellger, Martina Kumlehn, and Marco Gutjahr in Rostock; Tarald Rasmussen, Stine Holte, Trygve Wyller, and Sivert Angel in Oslo; Michael Moxter, Nina Heinsohn, Christoph Seibert, and Christian Polke in Hamburg; and my wise and friendly interlocutor David Tracy in Chicago. Thanks also for comments, discussions, and critique from Werner Jeanrond, Julie Clague, Merold Westphal, Ola Sigurdson, Sigridur Thorgeirsdottir, Asma Barlas, Sturla Stålsett, Bård Norheim, Jan-Olav Henriksen, and Atle Ottesen Søvik. For excellent linguistic and editorial assistance, my warm thanks go to Dee Mortensen and her colleagues at Indiana University Press and Jay Harward with colleagues at Newgen. I want to thank Taylor & Francis, Springer, and Maney Publishing and the editors for the permission to reprint parts of material published in journal articles. Further thanks go to my excellent students and Ph.D. students for good, surprising, and thought-provoking questions and papers—and vigorous debates.

A few people have contributed even more substantially to this work in various forms. The irreclaimable apocalypticist Joar Haga has not only read through the entire manuscript and given some significant corrections and suggestions, he has also supported the author in hard times, for instance with an excellent meal and a glass of old, clarified wine, when needed. My family has been extremely patient, day and night, on working days and holidays, year after year, and I guess Sara, Tim, Maria, and Jonas can hardly think of a life without papers and notes on the *deus absconditus* dwelling in some corner of the house. Finally, Angela, this book would not have been realized without your tireless support, your sharp and intelligent commentaries, our endless discussions by the fireside, and small signs of love in everyday life. These signs that make it worth the effort, make it worth all the work, since after all, in the final analysis, it all comes down to what is received, in passivity, without works and efforts, without . . .

THE HIDDEN GOD

Introduction

A philosophical approach to Martin Luther allows a less doctrinal access to some of his controversial but rather original ideas and methodological insights. The challenge is that such an approach has hardly been ventured before, at least not in the English-speaking literature: to analyze the seminal work of the *philosopher* Martin Luther. Many studies of Luther from a comparative philosophical perspective have been written over the years, for instance, his relation to Plato or Aristotle, Kant or Heidegger; but it is difficult to find contemporary efforts at reading Luther philosophically.[1] The point of such an approach is not to reject his explicit theological agenda and continuous theological significance, but to take one step back from these theological positions in order to disclose and discuss the critical insights that often remain hidden within his texts, although they are crucial for his argument as a whole, and thus eventually draw them into contemporary debates in phenomenology and political theology.

Is Luther, then, a philosopher at all? His many denunciations of philosophers and "sophists" among the Scholastics of his own time apparently speak against such a perspective. But this critical involvement with the philosophy of his time, based on profound and extensive knowledge and training in Augustinian, Thomistic, and nominalistic philosophy, makes him both a subtle critic of philosophy and a philosophically innovative thinker who paved the way for a radical critique of reason and the conditions for doing philosophy, which later became the hallmark of true—critical—philosophy. Admittedly, Luther considered this a theological rather than a philosophical task. The critique of reason has nevertheless remained a philosophical ideal, from Descartes and Leibniz up to contemporary Continental philosophy.

The *Heidelberg Disputation* (1518) is a programmatic text for Luther's opposition to the dominant strands of thought among his contemporaries. He coined at least one critical term, which later became a key term for philosophical inquiry—indeed, for a way of doing philosophy—namely, the notion of destruction. He presents an intriguing argument for the *destruction* of metaphysics, beginning with a destruction of Aristotelian anthropology in the "crucifixion" of old Adam. More precisely, he argues that *crucifying and destroying man* is necessary in order to acquire truth and unveil illusions: Since human beings naturally tend to be self-possessed, self-assertive, and potentially destructive to others as well as to themselves, they simply *need* this destruction of their illusions.[2] A redefinition of subjectivity is thereby introduced, based on the oppositions between speculation and destruction, active and passive, spirit and flesh, visible and invisible, powerful and suffering.[3] The hierarchy between the opposites is in each case overturned and destabilized by Luther's destruction, thus introducing an understanding of the subject that is based in *scripture* and not in *things* insofar as these are "essentially" defined by ontology. Implicitly, this is also a substantial critique of the hubris and the self-assertion of man, which Luther sees as the basic reason for the violent behavior of human beings in the world. Hence, the destruction, or re-formation, of the self is necessary in order to prevent the human potential for destruction and self-destruction as political subject. In our context, this is a key text for reconsidering his theory of the subject, its foundation and restructuring as *scriptural* subjectivity, and his understanding of God.

Finally, in order to avoid misunderstandings: A philosopher who insists on a strictly secular or atheistic understanding of his field will presumably define this book as merely theological. I have no problems with such an assessment, and there are indeed a number of theological issues at stake in the following discussions. This is not surprising when it comes to Luther, though. What distinguishes this book compared to more conventional studies of Luther are the frequent references to philosophical discourses by such as Kant, Descartes, Heidegger, Nietzsche, Derrida, Arendt, Schürmann, Marx, and Engels. Their philosophy is not merely discussed for the sake of comparison. On the contrary: They represent the basis for the philosophical approach adopted here, that is, for a different kind of analysis when we examine Luther's texts and a *repetition* of these texts in order to include them in a constructive argument. That is the case when, for example, Kant's transcendental analytic, Heidegger's notion of *destruction*, or Derrida's notion of *writing* are applied as conceptual framework and analytical tools for a critical engagement with Luther's thoughts—historically informed, but within a contemporary theoretical framework.

In a planned second volume, I will follow this set of problems (connected to "the hidden God" in the wide sense) via Pascal, Kant, Hegel, Feuerbach, and Nietzsche (comparing the topos "God is dead") up to the contemporary post-secular discussions on political theology and phenomenology. In the present volume, I focus on Luther's texts and those of some of his adversaries: first of all Desiderius Erasmus, but later also Thomas Müntzer and Ambrosius Catharinus Politus. Some of their debates have relevance for contemporary discussions, too, such as the problem of text interpretation, the destruction/recovery of metaphysics, and the emergence of a public sphere for political controversy. Yet I find that the most intriguing and challenging philosophical problems of Luther are found in his unresolved theological dilemmas, when we critically discuss the linguistic, epistemological, ethical, and metaphysical *preconditions* for his theology.

Hence, I believe that the philosophical discussions that follow are also of theological relevance, even for the formulation of Christian doctrine (a discipline in deep crisis). The focus and emphasis of my inquiries here are put somewhere else, namely, on philosophical questions detected within the texts and repeated as questions within a contemporary philosophical and political context. These tensions due to overlapping but also conflicting research interests will not be unfamiliar to someone acquainted with the essentially hybrid field called "philosophy of religion." The sympathetically minded reader may find new insight from these crossing perspectives for the study of philosophy, theology, political theory, or intellectual history, whereas the more critically minded reader may find reasons for further controversy.

PART I

The Topology of Texts and Destruction of Metaphysics

[I]t is difficult to begin at the beginning. And not try to go further back.

—Ludwig Wittgenstein

ONE

History, Hermeneutics, and Political Theology

Authors from the early sixteenth century have often been interpreted along confessional lines of division. In this book such differences play only a minor role, when any at all, and I have no ambitions of continuing or enhancing the old confessional discussions on Luther and Erasmus. Since Oberman, it has become more common to see both the Reformation (Lutheran, Calvinist, Radical) and Counter-Reformation as parts of a major historical and intellectual shift in the history of Europe, and thus to transcend the more narrow-minded apologetics in favor of one side or the other.[1] I even find it necessary to transcend the more or less strictly *theological* approach outlined by Oberman, in order to study the close relationship between theological ideas, philosophy, and political changes that occurred in this period, like James Tracy and Carter Lindberg do with their more general approach to the history of ideas.[2]

Historical Background

Five centuries after the texts were published, Martin Luther's writings still cause polarization and controversies. One reason is the confessional polemics that have been going on for centuries and the quasi-normative status of these texts among the Protestants. Another is their extremely sharp and polemical tone. They bear traces of an author who was witty, pointed, and sarcastic, although not exactly fair to his adversaries. His Bible translations contributed to the formation of a common German language, and he was the first author who was able to apply the printing medium to mobilize a wider public readership. His series of pamphlets was extremely popular and has been characterized as the first successful mass media propaganda in world history.[3] Even today his texts are astonishingly readable, mainly due to a large number of lucid examples, humor, polemics, and sarcasms, and a vivid and precise prose.

The unexpected success of the Reformation movement is not explainable by Luther alone, let alone by theological issues. A number of social issues and political tensions in Europe contributed to the schism of the church and the subsequent political destabilization of Europe. Because of general dissatisfaction with the popes in Rome and abuse of power within the ecclesiastic hierarchy, the discussions on church authority and dogmatic issues had already been going on for centuries. Moreover, a number of philosophical questions that came up during the Reformation have their roots in the long academic debates at the universities, from Anselm of Canterbury, Thomas Aquinas, and Bonaventure, via John Buridan, John Wycliffe, and Duns Scotus, up to the so-called modern thinkers (following the *via moderna*), William of Ockham and Gabriel Biel.[4] In a certain sense, all the significant problems Luther discusses are traceable back to other thinkers in late-medieval theology. Hence, some church historians see it as an anachronistic misconception to read Luther in the light of problems coming up in modernity.

They have a point, but there are also limitations to the historical approach, which often reflect modern reconstructions of late-medieval academic debates. In Germany, a sharp debate was provoked by Volker Leppin's biography on Luther (2006), which demonstrated how deep the controversy between systematic and historical approaches still runs.[5] Such inner-theological disputes, predominantly written in German, have contributed to the alienation of scholars from other disciplines, including philosophers, who rarely discuss Luther's contributions to the history of philosophy. Contemporary or more-systematic philosophical readings of his work are so rare that they are virtually nonexistent, at least in the English-speaking world. This shortcoming is all the more surprising if Luther played a key role in the political and philosophical development of modernity.

For myself, it has been necessary to take one step back from the ideological conflict between church historians and systematic theologians, which seems to have reached an intellectual dead end. The analytical and textual approach of contemporary Continental philosophy appears to be more promising for the development of new perspectives on the works of Martin Luther. A few recent publications in German indicate that there might be an intellectual shift coming up prior to the five hundredth anniversary of the Reformation.[6] Not that the historical studies have become superfluous; but the post-secular debate on the significance of religion for understanding contemporary society and its basic structures of thought has opened new interdisciplinary fields of discussion in metaphysics, politics, culture, values, and belief systems.

Among the pioneers of intellectual history, we find the by now classical contributions by scholars like Alexandre Koyré and Norman Cohn dealing with this fascinating period from a historical point of view, while focusing on the interplay between theological ideas, philosophy, and political movements.[7] Cohn gives an intriguing argument for the influence of apocalyptic ideas and movements from this period on the imagination of political movements in the twentieth century, including communism, fascism, and liberal capitalism. Lucien Goldmann belongs to the same strand of historical inquiry, although with a more explicit Marxist agenda, and his study on *The Hidden God* (*Le Dieu caché*) from 1955 represents a significant point of reference for the analyses presented here, not only because of its title, but also because of its novel approach to Pascal as a tragic thinker.[8] Although it is easy to criticize his programmatic and ideological Marxism (thinking "from below" and rephrasing all ideas in terms of social and political class structures) and his somewhat confusing methodological considerations, his original approach to the concept of God as politically and sociologically decisive remains relevant to our inquiry, in particular when it comes to understanding revolution and political theology.

Secularization and Post-Secular Political Theology

The historical process commonly referred to as "secularization" has been the topic of a number of studies since the turn of the millennium, arguing for a more differentiated understanding of secularization. Rather than being a process which simply determines various discourses of politics, philosophy, law, and religion, secularization has itself become an object of study, and many of the premises that were taken for granted have been jeopardized. A secular interpretation of political processes serves particular power interests, whereas others are disadvantaged. Claims of secularism as a "neutral" and rational sphere, as opposed to the prejudices and myths of religion, are therefore hardly defensible any longer.[9] When studied from different perspectives, secularization turns out to be a complex process involving religion, politics, law, philosophy, theology, literature, and sociology. Hence, the so-called secularization thesis dominating the social sciences since the beginning of the twentieth century, indicating that religion will be marginalized, privatized, and eventually disappear, has been jeopardized in favor of more-complex approaches.[10]

The so-called post-secular condition proclaimed by Jürgen Habermas in 2001 has been followed by a number of significant contributions by, for instance, Canadian philosopher Charles Taylor, Arab-American anthropologist Talal Asad, and German sociologist Hans Joas.[11] These three contributions reject the presumption that secularity represents some neutral common sphere, whereas religions represent superstitious or anti-modern survivals from a remote time. On the contrary: A scholar like Hans Joas underscores that a number of significant *modernizing* changes are driven by religious movements and depend on a sacred rationale. Moreover, historical analyses show that a period of secularization is often followed by a period of resacralization. Asad argues that these opposite processes may even be intertwined, and more-detailed comparative studies demonstrate that they do so within different religious contexts. He demonstrates that just as there are different religions, there are also different *secularities,* which often depend on the religious context of their origin.[12]

Paul W. Kahn raises significant methodological questions concerning the relationship between religion, law, and politics in *Political Theology: Four New Chapters on the Concept of Sovereignty,* while continuously referring back to Carl Schmitt's celebrated and controversial book from 1922.[13] His argument is not normative but descriptive. He argues that when concentrating exclusively on pre-modern political theologies, we miss the entire problem of political and cultural imagination, which dominates political decisions without any institutional foundations. Hence, this is not a question of state and church but of the politico-religious rationale for the question of sovereignty. Kahn returns to the question of sovereignty raised by Schmitt and concludes that it remains a religious issue even within Western, so-called secularized, societies when it comes to the question of sacrifice. Most of his examples refer to the United States, where political rhetoric and discourse have always been open to religious perspectives and sacred values. Yet even European democracies have the tendency to construct their own sacred sphere in order to justify their sacrifices, he argues, which demonstrates the ultimate values, the paradoxes, and the limits of the political decisions.

Other intellectual historians, such as Mark Lilla and John Gray, have chosen a different path for their studies of secularization, politics, and apocalypticism. They intend to develop a more subtle historical understanding of the relationship between religion and politics in the West.[14] Both contribute with interesting historical cross-references to the discussion and demonstrate the intimate relationship between politics and theology—which still is the rule rather than the exception from a global perspective. Both authors warn against a future collapse of the limits between the religious and the political spheres, with the possible consequence that religious ideas, including the apocalypse, once more will dominate our political imagination. This fear of religion seems to dominate their approach normatively, though, and apparently it hinders more-audacious and innovative theoretical discussions concerning a redefinition of the relationship between secularity and religion in the post-secular society.

Two publications by Giorgio Agamben add to the methodological complexity of the field: his analysis of Paul and political theology in *The Time That Remains* (2005) and his considerations on method from 2009, where he defines the secularization of the West as a generic *signature* changing the way we perceive the world in modernity—including society, history, and philosophy—rather than a new set of ideas that presupposes a rejection of the previous ones.[15] Agamben's approach is based on Foucault, in particular his genealogy of knowledge and power, but it also corresponds to Heidegger's understanding of modern philosophy as *repetition* of earlier topoi within a new context.[16] Heidegger's notion of repetition is closely connected to the problem of a *destruction* of metaphysics.

TWO

Philosophy

The Grammar of Destruction

The destruction of metaphysics is a favored topic in twentieth-century philosophy, in terms of a positivist critique, an overcoming, an *Abbau*, a rejection, or a deconstruction of traditional metaphysical notions and concepts. But where and when does this discussion of a general destruction of metaphysics start? I argue that the *Heidelberg Disputation* plays a key role here.[1] In this short disputation, Luther presents forty theses giving a principal justification of his position, twenty-eight of them theological and the other twelve philosophical. In the explanation to thesis 21, he argues that the cross is a good thing, since it *destructs* (*destruuntur; destructus*) the good works and thus crucifies old Adam.[2] A double work of destruction is thereby indicated: first, a self-centered and inflated (*infletur*) ego is demolished until it realizes that it is *nothing* (*nihil esse*), and second, the speculative metaphysics of scholastic theology is unveiled as a seductive illusion when confronted with the notion of God as crucified in Jesus Christ.

Heidegger and Luther on Hiddenness and Destruction

The double process of destruction, including the notion of human being (*Dasein*) on the one hand and traditional metaphysics on the other, is picked up four centuries later by Martin Heidegger, first in his lectures on phenomenological interpretation and then in a guest lecture on Luther and the concept of sin. The notion of destruction is again applied somewhat differently in *Sein und Zeit* (1927) and later works. Heidegger's reading of Luther had major influence on his general philosophical orientation, as recent research has shown.[3] In a lecture from 1922 on phenomenological interpretations, he writes:

> *Hermeneutics carries out its task only on the path of destruction,* and [. . .] the Graeco-Christian interpretation of life [. . .] determined the philosophical anthropology of Kant and that of German Idealism. Fichte, Schelling, and Hegel came out of *theology* and received from it the basic impulses of their speculative thought. This theology is rooted in the theology of the Reformation, which succeeded, only in very small

> measure, in providing a genuine explication of Luther's new fundamental religious insight and its immanent possibilities.[4]

The relationship between hermeneutics and Luther's insight is the *path of destruction,* which means a repetition of the immanent *possibilities* of Luther's thought in a different philosophical context, in particular by Kant and in German Idealism. The final claim, that the theology of the Reformation was unable to provide a genuine explication of Luther's insight, is also significant. Heidegger sees a *surplus* in Luther's texts that was not quite understood, perhaps not even considered significant by the subsequent theology, which soon returned to Aristotelian metaphysics.[5] The unacknowledged possibilities recurring in the period of the Enlightenment and German Idealism are not merely found in Kant's ethics or his religious reflections. It is a more general question of the structure and *place* of his thought: Is Kant's critique of metaphysics, and thus the basic structure and critical consequences of his transcendental turn, included in this path of destruction? Has Luther identified a *site* of reflection which is further explicated by Kant, Fichte, Schelling, and Hegel? However this relationship may be analyzed in detail, we see indications of a genealogy in this remark. Heidegger's comment could also be viewed more critically: If he is basically right in this regard, should Luther even be called a speculative philosopher in the sense of German Idealism? That would indeed be an irony of history, since Luther harshly criticizes the speculative theology and philosophy of his time, the so-called theologians of glory.

Heidegger's destruction of the history of metaphysics is a complex undertaking. In his early period up to 1927, there is a close nexus between destruction and authenticity, echoing a major concern in the early texts of Martin Luther.[6] In his later philosophy, after the so-called *Kehre,* this term is once more reversed, and then applied in order to *destruct* the kind of authenticity he earlier endorsed. In this period, he focuses on a *topology* of being, setting out from the relationship between Nietzsche's nihilism and the language of metaphysics, that is, destruction as *Abbau* and *Verwindung* of metaphysics. This is not necessarily an approach which deviates from the *destruction* found in Luther; rather, it delves deeper into the problem of *destruuntur* once formulated by Luther. Whereas Nietzsche identifies the *site* of God as *empty* and void of sense: "Gott ist todt! Gott bleibt todt! Und wir haben ihn getödtet!" ("God is dead! God remains dead! And we have killed him!"), Luther identifies God as *hidden* and thus void of sense. In Heidegger's later philosophy, the two sites are contrasted and compared, and the former is perceived as analogous to the latter. Discussing this site of the *deus absconditus* (hidden God), of which he is decidedly critical, Herman Philipse points at various forms of divine hiddenness:

> In Heidegger's later discourse on Being, the postmonotheist analogue of this theme of the hidden God (*deus absconditus*) expresses itself in

> a great many ways, which a reader of the late Heidegger will easily recognize. Being is forgotten (*Seinsvergessenheit*) because it conceals itself (*Seinsverborgenheit*). This means that Being has abandoned us (*Seinsverlassenheit*) so that we live in abandonment by being and are homeless. Being withdrew itself (*Entzug*) in the beginning of the history of Being, and it refuses itself to us. Being is hidden, it is like a shadow, so that we are doomed to err (*Irre*), and our life is meaningless. Being is not a ground (*Grund*), but an abyss (*Abgrund*), which hides the real ground. It is a mystery, which does not betray itself. It turns away from us. Yet, Being is *das Fragwürdigste,* both in the sense that it is the most problematical (*fragwürdig*), because it is hidden, and in the sense that it is the most worthy (*würdig*) aim of our quest (*Fragen*).[7]

Being aware of the significant displacements of conceptuality from Luther's early modern to Heidegger's post-monotheist discourse, our inquiry on the hidden God ventures to follow a similar line of thought, albeit with a point of departure that slightly differs from Philipse's explicit atheism. Within the more general discourse on *phenomenology,* I emphasize a topological analysis in order to better understand the displacements of the *deus absconditus* throughout the modern era—not in order to neglect or reject Luther's theological achievements but in order to analyze them from a different angle and thus let *other* aspects of his theology come to the fore. As Heidegger suggests, there are indeed some crucial insights of Luther's theology that were more profoundly understood by philosophers than theologians, and I believe that there are still significant parts of his theology that have not yet been recognized and explicated. With Derrida we could speak of a "nondogmatic *repetition*" of dogma, which studies Luther's notions of scripture, of God, of revelation and hiddenness from a contemporary perspective.[8]

I see Luther's reference to the *deus absconditus* in *De servo arbitrio* as more of a metaphysical than a theological argument. Hence, it transcends the limits of theology in the strict sense. The rejection of these references to the hidden God in favor of the Christological mystery which *resolves* the problem is typical for scholars like Karl Barth and Rudolf Bultmann, Paul Tillich, Eberhard Jüngel, and Dorothee Sölle. Partly it stems from a rejection of metaphysics and skepticism toward traditional philosophy and so-called natural theology. But the reaction also betrays an element of anxiety in the face of nihilistic relativism. Although they are deeply occupied with Luther, they avoid the most *questionable* premises of their own theological discourse—both in the sense of the most problematical and the most worthy aim of inquiry. Whereas Gerhard Ebeling, who insists on the continuous relevance of the hidden God, ends up with a pre-modern monstrosity of transcendent essence, Eberhard Jüngel's treatise on the *deus absconditus* in "Quae supra nos, nihil ad nos" is exemplary in this respect, by excluding and rejecting the *absolute* hiddenness as irrelevant to "us."[9]

Jüngel is troubled by Luther's notion of the hidden God and even more troubled by the way this notion influences Protestant theology in the twentieth century. He argues that the notion is useless and senseless unless it is identified with God's presence in Christ, who is suffering at the cross. In all other respects it ought to be rejected and excluded from theological discourse, since it is "no concern of ours." There are obvious correlations between Heidegger's hiddenness of being and Jüngel's discussion of the hidden God, but the latter takes the opposite direction from Heidegger: He seeks to avoid the question of hiddenness in order to declare the fulfillment of *revelation* in Christ.[10] Heidegger, conversely, insists on the need to dwell on the most problematic point of discourse. At this point, where the problem threatens to dissolve, he looks for the question which is most worthy of being raised; indeed, the question which keeps on disturbing us and therefore unavoidably *is* of our concern. The problem thus discussed by Heidegger has far-reaching theological consequences; but rather than dwelling with Heidegger, we excavate the sources of this problem as formulated by Luther in the *Heidelberg Disputation* (1518), *De liberio arbitrio* (1525), and further texts, predominantly from the early period of the Reformation.

Scripture, Writing, and the Theory of Texts

The authority of scripture is a decisive argument for Luther's critique of tradition. He sees scripture as more trustworthy than the opinions of men and a final argument against the tendency of institutions like the church to create new moral obligations and measures of control. In his radical quest for freedom, he is suspicious of the human propensity to control other human beings through ecclesial authority, additional ethical demands, or letters of indulgences. A significant power is thereby ascribed to scripture, that is, to reveal the truth by letting the world proceed in a different light, according to the grammar and meaning of the text. He compares scripture to a shining torch, which gives light to the otherwise confused or blinded eyes.[11] Whereas Erasmus argues that the controversy between Luther and himself is a question of interpretation—and thus the result of conflicting interpretations by qualified readers of the same text—Luther rejects this argument as irrelevant. The question is *not* solved by a discussion of interpretations, he argues, since they would then presuppose the superior position of a reader in relation to the text. Luther insists on a change of perspective: Reading and understanding a text is not a question of *what* you understand, but of *how* the world proceeds *in the light* of scripture.

The difference may be illustrated by reference to Plato's parable of the cave: Either you try to understand the movements of shadows in the light of a fire inside the cave, or you move outside and discover the true clarity of the world—proceeding in the light of the sun. The difference is indeed a phenomenological one. Translated into Luther's terminology: There is an absolute difference between the (shadowy) world as nature and the (clear) wor(l)d according to scripture. A similar difference is established between the human being as defined according to Aristotelian anthropology and the human being as circumscribed by scripture.[12] Finally, there is a crucial difference between the metaphysical definition of God's nature and the God who is made accessible, who is *revealed* and thus *given,* through the word of scripture. At this point, Luther is not willing to accept any compromise.

The theoretical point thus sketched out can be analyzed either as a theology of revelation where "scripture" is applied in its theological sense or as a general philosophical and linguistic theory of writing, where "scripture" or "writing" refers to the way phenomena are qualified and described through texts. The Latin term *scriptura* covers both. And the expression *sola scriptura* explicitly puts the emphasis on the *written* form of scripture, its grammar, its literality. Martin Luther is cautious not to ascribe the same *authority* to any text; for him, it is the "Word of God" that is qualified as revelatory, although he is surprisingly liberal when it comes to the limits of canon. This traditional point with respect to authority is by no means a decisive argument against the *generic* analysis of his procedure, however. On the contrary: It should be perfectly possible to study his linguistic procedures of text analysis, which have been overlooked for centuries, and on a different level than the studies of Luther's rhetoric which are now available.[13] Indeed, it would be a theoretical advantage if we could discuss the general procedures of his arguments and text analyses without slipping directly into theological controversies on the doctrine of grace, of justification by faith, of free will, and so forth.[14]

In my analysis of Luther's theory of scripture, I emphasize the latter point: the way he approaches the literal expression in its grammatical form in order to discuss, problematize, and clarify its meaning. The point is not to reject or overlook the theological exegesis of the text, nor that Luther considered the authority of the Bible to be absolute and unconditional, but rather to better understand *how* these readings are based in the text and *why* Luther argues as an assertor, without compromise, for the reading he finds most plausible.[15] By raising the question of scripture, I also suggest that the world proceeding from a contemporary reading of the texts may look different from the world Luther discovered, although the texts are more or less the same.[16] The written text is given priority rather than the many theories that defend a Lutheran position or see Luther as guarantor for their own position. The latter has been a popular theological exercise throughout the twentieth century, beginning with the scholars of the so-called Luther Renaissance. Rather than defending a position because it allegedly represents Luther, we examine the procedures of the text theory at work in Luther's texts and discuss what a contemporary version of this theory may look like.

The emphasis on writing is here applied in the linguistic, or rather philological, sense Derrida adopts in the second half of *On Grammatology* for his analysis of Rousseau's essay *On the Origin of Language*. He there discusses the premises for a detailed, rigorous analysis of the text that is conservative in emphasizing the grammatical expression and written form of the essay. In certain respects it contradicts the explicit intentions of Rousseau, but these contradictions are based on a rigorously grammatical and thus *literal* reading of the text.[17] Derrida points at the equivocal usage of key terms such as writing and speech in Rousseau's essay, which breaks this text open for a different reading. In significant respects this second reading contradicts the traditional reception of the text, and Derrida underscores this *difference* as the origin of the question of meaning and phenomena. Rather than proclaiming this new, grammatological reading to be correct, whereas the traditional one is rejected, Derrida emphasizes the inherent tensions between the two readings, which open up a space of interpretation and understanding, within the text.[18]

This textual space, established by new readings of old texts, is decisive for the construction of sense in general, according to Derrida, insofar as language unavoidably structures our experiences, including our memories and expectations, our past and our future. However, as opposed to the philosophers Derrida criticizes for giving priority to speech and presence rather than writing and absence, such as Plato and Rousseau, Luther is himself a *scriptural* thinker and a grammatologist. Luther actually applies the term "Grammatica Theologica" as a methodological device for his own exegesis of the Psalms.[19] Hence, a deconstruction of Luther's theology is out of question, at least in the sense this term was popularized within literary studies, philosophy, religious studies, archeology, and other disciplines during the last two decades of the twentieth century. Derrida admits that there is a certain historical link, a genealogy, which connects his own notion of deconstruction to Luther's theory of destruction and his emphasis on writing, yet at the same time he argues that he does *not* belong to the same filiation as Luther, Pascal, and Heidegger:

> One must not only say, as was said, and not without audacity, *"Luther qui genuit Pascal,"* but perhaps also *"Luther qui genuit Heidegger."* Which has completely other consequences. I have recalled in several different places that the theme and the word *Destruktion* designated in Luther a desedimentation of instituted theology (one could also say ontotheology) in the service of a more originary truth of Scripture. Heidegger was obviously a great reader of Luther. But despite my enormous

> respect for this great tradition, the deconstruction that concerns me does not belong, in any way, and this is more than obvious, to the same filiation. It is precisely this difference that I attempt, although not without difficulty, to be sure, to articulate.[20]

It is worth noticing and emphasizing this difference before we draw any conclusions concerning similarities and influences—claims that are often difficult to demonstrate and almost impossible to prove. Even for the textual theories discussed in this book, it would be a failure to overemphasize the proximity between the notion of scripture discussed on the basis of Luther's texts and Derrida's notion of writing. Derrida's philosophical analysis of writing has been seminal for the approach adapted here, in particular the rigorous analysis of texts according to their grammar, but this makes his emphasis on the *difference* all the more important. Identifying and discussing the significant differences between Luther and philosophers like Kant, Nietzsche, Heidegger, or Derrida is more challenging, more demanding, but also more rewarding than the demonstration of influences and commonplaces.

Characteristic of Derrida's *grammatology* is not only his focus on the problem of *writing* as prior to questions of being and presence, but also a phenomenological approach emphasizing the grammatical expression prior to the presumed *intentions* of the author.[21] The written text analyzed in its scriptural form makes one aware of the problems raised by the *absence* of the author, which may nevertheless be decisive for the perception of a certain moment as *present*. Religions in general—and the three Religions of the Book in particular—depend on the *structuring* language of the written text, which makes possible a certain specter of significations and experiences, whereas others are excluded. Thus, the narratives of the Old and the New Testaments function as structuring patterns of experience: Paul's theoretical reflections on sin and justification, death, guilt, bondage, freedom, law, and grace make possible a structuring of human reality and perception, whereas other alternatives are excluded. Luther's emphasis on *scripture alone* can be read as such a rigorous methodological device for studying the written text in its precise grammatical form. Following this line of thought, the grammar of scripture *structures* the basic conditions for the perception of phenomena and the construction of the past (memory, history) and the future (expectations, promise), through the *letter* of the law and the freedom of grace.

The dynamic of this scriptural method, which may otherwise fall into legalism or fundamentalism, follows from the sudden possibility to which the texts gives access: an unconditional gift, the surplus of grace, or whatever names are given to this radical possibility proclaimed by the text, and thereby structuring the perception of the reader. The argument Luther returns to again and again is that only the rigor of detailed exegesis will make the reader aware of this radical possibility, and thus make the *repetition* of that gift possible. The classic example is the grammatical construction of *iustitia Dei* in Romans 1:17, where Luther after years of detailed exegesis discovers a *double* meaning: first the genitive objective, and second the genitive subjective, which opens the scriptural space to a complete reinterpretation of Paul's Letter to the Romans—indeed of scripture as a whole, according to this double structure.[22] It is the equivocal meaning of the term *iustitia Dei* discovered *within the text* which makes this reading possible, and thus opens up for the re-formation of experience, of anthropology, of phenomena. And in this respect, an equivocal reading of the term *scriptura* also seems to be justified, if not even required for a rereading of the works of Martin Luther. The emphasis on scripture in this formal or literal sense of the term is already there, in the texts; it only needs to be spelled out in a different philosophical and historical context.

Luther's assertoric argument for *scripture alone* indicates that he must have expected a certain stability of texts that may resist the chronic dissolution and corruption of their meaning through time. He is aware of the problems raised by historical distance to the texts, yet his view of history is not one of continuous progress, but rather a history of decline; *Verfallsgeschichte.* Within this historical instability of sense, the grammatical structure of language represents a relatively stable structure, and thus may be more trustworthy than the shifting opinions and interpretations of human beings. Accordingly, Luther claims that he always doubts his own power of judgment and therefore keeps returning to scripture in order to test his own opinions.[23] Occasionally, as in the *Heidelberg Disputation,* this gives his argument a paradoxical form, aimed at *destructing* the reasoning of the reader (that is, the wisdom of this world). This persistent hesitation and doubt is significant for Luther's theory of scripture. It is as if he is constantly looking for a breach point where the compact text is fracturing and therefore allows the light to break in. A double movement of destruction and construction introduces this critical and productive force of Luther's theory of texts. In part II (*Sola Scriptura*), this theory is analyzed and its ambiguities explored. I thereby also establish a theoretical (scriptural) apparatus for the subsequent chapters.

I have already indicated that this textual theory is discussed in relation to contemporary theory of texts rather than an effort at historical reconstruction. It is not quite self-evident, though, how Luther's textual approach should be related to the various hermeneutical and textual theories in Continental philosophy of the late twentieth century. There are significant philosophical differences between, for example, the hermeneutics of Gadamer and the grammatology of Derrida, although both emerge from Heidegger's phenomenology. Whereas the former emphasizes the constructive role of tradition and its inherent authority, the latter rephrases Heidegger's destruction of the history of philosophy in terms of a deconstruction of texts. A reconsideration of Luther's textual theory may imply critical aspects in relation to both Gadamer and Derrida. In any case, critical analysis of Luther's generic theory of scripture should be possible and allows us to develop a new approach to some of his most polemical texts. I have addressed key issues in some of Luther's controversies and discovered that a number of them may still be relevant—and even raise controversy—within contemporary philosophy. This is no disadvantage for a more thorough analysis of other aspects of his thought, including notions that seem to be more alien to contemporary philosophy, such as the hidden God.

Throughout the book I emphasize the problem of place, and thus of topology, as a basic question in Luther's controversies and disputations. If Luther's critique of philosophy has paved the way for philosophical inquiry in the modern sense, we should at least consider whether it has something to do with this questioning of place. This means that the problem of hiddenness cannot merely be located to the doctrine of God, as was often the case within theological discussions of the issue.[24] The problem should at least be *articulated* as a more generic one, a problem concerning the origin and place of *theory,* including philosophical inquiry and the theory of texts.

THREE

Topology

The questions of place and topology require separate consideration. The use of topics as an analytical approach goes back to Aristotle's *Topics,* where he defines the conditions for the art of dialectics. The topological approach is reserved for arguments based on commonly held opinions, Greek *endoxa.* Thus, they differ from the *questions* that are treated by way of syllogisms. Aristotle gives no definition of a topos, but the topoi are referred to as places from where his arguments can be invented, elaborated, or discovered.[1]

Topology in Melanchthon and Luther

In the early 1520s, topics as a philosophical and theological approach was rediscovered by humanist and Reformer Philipp Melanchthon, Luther's closest ally at the University of Wittenberg. His *Loci Communes* (1521) represents a new type of theology, based on common topoi in the scriptures, in particular from Paul's Letter to the Romans. Hence, it is written according to the principle *sola scriptura,* but with due respect to traditional rules of dialectic and rhetoric. Günter Frank points out that Melanchthon applied the same principle of topics to the interpretation of a variety of texts in his *Tübinger Rhetorik* (1519), but developed a specifically *theological* method in the *Loci.*[2] Frank argues that the concept of topoi is ambiguous from the beginning, for example, through the different usage of the term in Aristotle's *Topics* and the *Rhetoric,* and it oscillates between various meanings in Cicero and later in medieval philosophy up to the Renaissance. According to Melanchthon, the notion describes *places* of arguments (like in Cicero), but also a semantic field, a "signature" of things, which makes it possible to organize general thoughts under a common heading. Finally, he applies the term *loci* for generic propositions concerning a specific question, achieved through systematic analysis of texts.[3] Hence, Melanchthon is basically faithful to Aristotle's prescriptions, but he applies the method in a way which emphasizes the authority of scripture and thus remains faithful to the principles of the Reformation, including *sola scriptura.*

Luther occasionally refers to Melanchthon's *Loci Communes* as an exemplary way of doing systematic theology.[4] Still, he did not develop any methodology similar to the topology we find in Melanchthon. His discussion of the clarity and obscurity of texts in *De servo arbitrio* is compatible with this approach, but Luther is not visibly interested in common opinions (*endoxa*). He is fixed on the clarity of scripture, according to the rules of grammar and common rules of speech (*usus loquendi*), but his arguments may include paradox and counterintuitive opinions. There is one place of clarity in scripture which, according to Luther, overshadows all other places or, rather, gives light to these other places as their organizing principle, and that is the *logos* referred to by John in the Gospel (John 1:1–14), which nevertheless is a mystery, deeply hidden, and definitely *remains* a mystery.[5] Still, when the mystery approaches as revelation, then the inner connection in the scriptures is established: the semantic field that makes sense of the otherwise obscure doctrines and affirmations.[6] This is the sense Luther ascribes to "clarity" (*claritas*), and it conforms to the *topical* ideal presented by Melanchthon. Still, the discussion of places is more problematic in Luther.

It is not quite evident that Luther subscribes to the *Aristotelian* sense of the topoi, that the arguments are based on *endoxa*—on common sense. Contrary to Aristotle, Plato had rejected the thought that philosophical arguments can be based on *doxa* (meanings) or *endoxa* alone. He argued that philosophical ideas run counter to common sense, and only the perplexing experience of a difficult problem, such as paradox or aporia, may uncover the deceit. The problems thus being raised when it comes to the most basic principles of thought, such as the One, the Good, identity and difference, time, place, and being, may be studied in some of his main dialogues, above all in *Parmenides* and *Timaeus*. In the former, Plato addresses the question of the One, the origin and simplicity of being, which is therefore *older* than all other beings and ontologically prior to other ideas.

Timaeus is the dialogue wherein Plato discusses space and place as conditions for something to come into existence. Hence, what is the "receptacle (*hupedochē*) of all becoming" where the world is created?[7] Plato describes it as a third kind (*triton genos*), and gives a few examples indicating what it means (a womb, a lump of gold, a plastic stuff), while apologizing for the obscurity of the concept.[8] It is void of any specific characteristics except for its plasticity and its receptivity, yet it remains the enduring condition for something to become or take place. Plato simply describes it as *chōra,* that is, "space" or "open place." It is hardly a specific topos in the Aristotelian sense, and yet it provides a *site,* that is, a "spatial location for things that enter it and disappear from it."[9] The space thus indicated represents a condition of possibility for something to become.

If we can take it for granted that *space* is the general condition for something to become, even an idea or a discourse, then the whole discourse is *spatialized.* It is the space between the categories which makes sense possible, through differentiation and opposition. Yet this difference is opened up and made possible by a *third,* which is neither the one nor the other, that is to say, the *triton genos* of *chōra* which therefore also enables change and displacements, indeed also an *event* to take place. Whereas the event is basically a temporal category (kairos), *chōra* remains passive, receptive, and open for redefinitions. In Plato's dialogue, this receptive *place* of thought apparently remains unaffected by temporal distinctions, and yet it *gives space* to the perception of time in terms of movement and change.[10]

Although Luther's references to scriptural topoi in general follow the Aristotelian pattern, his effort at approaching the *deus absconditus* as a topos of thought seems to burst all limits for Aristotle's definition of topics, dialectically as well as rhetorically. This is the main reason why *De servo arbitrio* by far transgresses the rather limited scope of Melanchthon's *Loci Communes.* The *deus absconditus* may thus be referred to as a place, a place which Erasmus and Luther alternately describe as a "Corycian cave"—but this is definitely not a commonplace. Luther is aware of the difference, and he draws a distinction between these two kinds of topology, respectively, inside and outside of scripture: "The distinction I make—in order that I, too, may display a little rhetoric or dialectic—is this: God and the Scripture of God are two things, no less than the Creator and the creature are two things."[11] The commonplaces may simply be found in scripture and their mutual relationship is elaborated according to the *logos* of the scriptures, in particular as displayed in the letters of Paul. Hence, both Melanchthon and Erasmus display "rhetoric and dialectic" while referring to topoi in the Aristotelian sense. Such topology is possible as long as the criteria are defined according to Holy Scripture or any other clearly defined text corpus. With God *outside* scripture, as Luther points out, the conditions of rational discourse are very different. Hence, according to this basic distinction between God revealed in scripture and God outside scripture, the notion of the *deus absconditus* approaches us as a question, or rather a *questioning,* of reason itself—an open space which remains *paradoxical* and undefinable, despite the clarity of scripture.

Erasmus and even Melanchthon argue that this undefinable place, this obscure notion of ultimate hiddenness, ought to be excluded from the discourse.[12] Unless it is excluded, the rationality of the debate threatens to collapse. Although Luther agrees that the distinction is necessary, he rejects the *exclusion* or *elimination* of the topic as illusory. Even though the *deus absconditus* is difficult to define, it remains a *topic* of discourse and controversy, he argues. He reproaches Erasmus for his ignorance, since he lacks the distinction between the hiddenness and the predicates of God.[13] When the difference is *lacking,* Luther finds that the discourse in the final analysis becomes dishonest, confused, and thus intellectually untenable: It would imply an impossible hubris on behalf of philosophy and even theology. Hence, Luther vehemently rejects the exclusion or leveling of this term for some good purpose, for instance, to make the discourse more comprehensible or avoid confusing the general public.

Although Luther argues that *excluding* the term *deus absconditus* as if the problem did not exist would be intellectually dishonest, it gets equally problematic to *include* the notion of *deus absconditus* by defining its meaning univocally, since it eludes precise circumscription. Hence, it seems like the topos or *place* indicated by the "hidden God" suspends the limits of rational discourse and forces us to reconsider these limits, just as they once jeopardized the limits of philosophy in Plato. The distinction between outside and inside scripture, between hiddenness and revelation, between the pre-phenomenal and the phenomenon is at stake; and to a certain extent it is undermined and displaced by this *third term,* which neither is simply outside nor inside scripture. A problem of hiddenness and obscurity has caught our attention, but it remains an open place, a place of becoming. Could the hidden God even be the topos of the text which reopens the space of the discourse for a different reading or interpretation?

If we are right in identifying Luther's notion of the hidden God as a topos of discourse, indeed also a topos of much controversy, then the inquiry can hardly remain satisfied with an Aristotelian understanding of its topology. On the contrary: Luther's effort at describing the term betrays it as an open and indefinable space, and thus a different procedure of analysis is required. With reference to Plato, I have indicated that this is not merely a theological notion, but in the first instance a metaphysical term and a notion raising the problem of space within metaphysics; in other words, as the ambiguous condition of metaphysical discourse. Moreover, it also raises a problem of political power and political space, hence becomes a topic of political theology. Finally, it is related to the logos of discourse, to scripture and justice, including Luther's reinterpretation of the term "justification by faith."

The Question of Scripture

An inquiry concerning the hidden God presupposes a formal deliberation on the question of scripture: its origin, its limits, and its clarity. *Sola scriptura,* the principle formulated by Martin Luther, is well known, but its meaning is obscured by the course of time. I therefore attempt to reformulate the principle in terms of a repetition. Whereas Luther was focusing on the Bible as Holy Scripture, our repetition focuses on the question of scripture as a generic one, not bound to the Biblical corpus: Could *sola scriptura* thus once more enable us to adopt new perspectives on the texts by emphasizing their written form?

Sola scriptura was introduced as a principle of interpretation and authority in the early sixteenth century and soon became a popular slogan. The expression has often been taken in the literal and solely theological sense, pointing at Holy Scripture as the single authority and only source of true knowledge. It may thus be used as a pretense for an exclusively religious truth claim, in order to avoid serious rational confrontations with other disciplines. However, what if *sola scriptura* originally initiated a critical, interdisciplinary discussion about the conditions for both philosophy and theology? What if its most provocative sense was political and the most significant consequences were philosophical? What if *scriptura* here must also be taken seriously in its even more simple, literal, and common sense, namely, as writing, and thus allows for a way of reasoning which is neither based primarily in metaphysics nor in nature, neither in the subject nor in the spoken word, but in a particular grammar or *logos* found in the written text?

Such basic deliberations represent a challenge to traditional scholarship. However, if their bearing is sustained by a more rigorous examination of the texts in a contemporary context, the consequences will be far-reaching, in particular if the analysis is included in an interdisciplinary discussion of text and interpretation. For a reconsideration of historical, philosophical, and theological texts, including the ones discussed in this volume, the principle could once more open up the scriptural space for new readings. Compared to traditional applications of *sola scriptura*, it would then acquire a more distinctively *political* significance. Thus, it is possible to read Luther's appeal to focus on *scripture alone* not only as a procedure for Bible interpretation, but also to apply it in a careful analysis of Luther's texts and the writings of his contemporaries as contributions to a discourse on the genealogy of political sovereignty.

Sola scriptura was a slogan with the purpose of liberating the text from the institutional control of its meaning. Hence, the established civil and religious structures of governance were jeopardized in terms of an egalitarian subversion of power. It is not quite insignificant that this subversion begins *within* the text, for example, with a detailed and rigorous analysis of the expression *iustitia Dei* in Paul's Letter to the Romans.[14] The *double* grammatical reading of this term, as objective and subjective genitive, turns out to have consequences for not only the understanding of justice, but also of interpretation, of power, and of faith. Hence, the scriptural strategy is not merely of historical interest. It challenges contemporary political theology, which is concerned with the historical basis for contemporary political philosophy. As Carl Schmitt once pointed out, theories of power and governance betray a certain dependence on theological conceptuality.[15] This dependence goes back to early modernity and even antiquity. However, our focus in part II is on examining texts and textual theory in Luther's writings, in terms of an interdisciplinary analysis of the principle *sola scriptura*.

PART II

Sola Scriptura

I have no dispute with any man concerning morals, but only concerning the word of truth.

—Martin Luther

FOUR

The Quest for Immorality

Right from the beginning, there was a remarkable moral tenor in Luther's criticism of the church authorities.[1] From 1517 onward he criticized the church for operating with double standards and undermining the prayers of penitence.[2] He accused the responsible authorities of organizing the confession of sins economically through the production and sale of indulgences. Hence, the moral emphasis of his criticism is striking when he attacks the praxis of exploiting poor people and their fear of Hell to the benefit of the church, the pope, and the clergy. His attacks on immorality within the church have contributed considerably to the popularity of the movement he initiated. Luther not only addresses the dubious motive of earning money from people's misfortune and religious fears, though. The more substantial argument is concerned with the economic logic that invades theology, thus consuming and taking over the most basic theological concepts, including the concept of God.[3] Within such a system of calculable exchange, Luther saw virtually no space left for the unconditional gift.

These descriptions mirror a popularized image of the church in late-medieval Europe, occasionally more of a caricature than a characterization, but this is nevertheless the image Luther refers to and attacks throughout his early texts. And the dangerous popularity of his texts, raising concerns not only in Leipzig and Cologne but all the way down to Rome, indicates that there must have been some kernel of truth in the description and his analysis of the consequences. He warns that the result of this praxis is a cost-benefit rationality that makes man self-centered, even in his relationship to God.[4] Moreover, such self-centeredness runs counter to the principle of forgiveness, and thus the letter of indulgences undermines and betrays the very rationale that made it attractive for sale in the first place. It becomes the iconic symbol for man's self-deception and for the alleged "captivity" of the church. Hence, the consequences of such immoral praxis go far beyond the moral issue as such.

Morality and Immorality

It was not immorality, however, but rather the opposite—an immense pressure toward *moral perfection* combined with a lack of absolute and unconditional grace—that was the direct occasion for Luther's confrontation with the church and with the theologians of the time. He fiercely attacks the anthropology and the understanding of God implied in the praxis of penitence. When he published *Ninety-five Theses* on the question of indulgences in October 1517, this was the main target of his criticism.[5] Luther never argued against penitence (*Buße*) as such, but against the *lack* of true penitence within the practice of indulgences and confession of sins. In the text initiating these dramatic events in the history of Europe later called the Reformation, he argues for more earnestness and thus a more authentic and radical understanding of confession and repentance: The entire life of a believer should be determined by penitence.[6] All through the ninety-five theses we hear a loud and clear, in modern terms also foundational, cry for authenticity against institutionalized forms of life-lies and bargaining with the truth.

It is astonishing how determinant this discovery of a deception becomes for Luther's approach: Just like the sophists define the counterpart to Plato, but thereby also influence his thought, this *economic* anthropology, based on a barter economy, becomes the negative counterimage to Luther's own thinking.[7] Yet as negation it is also a starting point. He claims that the deception he discovers is everything but a coincidental fallacy. He sees it as a systematic failure, deeply rooted in the ethical and philosophical convictions of his times. The sale of indulgences is therefore only an extreme token of the dominant structure of thought pervading his contemporary church, society, and academy. This prototype remains one of the decisive coordinates of his theology, anthropology, and even of his thoughts on text interpretation.

In the debate with Erasmus, Luther gives his opponent credit for having identified the key question of his critique, namely, the question of free will.[8] Erasmus is the only critic among theologians, philosophers, lawyers, and clergy who has understood the importance of this question for both anthropology and theology. Still, Erasmus argues that the question of free will is completely dependent on interpretation.[9] Luther disagrees, but he nevertheless bases his own argument on an interpretation of the Bible texts that differs clearly from the one of his opponent.[10] Already in the introduction to his *Diatribe,* Erasmus questions the superiority of Luther's approach, though, and with good reasons. He points out that they both agree on the authority of scripture but that the controversy begins as soon as they start interpreting it.[11] He blames Luther for his lack of sufficient criteria or rather for not even reflecting upon the question of criteria. When the scriptures, as Erasmus concludes, are so unclear at this point, how can Luther be so self-assured that his reading is the right one, against the majority of the tradition to which he belongs?

Luther's counterargument is simply that scripture is clear and scripture is its *own* interpreter, as he had argued in *Assertio* five years earlier.[12] The smart turn here is to make scripture into the *subject* of interpretation, but the formulation is circular, elliptic, and the reader somehow remains *outside* this circle of interpretation. In his controversy with Erasmus, we can study how this strategy is applied in order to present a series of double readings aimed at undermining the arguments of his opponent. Hence, it appears to be a first move in order to establish a relative autonomy of the text as opposed to the total hermeneutic *control* of the reader.[13]

After discussing the criteria for judging between good and bad interpreters—rather than a particular method for interpretation—Erasmus arrives at one of his most decisive objections to his opponent: Luther breaks down the morality of the common people with his babble against the freedom of will. His argument is, according to Erasmus, doomed to be misunderstood as soon as it becomes public and will then be taken as an excuse for crimes and excesses.[14] Luther is thereby (like Socrates) directly accused of promoting impiety and immorality, an accusation with more dramatic consequences than his alleged moral deficiencies.[15] This is a recurring issue throughout the *Diatribe*. However, is this analysis presented by Erasmus correct? Does Luther, either on purpose or against his better judgment, promote immorality and undermine the piety of common people?

Erasmus on Luther's Contradictions

Moral annoyance is certainly one of the reasons why Erasmus has chosen free will as a topic of controversy. His point is convincing: Luther's public argument against the freedom of will might be taken as a pretense for not following ethical rules. Whether that is a deliberate consequence or not is less important. The question of morality is interwoven with the question of interpretation, and both are interconnected with the problem of free will. And if Erasmus argues for a moral reading of the text, then is Luther perhaps rightly accused of *immoral* reading? The question is arguably a bit more complex than that, but both morality and immorality are at stake within the question of interpretation. One of Luther's strategies when faced with the charge of immorality is to show what happens when scripture *in its totality* is read from a *moral* perspective. Albeit the so-called *tropological* or moral reading of scripture is only one out of four approaches within the Quadriga, the fourfold method of interpretation widely used in the Middle Ages, it gives the entire construction of the text a moral tenor.[16] Together with the two other spiritual senses it safeguards the reader against contradictions.[17] In case of interpretive difficulties, the allegorical and anagogical approaches allow figurative and mystical interpretations, but they do not transgress or contradict the moral admonitions set up by the tropological reading and supported by the teachings of the church.[18]

Erasmus is faithful to this pattern when he argues against Luther's understanding of will in the polemics of the *Diatribe*. His definition of will is based on the assumption that without freedom of will, humans would be unable to fight against evil; they would even a priori be unable to strive for good and turn away from evil.[19] Therefore, he argues for the necessity of assuming that we have a free will in order to understand the basic logic of biblical anthropology:

> But if the distinction between good and evil, as well as the will of God, had been hidden for man, he could not have been blamed for making the wrong choice. If the will had not been free, he could not have been charged with sin, because it ceases to be a sin if it is not done voluntarily, except when error or constraint of the will is the result of another sin.[20]

Admittedly, the argument is based on a particular *interpretation* of responsibility, in that it presupposes a relatively free choice and knowledge about the alternatives; but that interpretation was not so far from the dominant common sense in sixteenth-century philosophy and theology—and possibly not so far from common sense five centuries later. It is still a truism within moral philosophy that if an act is not done voluntarily, one can hardly be blamed for it.

Erasmus argues that an important function of the Bible text is to justify the church's teaching about the good, thus establishing a particular moral order. The interpretation of the Bible serves the purpose of disciplining the reader or (illiterate) listener within that order.[21] This view has clearly influenced his selection of Bible texts and Erasmus's emphasis on moral duty. When the texts are expounded, he consequently infers from commandment to ability; hence, if the commandment tells that you "should" do something, or even that you should choose *the good,* it would make no sense unless you "could" do it voluntarily: "It would be ridiculous to tell someone to 'choose' if it were not in his power to turn this way or the other, as though someone standing at a crossroads were to be told 'you see the two roads—take whichever you want,' if only one were open."[22] It is perhaps not a necessary inference from should to could, but it is not exactly far-fetched, either.[23]

In consequence, moral reading of the Bible makes sense of the text and gives a coherent impression of the biblical corpus as a whole. According to such a reading, Luther's accusations of moral decay within the church may be perfectly right, since a moral assessment of the sale of indulgences hardly would be favorable for the seller. Hence, the indulgences are not a point of disagreement. But Erasmus reacts against the self-contradictive tendency in Luther's argument: How can he attack immorality when he undermines the criteria for judging between good and evil in the first place? And this is indeed a convincing argument. If the German theologian argues against the very principle of morality, has he not disqualified the basis for his own judgment even when the statement as such may be perfectly true? Here Erasmus has identified a weak point and an inner contradiction within Luther's position. The accusations of immorality within the church thus hit back and strike the accuser himself.

Thus far the discussion stands without any prospects of solution. The accusations of immorality go both ways, supported by insulting comments concerning the moral character of the opponent, in particular from Luther's side. Erasmus is accused of being a coward and a fool, and, more severely, that he is willing to bargain with the truth in order to save his own skin.[24] Luther, conversely, is accused of pride and stubbornness by insisting on his own private meaning instead of listening to others. Erasmus complains that Luther does not accept the judgment of anyone else and identifies his position with that of the Holy Ghost. Ironically, when Luther is writing one could almost speak of ghost-writing in the literal sense.[25] Still, the most provocative claim is that the will is bound, and therefore unable to choose good instead of evil, and equally unable to act accordingly.

Erasmus may therefore be right after all, in that the controversy is impossible to settle because it is a question of interpretation—and both sides have good interpreters, both sides have holy men, both sides can find support within other texts, indicating that their interpretation is right.[26] The *moral* question, at least, seems to end there—but not necessarily the question of *morality.* And even less the question of *immorality.*

Luther on Morality and Interpretation

The mutual accusations of immorality, of having a deficient moral character, of deceiving the readers and falsifying the truth, belong to the logical structure of immorality and the rhetorical play of the disputations.[27] The more interesting question, however, is whether the discussion moves beyond this dead end and scrutinizes the basis for morality as such, as a system of values and interpretations. At least in Luther's contribution, such a more radical project seems to emerge, possibly destabilizing the whole system of what was perceived as *traditional* ethics. This is what Erasmus fears and criticizes, and at this point Luther seems to accept that he is right.[28]

Immorality is thus not an accidental or peripheral question in this debate; it goes to the core of the issue. Moreover, Erasmus's objections and characteristics are directly based in Luther's main position, the argument about the bondage of will. Why would Luther insist on a position that seems so difficult to defend? Which arguments does he have for raising such radical questions concerning the logic of the ethical rationale to which he ascribes? Does it only represent his "private" meaning as a result of his personal experiences with the impossibility of fulfilling the moral rules, and if so, is it not just another consequence of his pride? Luther's personal experiences in this respect are conspicuous and to a certain extent they have become paradigmatic for his view on moral improvement and the futility of striving. In a rather odd way they later became paradigmatic and formative for a whole tradition of faith called "Protestant" or "Evangelical-Lutheran." Luther describes the process in *De servo arbitrio* as he has done in other texts:

> It has been regarded as unjust, as cruel, and as intolerable, to entertain such an idea about God and this is what has offended so many great men during so many centuries. And who would not be offended? I myself was offended more than once, and brought to the very depth and abyss of despair, so that I wished I had never been created a man, before I realised how salutary that despair was, and how near to grace.[29]

I find no reason to doubt Luther's descriptions of how he made hard efforts as a dutiful monk in order to achieve perfection. Yet the result was the opposite of what he strived for: He did not become a better person. In judging himself harshly, he describes how he became hateful and depressed, falling into the "depth and abyss of despair." He was torn between ideal and reality, between unachievable demands and insufficient striving, between the words of a loving God and the confrontation with a divine Judge who was strict and merciless. The effort at moral improvement seemed doubly futile because he ended up in a state that not only psychologically but even morally speaking was to the worse rather than to the better. He thus discovered a big gap between the words he professed and his own experiences. The reason for his suspicion of morality thus seems to be the disproportion between the words and their content, between the good intentions and the actual results. The inadequacy undermines the credibility of the words and thus the very connection between the words and the "thing" or state of affairs (*res*), between *signifier* and *signified*, but also the credibility of the individual as morally responsible.[30]

Luther's argument *against* interpretation could thus be read from this point of view: "Interpretation" is an apt word for the construction of sense within a certain framework. For the change of perspective he finds necessary, however, such an approach is insufficient, or even counterproductive, since it confirms the alleged deception. The conditions of reading ought to be altered—and this basic change has its origin not inside the reader or in the discussion between readers; it originates from within the text. Therefore, his analysis of Christian anthropology and moral philosophy is a scriptural analysis; grammatically detailed, based on rhetorical structures, and focusing on a particular dilemma connected to the described problem of striving for good. When Luther analyzes and dissects this human activity, the striving as such, he finds it comparable to an autoimmune disease.[31] As soon as it gets going, it functions as a self-supportive system, dominating the evaluation of actions and the definition of further goals for moral perfection. It follows its own inherent logic, which is then applied to text interpretation and once more reflected in the praxis of moral improvement.

The interpretation of texts is thereby included in the same order of moral improvement as the futile striving for moral perfection. Hence, it is not difficult to see why Luther intransigently denies the possibility of explaining the differences between Erasmus and himself in terms of "interpretation." For him, the term "inter-pretation" as a kind of mediation between two contexts or horizons remains *inherent* to the self-sufficient logic of morality and moralization.[32] Seen from Luther's perspective, the system of thought is self-contradictive but also self-sufficient: Moral activity implies striving for improvement that again fosters pride. The moral interpretation of the text is so extensive that it is even applied as criterion for defining and delimiting the concept of God.[33] This structure of thought is therefore rejected and denounced by Luther and summarized under the label *'liberum arbitrium'*—in other words, free will.[34] And the entire structure, rather than the different aspects taken separately, is called an illusion, merely an empty word without reference or content.[35]

A Place for Something Other

It is conspicuous how often Luther returns to the dilemma of defining the true or proper meaning of a word, and he makes the reader aware of a distinction in this relationship (between concept and content, or sometimes *definiens* and *definiendum*) which is not self-evident and not even constant. *Language* and its sense—in particular the language dominating the sphere of reason and ontology—proves to be just as mutable, arbitrary, and in- or convertible as the *"liberum arbitrium"* itself.[36] Through an analysis of the contradictive use of the term by Erasmus, Luther ends up with a proposition concerning the contingency and mutability of language and sense, including the battle or fight (*pugna*) between different definitions of the same term: "Here, in fact, two definitions are fighting each other already at the outset: one definition according to the name and one according to the entity, since the voice [*vox*] signifies something other and something other means the thing itself [*re ipsa*]."[37] This literal translation from the Latin text illustrates how the instability and inadequacies within free will itself (*definiendum*) are linguistically reflected by the instability of the language defining free will.

Luther's analysis is detailed at this point, showing in grammatical terms why Erasmus's definition is caught up in inner contradictions. When faced with traditional arguments in favor of free will, Luther's strategy is to analyze the inconsistency of the terms *arbitrium* and *gratia*. Both presuppose a particular concept of responsibility and justice: The former is based on responsibility and moral improvement, whereas the latter is completely dependent on God's gift, which, according to the *Heidelberg Disputation* (1518), means a destruction (*per crucem destruuntur*) of the "illusion" of free will in order to redefine the conditions for ethics, justice, and selfhood.[38] As soon as each concept of justice is clarified in its relation to the others, he ventures to show how the latter (justice based on *gratia*) interrupts the rationality and the conditions defined by the former. Not only *beyond* but also *within* the logic of morality, this *other* rationality disturbs and destroys the distinction between morality and immorality, and it does so by way of a suspension of both.

In Erasmus's definition of free will, we find the opposite, since he explicitly defines the choice of the believer in terms of his or her decision to turn oneself toward (*se applicare*) or away from (*se avertare*) that which leads to salvation: "At this place we define free will [*liberum arbitrium*] as the power of human will [*voluntas*] by which a human being is able to turn himself towards that which leads to eternal salvation or turn away from it."[39] Hence, the question of justice remains within the sphere of morality and all actions and choices, including the *choice* of believing in God's grace, depends on the agent herself and her power of will.

In a passage toward the end of *De servo arbitrio,* Luther describes precisely how the definition of morality *as sin*—including morality in its entirety, as intellectual and willing endeavor for the good—opens up an undefined *space* for something other.[40] Within the moral self, declared to be immoral, a different self emerges, and that is a self which is made possible through "scripture." This is another example of how Luther applies scripture *qua* writing in order to develop new *theory*—in the philosophical rather than the theological sense of the word. Since he rejects the conditions for the philosophical rationality of his times, it was perhaps only to be expected. Still, it has not yet been given the attention it deserves. His formal, grammatical reflection on scripture makes it possible for Luther to dissociate from the contemporary readings of the text and deliberate on other options.

Alone, this distance from the contemporary church and his insistence on reading *otherwise* would suffice to brand him "heretic," as Leo X had done in his bull, and as did other defenders of the Catholic faith like Eck, Catharinus, and Erasmus. Still, what does "heretic" mean? It pertains to someone who has a choice, or believes in having a choice, a free and arbitrary will (*liberum arbitrium*). Hence, Luther can easily turn this term against the accusers, since they are the ones to believe in—and even *assert*—the existence of such a faculty that makes heresy possible. In this and similar ways he consequently *transcends* the dialectics of either/or: either moral or immoral, either good or bad, either free will or fatalism. He draws the distinction back to the question of the *conditions of possibility* for ethics, for justice, for free will, for unconditional grace. For a contemporary analysis and reassessment of this approach, however, the decisive question is not *what* he believes (such as whether there "is" a free will or not) but *how* he proceeds in order to achieve a new understanding of "scripture": How does he approach the linguistic and rhetorical challenges? What kind of philosophical arguments does he accept and defend, and why are other arguments rejected?

I suggest that his theoretical approach is intimately connected with the notion of "scripture" itself, although scripture not defined in relation to its *matters* but regarding what kind of insight scripture may convey, and how: When reading and understanding "in the light" of the scriptures, they may restructure any given reality according to the narrative, logical, and grammatical structures within the text. That is also a possible sense of the word "*re-formatio*": forming the principles for temporal and spatial experience, for activity and passivity, according to the paradigms fixed in writing.

Although Luther in his political and theological positions in many respects belongs to the late-medieval world, the rational structures of his thought are innovative, even revolutionary, especially his theory of scripture. The revolt consists in his immoral and unprecedented step *beyond* the given tradition, *transcending* the philosophical and theological framework within which he belongs. The grammatical destabilization of a particular understanding of theology and philosophy and their mutual dependence is therefore a decisive theoretical condition for the political and religious movement we call the Reformation.

Some possible consequences are already anticipated within Luther's texts: The temporal structure of the promise and the unconditional qualification of the gift open up a new space for the human self within and beyond more traditional patterns of understanding. This step *beyond* the tradition (although he insists on remaining within the tradition by seeking to maintain the tradition through a radical break, through the emancipation of each singular human being) appears to be a profoundly *modern* thought. Here I think Luther has identified what eventually became basic conditions for philosophical and theological reflection, an ambiguous understanding of the self that later plays a crucial role in the history of philosophy in early and late modernity.[41] The interesting point is that he does not present some kind of modern synthesis or system of thought but that he insists on the very *division* of the self into active and passive, living and dying, defined by causal necessity but distinguished with an outrageous freedom.

The accusations of immorality are significant here because they illustrate the inherent contradictions and infinite possibilities of *scriptural* reasoning by challenging the idea of morality as an appropriate perspective on the text. Again, this is a question of grammar, but the logic of this grammar opens up the space for different and opposed interpretations within the same text, regardless of whether all the scriptures or just a single passage is taken into consideration. Luther ventures to prove that all definitions of human beings as morally accountable run into contradictions, since what is expected is moral perfection and what is achieved is failure, imperfection, immorality.[42]

The notion of immorality plays a double role in this analysis. On the one hand, it is the conclusion to the question of what humans can achieve in ethical respects. On the other hand, it is the turning point for a different approach to the problem of responsibility. The second sense of the term *iustitia Dei* discussed in chapter 6, the "passive" reception of God's justice *without* works, is indeed immoral, but in a way that surpasses the distinction between morality and immorality. The *amoral* grammar of possibility thus breaks up the moral limits, the moral order, the moral commandments, and the moral principle of interpretation from within. Indeed, immorality in the first sense is nonetheless presupposed in order to *make space* for justice as unconditional gift, beyond the logic of merit and calculable exchange.

The significance of immorality is thus widely underestimated and commonly misunderstood, not only in practical life but even more by philosophers and theologians of early modernity and the period of Enlightenment, who had a tendency toward moralization. The same applies to the Luther research of the twentieth century, for instance the proponents of the Luther Renaissance who justified their approach in terms of Neo-Kantian ethics.[43] In Luther's reading of the scriptures, however, immorality emerges as the *conditio sine qua non* for a rejection of moralism in general, and the moral paradigm of text interpretation in particular.

The sense of the scriptures is redefined according to the double grammatical structure of imperative and future tense, of admonitions and unconditional promise.[44] Luther's decisive and still valid point is that as soon as the *difference* between the two is leveled, then the latter is consumed by the former and the concept of God is subsumed under an economic rationality. Admittedly, the rejection of morality as a valid condition for the interpretation of scripture requires some qualification, as demonstrated by Luther's controversy with the Antinomians.[45] The *amoral* reading does not imply that the words of the law are simply overlooked or rejected—or that the law is excluded as superfluous.[46] Luther has nothing but sarcasms left for such a simplification and leveling of the decisive *difference* between law and grace, justice by the law and justice by grace. The latter fulfills and surpasses the former, but only in order to institute a more profound responsibility with and without the law. This is what he considers to be the sovereignty of scripture and of *iustitia Dei*—counter to moralism and to the moral reading of scripture.

When Luther emphasizes the original immorality prior to morals, he suspends the limit between good and evil, moral and immoral. The limit is questioned and ought to be drawn according to the situation. Each person is facing the moral imperative in the face of the other: the neighbor, the kin, the friend, and the enemy. It is indeed a question of interpretation, where the freedom given is disquieting, disturbing. There is an implicit imperative of being most immoral, in order to become moral. And there is always a risk that the most moral alternative turns out to be completely immoral. Moreover, becoming immoral by recognizing the abyssal potential for evil within the best of intentions would be necessary in order to escape the most common (and dangerous) illusion of human perfection. Hence, as opposed to universal moralists like Kant, there is not only an ethical imperative in Luther, but also the opposite, an immoral imperative: Sin boldly![47] The inherent ambivalence of good and evil, of morality and immorality, is a frequent occasion of humor and offensive talk. And the only remedy for the deadly earnestness of moral responsibility would be a good portion of self-irony.

FIVE

The Quest for Destruction

Luther and philosophy is a topic that requires careful consideration, since there is a certain discrepancy between Luther's rhetoric and his actual involvement in philosophical issues. His many more or less uncouth comments on philosophers as sophists, mad, or impious, of reason as a whore, and so forth, should be treated with a grain of salt and ascribed to his image as a barbarian and simple spokesman of the truth from the northern provinces of the Roman Empire. This is an image ascribed to him by his opponents and enemies and exploited in lampoons and caricatures, but it is also an image he cultivates in his raw and subversive style, sometimes with burlesque self-irony.[1] The arguments against philosophy and the mockery of the philosophers should therefore be considered rhetorically before we proceed to a discussion of their impact and consequences. If not, there are sometimes conclusions drawn concerning Luther's alleged rejection of philosophy in general and Aristotelian metaphysics in particular, which have limited foothold in the texts. The barbarian image is deceptive insofar as Luther is an extremely subtle critic of philosophy and thus he cannot avoid getting involved in philosophical arguments. Some of the key arguments will here be discussed, with emphasis on Luther's destruction of metaphysics in the *Heidelberg Disputation* (1518) and *De servo arbitrio* (1525).

It would be incorrect to say that Luther rejects metaphysics and metaphysical arguments altogether. On the contrary: He struggles with metaphysics in many respects, and the passages where he struggles most intensively with metaphysical notions are also the ones that are philosophically most interesting. Luther's approach in the critique of metaphysics follows a similar pattern as what we have already observed in his critique of morality. The notion of destruction is a key to this form of critical involvement with philosophy: The conceptions of God and man that are based in Aristotelian metaphysics, including the essence and properties of God and the free will of human beings, are jeopardized and thus attacked, either in polemics and frontal attack or in ambush. Luther does not only confront the one or other notion in philosophical discourse, though; he attacks the very procedure for discovering truth, the speculative discourse of metaphysics which he labels "theology of glory" in the *Heidelberg Disputation*.

When questioning the first premises of this discourse, he gets involved in an effort at recovering their meaning within another theoretical framework, not according to *things*, but according to *scripture*. What options are there for analyzing this significant difference of rationality? The common strategy has been to separate Aristotle's "philosophical anthropology" from the pure and "single foundation" of all biblical hermeneutics, namely, the cross of Christ, as both Gerhard Ebeling and Walter von Loewenich have argued.[2] Thus, the *question* of metaphysics may be excluded. However, the confrontation between metaphysics and scripture is theoretically subtle in the *Heidelberg Disputation*, and I am not convinced that we understand it *better* if we take the conclusions as dogmatic prescripts rather than analyzing the problem and questioning the conditions of Luther's rationality. It is, as far as I can see, this *difference* which is puzzling, as if two ages or two paradigms are confronted within one short and extremely dense text. In this case we will leave the conclusions to the two theologians and raise a few questions instead. These questions are inherent to the text, and they are coming to the surface at the intersection between the two alternatives. Hence, we approach the text through a double reading, rather than rushing to the conclusion by prima facie excluding the one in favor of the other.

In the *Heidelberg Disputation*, this procedure is given another twist when Luther unfolds the logic of the cross: Suffering is preferred to works, weakness to power, madness to wisdom, evil to good. He apparently sees the need for overturning the hierarchy of values, indeed a *transvaluation* of values, as a logical consequence of the confrontation between glory and cross. But does this subversion of the categories influence the procedure of reading and understanding? Is it a stable and permanent change, or a permanent challenge to the linguistic system of conceptual differences? I will not only discuss philosophical and ethical but also the possible political consequences of this subversive logic of the cross.

Luther is reluctant to draw inferences from theology and metaphysics to politics, in particular because he fears the accusation that he is instigating turmoil or disobedience toward the rulers. It belongs to the puzzling paradoxes of Luther's argumentation that he ruthlessly criticizes the ecclesial authorities in Rome, accusing them of fraud and abuse of power, while preaching obedience and subordination to the princes in Germany. Still, there may be reason to ask whether we can accept Luther's normative separation of theology and politics as valid when it comes to the actual impact of his writings: Is there no connection between the critique of philosophy and the subsequent critique of political authorities which spread in Germany at the time? At the intersection between metaphysics and politics, the question of religion and thus political theology comes up, and thereby also the notion of a certain hiddenness of God—on the cross (*theologia crucis*) and in majesty (*theologia gloriae*). Hence, we have identified two topoi where this struggle on metaphysics takes place.

Per Crucem Destruuntur

In thesis 21, at the heart of the *Heidelberg Disputation,* we find this enigmatic expression: *per crucem destruuntur*—destruction by the cross. The cross is commonly referred to as a sign of suffering and death, and it still is: probably the most universal sign of suffering and death, not only in a Christian culture but cross-culturally, as they say. Paul the apostle identifies the cross as a place for the hidden God. Hence, according to Luther, the Christian *logos* begins with annihilation, with humiliation, with suffering, with death. The point of departure is thus identified as deformation and destruction. This is the place where God encounters the world, although, in Luther's words, "only showing his backside." No one can see God's face and live, Moses is told. And Luther refers to the story in Exodus 33 where Moses is only allowed to see the backside of God, *posteria Dei.*[3] He argues that God comes as an *alien,* in hiddenness, and the destruction is called God's alien work (*opus alienum*).[4] Luther underscores this hiddenness with a quotation from the prophet Isaiah: *Vere absconditus tu es Deus.*[5]

The logic Luther refers to as the logic of Paul, developed in scripture, is structured by some basic oppositions: action and passion, glory and humiliation, power and weakness, wisdom and folly, good and evil.[6] According to Paul's First Letter to the Corinthians and his Letter to the Philippians, both quoted here, these are elementary oppositions in various linguistic systems—Greek, Hebrew, or Latin. Similar patterns may be found in virtually all human languages, ancient or modern. In most cases we find that the linguistic structures give priority to the former at the expense of the latter; action rather than passion, power rather than weakness, good rather than evil, and so forth. However, in the logic of Paul, the cross overturns this hierarchy and becomes a sign of contradiction, of loss, of reversal. In Luther's reading of Paul, he points at the cross as the sign which institutes a *reversal* of opposites; it destructs and destructures the natural way of organizing the differences. It offers a different logic, a different way of reasoning. It draws a division that separates friends and enemies: Friends of the cross accept this reversal. Enemies of the cross reject it.[7]

Luther's argument is rhetorically structured as a controversy, with a clear opposition between true and false, good and evil, acceptance and rejection. The cross plays a key role in this opposition, yet at the same time it undermines the clear opposites of the controversy. The logic of the cross is different, since it *subverts* the very difference that was established between the "theology of glory," of which he accuses his opponents, and the "theology of the cross," which represents his own, paradoxical way of reading Paul. If we look for a genealogy of the notion of deconstruction in Derrida and *Destruktion* or *Abbau* in Heidegger, which strangely have become technical terms even beyond the limits of Continental philosophy, this is the place to start searching. Heidegger's dependence on this notion in Luther is well documented, and Derrida explicitly points at this conceptual background of the term, although he indicates that he belongs to a different "filiation."[8] If we consider the text as an example of *destruction* in the way Heidegger applies the term, there is indeed an effort at *destroying* notions which cover over a problem rather than opening it up *as* problematic, such as power, glory, wisdom, and goodness. Glory becomes the blending image of power, which blocks off the distinctions and the *differences* within the notion of God.

Beyond Good and Evil

After publishing the *Ninety-five Theses* in October 1517, Luther was overwhelmed by various and contradicting reactions, from vigorous support to harsh condemnation. Whereas he had discussed the theological basis for the praxis of penitence, his text was read as a massive attack on the church authorities and support of the common people. As soon as the discussion became public, the political issue got delicate and the need for clarification became urgent. This was the direct occasion for gathering the Augustinian friars in Heidelberg in April 1518. Luther had been asked to clarify and specify his position in order to avoid theological split and further conflicts within the order. Hence, many of his fellow friars had expected a strategic withdrawal to an orthodox position. They could not have been more mistaken. The disputation is no withdrawal but a polemical attack on speculative theology and philosophy.

The first twelve theological theses discuss the decisive difference between the works of God and the works of humans. The following six theses (13–18) reject the philosophical concept of free will and the ability of human beings to do good unless they act *in Christo* and are guided by the Spirit. The third part (19–24) is the most complex and in our context the most significant. Here Luther discusses the difference between *theologia gloriae* and *theologia crucis* and offers a devastating critique of speculative theology and philosophy, in particular when it comes to the notion of God as *ens entium* and *summum bonum*. The fourth part (25–28) is a demonstration of the sovereignty of God's love, which is not dependent on humans but "creates the loveable" out of worthless and fallen sinners. Thus the paradox of sovereign and destructive power which is established as contrast to Christ's suffering at the cross. In theses 19–20 Luther writes:

> (XIX) Not the one is rightly called a theologian who comprehends the invisible being [*invisibilia*] of God as if it was "clearly perceptible through that which has happened"; (XX) But the one who

> comprehends the visible and manifest *reverse side* [*posteria*] of God, seen through suffering and cross.[9]

Suffering and cross thus function as the *prism* through which the world is perceived, or, rather, the grammar which structures thought and perception in the light of scripture. The philosophical theology Luther criticizes defines God as *ens entium* and *summum bonum,* with the attributes power, virtue, justice, divine knowledge, goodness, and more. Luther adopts the opposite strategy: Power is acknowledged in weakness, wisdom in folly, and so forth. There is a change of priority and a transvaluation of values at work here. According to Luther, the Christian *logos* begins with annihilation, with humiliation, with suffering, with death; hence, with the quintessence of what Nietzsche scornfully calls the "slave morality." Luther's polemic runs opposite to Nietzsche: Master morality is a clear sign of hubris and the illusion of being superior to others, whereas the slave or servant of the cross recognizes what the matter is (*quod res est*). This is the very point of Luther's *destruction* by the cross (*per crucem destruuntur*):

> This is clear: He who does not know Christ does not know God hidden in suffering. Therefore he prefers glory to the cross, strength to weakness, wisdom to folly, and, in general, good to evil. [. . .] God can be found only in suffering and the cross, as has been said [. . .] for the works are being destroyed by the cross [*per crucem destruuntur*] and Adam is crucified, who is further built up [*aedificatur*] by works. It is impossible for a person not to be puffed up [*infletur*] by his good works unless he has first been deflated and destroyed [*destructus*] by suffering and evil until he knows that he is nothing in himself [*seipsum esse nihil*] and that the works are not his but God's.[10]

According to this logic of the cross, metaphysical discourse defines God's properties as powerful, active, good, and superior in all things. The conventional reading of scripture, in theology as well as philosophy, follows the same lines. Emphasizing the logic of Paul in scripture, however, Luther points at a *different* reading, which is inscribed in the former but subverts and destabilizes the logic of superiority. According to this second reading, power is *hiding* in weakness, actions are *hiding* in suffering, good is *hiding* in evil, etc. This *hiddenness sub contrario* (under the opposite) is the key to a new reading of this text: The hidden God makes the difference, the infinite difference, between good and evil, being and privation, acting and suffering.[11] And the cross is the sign of the reversal between the visible and the invisible.

The verbs in the quoted passage are worth noticing. The destruction by the cross is not merely a singular event which gives a particular conclusion; it is the *dynamic* between building up and destroying, between inflating and deflating, which characterizes this scriptural space between a reading of scripture guided by metaphysics and a reading where not only Christ but even the reader is suffering under the cross. This tension corresponds precisely to the tension between construction and destruction of sense: The reader is again and again constructing a meaning within the text, which according to Luther (and I think he might speak from experience here) tends to confirm her own goodness and superiority, as well as the infinite superiority of God's power and justice. Yet this construction needs to be crushed and demolished, Luther argues, before the text can be perceived in mere passivity. Suffering and evil are the modes of perception, or rather reception, that according to Luther distinguish this receptivity to the cross. The difference between construction and destruction is thus qualified as a *pathetic* difference, where pathos and passivity come prior to activity and the reconstruction of sense.[12]

Thesis 21, which is explained by the reference to destruction, runs as follows: "The theologian of glory calls the good evil and evil good. The theologian of the cross calls the thing what it is."[13] We find the basic moral categories of good and evil in the first sentence, where Luther accuses his opponents of a category mistake. Although Luther and Nietzsche differ in many respects, Nietzsche's *Genealogy of Morals* may be helpful in identifying the logic of Luther's argument, namely, to raise the question concerning the *value* of values, and thus take one step *beyond* the immediate definition of good and evil in order to question its legitimacy.

When Luther describes the *glory* of God as the highest value (which is devalued, or transvalued, by the cross), he appears to have the Greek word for glory in mind, *doxa*. Curiously, this word has two different meanings. First, it is the word for opinion or common sense, and as such it is well known from Plato. The second meaning is peculiar to the *Septuaginta* and the New Testament, where *doxa* also means "glory," a translation of the Hebrew *kabod*. The double sense of *doxa* (meaning/glory) is invoked by Luther in order to deconstruct the opposition between good and evil: His opponents are thus accused of taking the appearance, that is, the commonsensical notion of actions and events at face value, whereas a theology of the cross will call the things "by their right name." Hence, in every instance, in every judgment, they will presumably arrive at opposite conclusions and there is an inherent battle or fight (*pugna*) concerning the definitions, in which both sides accuse the other of complete misunderstanding.[14] Luther's point is therefore not to *reconcile* or mediate between the opposites but to draw the line of separation, and it runs exactly along this subversion of the terms good and evil.

If we apply a terminology which is well known from later philosophy, Luther rejects the effort at defining transcendence and transcendent entities like God exclusively in abstract terms. Instead, he scrutinizes the conditions of possibility for understanding these phenomena *in the world,* thereby including questions of ethics as well as epistemology. Let me return to the argument he gives for this approach, where the *place* of hiding, destruction, and suffering is directly linked to the logic of reversal, in other words, an encounter with the God who is hiding *sub contrario:* "Who does not know Christ does not know the God who hides in suffering. Hence, he prefers works to suffering, glory to cross, power to weakness, wisdom to madness, and universally the good to evil."[15] Luther's redefinition follows a particular logic; let us simply call it the logic of difference. In many respects he presupposes the rationality he criticizes. Still, the difference separates two prisms of understanding that remain incommensurable, divided by this destruction which overturns the power structures inherent to the linguistic system: Suffering is preferred to works, weakness to power, madness to wisdom, evil to good.

This logic of hiddenness corresponds to a strategy of perplexity, of paradoxality: a statement that deliberately runs counter to intuition. Luther's argument is connected to the immediate danger of hubris, of becoming "inflated" and self-possessed by the thought of doing well unto others. As soon as this thought takes possession of a person and becomes the measure for judging between good and evil, he argues that the cross ought to come in like a sharp needle and let the inflated self collapse like a punctuated balloon.[16] The cross therefore becomes the key figure in this process of perception. The cross is drawn across the original cognition, the so-called natural assessment of good and evil, of power and suffering. Luther does not *leave* the sphere of action, of actualizing good and evil like speculative metaphysics may be accused of; he applies the cross deliberately in order to crucify wisdom, works, desire, and power. He rejects the notion of metaphysics, or, rather, the metaphysical framework for theology and anthropology, because it blows up the self.

But how should we label his effort at redefining *reality,* a proper understanding of being that says, "what is the case (*quod res est*)"? The criticism of metaphysics is an effort at *redefining the concept of reality,* and in that respect *it is itself metaphysical.* Still, Luther also redefines the *task* of metaphysics, its focus, and the criteria for judging between good and evil. What he suggests is a subversive metaphysics that continuously redefines the normal or natural way of defining "things," that is, phenomena, actions; the world as it appears to "us."

Between the world as "appearance" and the world "as such," between the word and the thing, between the eye and what it sees, between the self and its self-perception, Luther situates the cross and the logic of scriptural difference. Hence, he is always *suspicious* of metaphysical judgments but he cannot refrain from referring to them.[17] This hermeneutics of suspicion is guided by the principle of scripture rather than his own spirit, which he notoriously mistrusts.[18] Following the principle outlined in the *Heidelberg Disputation,* he would never be able to perceive the world, and not even perceive of himself, apart from this critical and subversive principle of cognition. Cross and scripture are the two conditions of possibility for this theory of knowledge. We could simply call it *scriptural* reasoning.

Two Economies of the Gift

The immediate historical context of the *Heidelberg Disputation* is Luther's attack on the practice of indulgences, and the first eighteen theses can be read as an explanation and principal defense of his position. I therefore take the practice of indulgences as an example to illustrate Luther's point. The system of indulgences is merely analyzed from a formal point of view, though, as an example of a particular way of thinking. It illustrates how this economy works and how it interferes with different kinds of logic.

The main question was not economical in the common sense of the term, concerned with cheating or the like—it was a question of theological rationality. When it became possible to pay off moral debt, the consequence was that questions of guilt and grace, sin and sovereignty, were organized within an economy of giving and taking, paying and receiving—in short, a barter economy. This is where Luther's protest intervenes: a protest against the system as such. Grace allows no calculable system at all, he argues, which means that the logic of the gift must be thought completely otherwise, in a total difference from the barter economy.[19] In principle, this thought of grace remains un-thought, or un-heard-of within the barter economy, owing to its absolute difference from the system of giving and taking. It remains incompatible with that system as a whole, and this incompatibility is the basis of reflecting upon the difference. Hence, rather than identifying the different characteristics of each economy, Luther underscores the difference which is already there, presupposed and taken as given, and the recognition or discovery of this difference is bound to revelation: a divine gift.

Luther discusses a theological difference between works and grace, but is it also possible to analyze the logical conditions for the difference spelled out here? It depends on how exclusively the "truth" and the "Word" of theology are defined. The difference may at least *also* be identified as a logical difference, structuring the logic of the gift. Accordingly, there are at least two ways of reflecting upon the logic of the gift, and according to our previous definition they remain heterogeneous.

The barter economy seems to work well without the other economy. The other economy, however, the non-economical or hyper-economical economy, seems to presuppose that first economy in order to make sense. Only in the moment when that other economy disturbs and rejects the first-order economy does it makes sense, by insisting on the absolute difference. Thereby the barter economy remains a presupposition for defining what the gift and the logic of grace mean in the first place. *Without* this system of giving and taking, of regulating guilt, punishment, and absolution, this absolute gift and the absolute absolution do not make sense. The gift makes sense only in presupposing the difference and expecting that the regular economy of indulgences as economical figure, or, rather, as example of a way of thinking, will always exist, that it will never collapse or be destroyed as long as there are human beings reflecting on their guilt. For similar reasons Luther cannot accept the general and permanent suspension of the law.

From a historical perspective, this is one of the points where Luther's disputation immediately interferes with the economic and political state of affairs in late-medieval Europe. The feudal system was based on faithfulness to the local lord, yet the *pressure* on this feudal system of mutual obligations had gradually increased during the fifteenth and early sixteenth centuries, due to a rising population. The system was also under pressure from a growing monetary economy within the cities. Hence, the loyalty to the lords and princes was gradually being felt as an unfair and unbearable suppression by the peasants, who on several occasions had revolted in Bohemia, Switzerland, and Germany. The web of mutual obligations between lord and servant, princes and serfs, followed a logic comparable to the economy of guilt, organized and extended by the letters of indulgences.

Hence, the system of indulgences became understandable to the common people and the economic bondage was recognizable. When Luther insists on a direct relationship to God, who gives grace and pays off the guilt without expectations of anything in return, this statement may have revolutionary consequences when transferred to the economic and political sphere. The argument follows the political logic of sovereignty: Debts may be forgiven and abolished because God is perceived as the absolute sovereign; hence, the entire system of mutual obligations and debts is suspended.

In the years after 1518, this logic was applied in political revolts, such as in the Twelve Articles of Memmingen (1525), which was the political manifesto of the rebelling peasants and miners.[20] Luther explicitly rejected such a *metabasis eis allo genos*, that is, a transference of his argument to the mundane and economic sphere, but it was nevertheless extremely popular and proved impossible to control. One aspect of this *metabasis* is the demand of canceling debt. The other is the image of God as sovereign ruler, suspending or even *crushing* the power of subordinate rulers, possibly even favoring the poor rather than the rich, the suffering rather than the powerful, the weak rather than the strong. When we read the quoted passage from thesis 21 of the *Heidelberg Disputation* once more, we may find it remarkable if this was considered a non-political statement by its author:

> This is clear: He who does not know Christ does not know God hidden in suffering. Therefore he prefers acts to suffering, glory to the

> cross, strength to weakness, wisdom to folly, and, in general, good to evil. These are the people whom the apostle calls "enemies of the cross of Christ" [Philippeans 3:18], for they hate the cross and suffering and love works and the glory of works. Thus they call the good of the cross evil and the evil of a deed good. God can be found only in suffering and the cross [. . .].[21]

It is not difficult to detect an immediate social background of the opposites thus mentioned in late-medieval Europe: Glory points toward the papacy, strength toward the princes, wisdom toward the universities and the dominant synthesis of metaphysics and theology; the "theology of glory." Hence, when the words of Paul are emphasized and read literally in this preference for the poor, for the weak, for the fools, it challenges the basic structures of the society in central Europe during the sixteenth century. This is at least the way Luther understands the development leading to political tumults and upheavals only a few years later.[22] If we adopted a Marxist perspective on the text, the social and political explanation would precede and determine the theological arguments rather than vice versa. Hence, when the social structure breaks up from within, it is gradually superseded by centralization of power and absolutism in this period. Still, the disputation gives us a glimpse of a more complicated interplay of theology and politics when Luther insists on a destabilization and reversal of the opposites instituted by the cross.

A political reading of the *Heidelberg Disputation* is therefore not exactly far-fetched but still politically dangerous. Although Luther later warns against such a *directly* political interpretation of theology, this rejection seems more ambiguous, given the dominant logic of the *Heidelberg Disputation*. In 1525 a similar way of reasoning justified the peasants' revolt during the German Peasants' War. The idealism and hopes were high, but the result was disastrous. Still, whereas Luther was revolutionary in other respects, he seems to be extremely anxious about the possible *political* consequences of his thought. Hence, he restricts the use of this *other* logic of the gift to *interiority,* to the spiritual and the inner man—whatever that means and however it may be isolated from the political.[23]

In the exterior and societal sphere, Luther claims, the normal economy and power structures remain valid, whereas in the interior sphere, everything is different. This is later called the doctrine of two kingdoms or two regiments. Its biblical foundation remains problematic and its political applicability contested, in particular after the experiences of the Third Reich in Germany. Still, it is not difficult to see why it soon became a pragmatic necessity during the upheavals in the 1520s. However justified it would be to separate the two discourses, I find it necessary to point out that the author is unable to control the impact of the texts, their limits of validity. When Luther proclaims a radical freedom, such control becomes all the more problematic. Hence, a text like the *Heidelberg Disputation* also functions as a political pamphlet, written during a tense political situation that ended with increased political conflicts and divisions in Europe.

When Luther's political legacy is discussed, it should not be restricted to the so-called political tracts but include the texts from the early Reformation that were written in a politico-theological context and respond to political as well as theological issues. That makes Luther's authorship and legacy less coherent but much more relevant for political history and philosophy. The inner divisions and contradictions in Luther's thought imply that the political legacy of the Reformation remains internally divided, pointing in the direction of further revolutions on the one hand, in 1525 as well as in 1848, but also toward centralization and enlightened absolutism on the other. For the history of the West, political theology remains a controversial issue that may merit from further inquiries into the period of the Reformations.

SIX

The Quest for Clarity

One of Luther's most portentous debates was his controversy with Pope Leo X. After the *Ninety-five Theses* and subsequent articles had been condemned by the pope in *Exurge Domine,* Luther wrote an apology in the form of forty-one theses with extended explanations in the pamphlet called *Assertio* (1520). It was published only a few weeks before Luther was finally excluded from the Roman Catholic Church on January 3, 1521. It is written by a man who is already more outside than inside the community of the holy and the orthodox. Thus almost excommunicated he communicates back *in,* to those who represent the authority of the tradition and the cornerstone of the church.

This polemical situation forced Luther to elaborate on his theory of scripture, with emphasis on its theological authority. I venture a double reading of Luther, as a non-dogmatic repetition of his text: On the one hand, I discuss Luther's approach to scripture, and thus introduce some theological theories of hermeneutics (such as by Ebeling, Jüngel, Beisser), which argue that we should continue reading and interpreting the biblical texts by following Luther's procedure for the interpretation of scripture: *sola scriptura.* On the other hand, I *question* three of the basic premises of their hermeneutical theory: the univocal authority of the text (the single reading), their emphasis on the true *sense* of the text (and consequently the rejection of non-sense), and the *dialectical* exclusion of hiddenness, including the most *problematic* topos of the text. All three methodological presuppositions correspond to the philosophical hermeneutics of Gadamer, and may thus be considered *ontological* presuppositions within the hermeneutical paradigm of dialectical understanding. Rather than presenting an alternative theory here, I will discuss alternative readings of Luther, since I think that there are certain traits of his theology that resist the kind of hermeneutic synthesis that has dominated the (traditional as well as liberal) polemics on Luther, and on Protestant theology, in the twentieth century. Hence, I focus on a few simple strategies of his textual theory and analyze them as examples of scripture with lower-case letters, that is, according to a more generic theory of scripture as writing. This is explicitly an invitation to further controversy on the issue.

Luther's Polemics: Rejecting Interpretation

In *Assertio,* Luther addressed the accusations of heresy formulated by Pope Leo in each of the forty-one theses, and they are mostly given in return. One of the papal concerns is that Luther reads the scripture according to his own spirit, which is strictly proscribed.[1] Luther counters this argument in the introduction with a general consideration on the relationship between the Holy Scriptures and the human commentaries that according to the pontifex are supposed to be normative for understanding them. If these commentaries are considered necessary for understanding, he argues, the clear words of scripture are subjugated to the disputed and obscure words of human beings. This must be an insight given to him by Satan himself, Luther claims, thus rhetorically well prepared for open and friendly dialogue, as always.

However, if these traditional texts of the fathers and the saints of the church represent the condition for understanding and the limits of access to the scriptures, then he argues that one would never understand the scriptures according to their proper spirit, the spirit of scripture (*spiritus scripturae*).[2] On the contrary, he claims, one has to look for the spirit *within* the scriptures *first*—and not by the church fathers or the commentators—since that is the place God has chosen as the secret haunt (*latibulum*) of his spirit. Consequently, this must be the *place* where an encounter with the spirit is most probable, although never guaranteed. Luther therefore turns the relationship between the tradition and scripture upside down: Neither the tradition nor the pontifex is in a position to judge about the scripture, and not Luther, either, for that matter. He thinks that *scripture* should judge about all things and thus be given priority in all issues of controversy.[3] This movement is decisive, since scripture is posited at the border line between two contrary interpretations and given the authority to judge between them. Scripture will have to be conferred when other meanings are divided, not the other way around. Moreover, *scripture* must be able to arrive at a decision in a situation of undecidability. And this is exactly Luther's point when it comes to scripture: "that it is, by itself, most certain, most simple, most open, its own interpreter [*sui ipsius interpres*]; probing, judging, and illuminating all in all."[4]

The relationship between tradition and scripture is therefore not only reversed, so that scripture is given priority versus the tradition and all the interpreters, but it is also established as its *own* interpreter, being interpreted by itself. The formulation is strangely circular, or rather elliptic, suggesting that the scriptures are able to interpret themselves apart from every interpreter. Does it imply that the scriptures represent a self-sufficient hermetic corpus, shining upon the reader in utter radiant completeness? Not exactly. I argue that this circular formulation indicates the need for a *double* reading of the text, one which basically follows a general and conventional rule of reading, be it moral, dogmatic, or traditional; whereas the second emphasizes the *grammar* of the text—and this is the decisive point: It is the grammar of the text that may open up the text according to decisive linguistic differences.[5] The subchapter "Justification by Grammar Alone" will serve as a concrete example of such a double reading.

Luther's approach to biblical texts was perceived as unconventional among his contemporaries and harshly condemned by his opponents. Erasmus, too, attacked Luther's interpretation of scripture, although in other respects he was a peaceable man who avoided controversy. Pope Leo and other adversaries seem to have been less peaceable, and the massive resistance forced Luther to develop a more elaborate theory of interpretation—although he explicitly rejects interpretation. At some level he is of course interpreting, but he is cautious to avoid the impression that the disagreement is merely a question of different opinions on the text—or more or less arbitrary procedures for text exegesis. This is not a question of procedures, he argues; it is a question of truth.

Assertoric statements about the truth are not necessarily true statements, though. The question therefore comes up: How to deal with these statements? There are basically three options in traditional scholarship on Luther: rejection, confirmation, and hermeneutic interpretation. The first two options were the standard positions during the first three centuries of confessional apologetics. The Catholics rejected Luther, the Protestants confirmed his statements, often with some adjustments or modifications, and thus the arguments went on. Nietzsche ironically comments that the religious wars represent the greatest progress of the masses up to his own days, since they indicate that the masses had started treating concepts with respect: "Religious wars start only when the finer quarrels among sects have refined common reason so that even the mob becomes subtle and takes trifles seriously, and actually considers it possible that the 'eternal salvation of the soul' might hinge on slight differences between concepts."[6]

Hermeneutic Philosophy and Theological Polemics in the Twentieth Century

The third option has dominated the field since the 1960s, namely the hermeneutic interpretation. The period corresponds to the heyday of hermeneutic philosophy, beginning with Hans-Georg Gadamer's *Wahrheit und Methode* (1960) and remaining a significant strand of phenomenology for the next four decades. Scholars from Habermas to Ricoeur and from Jüngel to Caputo and Vattimo have developed hermeneutic approaches within the human and social sciences. Although Gadamer's theory of language, art, and tradition has been challenged by critical theory, deconstruction, and discourse analysis, it has remained one of the dominant strands of so-called Continental philosophy. I will emphasize the close link between theological and philosophical hermeneutics in the following discussion of Luther's scriptural theory and its critical sting undermining the hermeneutic praxis of interpretation. Its relevance is by no means limited to theological inquiry, though. In a way similar to Luther's critique of metaphysics and morality, it raises the question of truth and method within philosophy, too.

Hermeneutics is originally more of a theological and juridical discipline than a philosophical one. The Protestant exegesis of the Bible has given significant contributions to its development in early modernity.[7] Schleiermacher establishes hermeneutics as a post-critical method of exegesis and understanding, whereas Wilhelm Dilthey develops it into a philosophical method and argues that it should become the theoretical and methodological foundation for all the humanities. The friends and colleagues Rudolf Bultmann and Martin Heidegger apply, respectively, theological and philosophical hermeneutics as theoretical framework for their existential anthropology, whereas Gadamer's *Wahrheit und Methode* becomes the standard reference work of hermeneutic philosophy in the twentieth century.

Hence, it is not exactly surprising that hermeneutics becomes the dominant approach in Protestant theology in the second half of the twentieth century. Moreover, the works of Martin Luther play a double role in this development: on the one hand as methodological legitimation of hermeneutics, because he emphasizes the clarity of scripture and the "Word of God" as the primary authority and theoretical basis for theology; on the other hand as a classical author whose texts are interpreted hermeneutically. If we add to this picture the exemplary role of the historical figure Martin Luther, a Protestant archetype, it is not difficult to imagine that there are several occasions for circular argumentation. Indeed, for theologians who simply agree with Luther and see his words as a testimony of the truth, there is hardly any reason to question the inferences from source to interpretation, from text to truth. Just as the alleged clarity of scripture, they appear to be self-evident.

Gerhard Ebeling was one of the dominant figures in developing hermeneutic theology in the 1960s, in a theory based on Luther, Gadamer, and later even the speech-act theory of Austin.[8] Ebeling's theory of hermeneutics is at its best when he remains close to Luther's texts, as in his close reading of Luther's first Lectures on the Psalms (1513–1515).[9] In a recent article, Volker Leppin discusses Ebeling as biographer in relation to his many text interpretations of Luther.[10] Leppin argues that "the man Luther" seems to disappear behind a theological construction of the ideal Dr. Martin Luther, as Ebeling perceives him. At the same time, Ebeling needs this ideal construction as guarantee for his own theological position.[11] For a historically minded scholar like Leppin, this is untenable. For mere methodological reasons, he is obliged to present a number of *different* contemporary perspectives on

Luther's biography: the voice of his enemies, of other contemporaries, perspectives contradicting one another—and then critically discuss each perspective from historical distance. The historical biographer can neither allow himself an atemporal idealization nor the central first-person perspective on his object of study.

A different but similar problem, namely, that of idealization and idealism, comes up when we read Ebeling's *interpretations* of Luther's texts. He is a careful and perceptive reader of the texts, and hence there is always a lot to learn from his exegesis.[12] Yet he often gets so absorbed by the sources that it becomes difficult to distinguish the voice of the reader from the voice of the text.[13] By less rigorous scholars than Ebeling, the same praxis may result in what I would call ventriloquism in scholarship: At an advanced stage, this means that the written source you study begins to speak from your belly or express itself directly through your pen. In these cases the second and third options above (confirmation and interpretation) tend to converge. Hence, there is no longer any need to distinguish between one voice (or text) and the other. The authority of the author (Luther) becomes your authority, and vice versa. This could happen to be the result of a perfect fusion of hermeneutic horizons, but it is not necessarily good scholarship. The by now classical work of Friedrich Beisser on *Claritas scripturae bei Martin Luther* (1966) is in my opinion an example of such circular argumentation. The book is discussed more thoroughly below. I could also mention *Theologia Crucis* (1970) by Klaus Schwarzwäller. The combination of scholars being convinced of the genius of their object of study, of its relevance, and of their natural role as apologetics against virtually all other positions is not optimal for open and critical discourse. Admittedly, this latter tendency by no means represents the general impression of Luther scholarship today; but hermeneutic interpretations are still dominating the field.

Like Martin Luther, Gadamer is first of all critical of scholars who believe that the truth is found by following a particular method of interpretation, which is based on a means-end rationality, what the Greeks called *technē*.[14] Instead, he advocates a procedure of questions and answers where the reader remains open to the message of the text and the intentions of the author. A successful understanding is described as a fusion of horizons, where the new knowledge is dialectically incorporated in the knowledge you already have: "In the procedure of understanding a real fusion of horizons takes place: with the outline of a historical horizon, its sublation [*Aufhebung*] is already accomplished."[15] As the term *Aufhebung* indicates, Gadamer explicitly subscribes to a Hegelian dialectic, which pertains to his notion of history and tradition as well as his notion of experience and the process of understanding. He even argues that language as such (*logos*) is structured speculatively in accordance with Hegel's dialectics.[16]

The *dialectical* theology of Karl Barth and his numerous followers also subscribes to a Hegelian understanding of dialectics and applies it as the basic rationality of theological inquiry. Hence, it is not far-fetched when an external critic like Graham White accuses the German Luther research for adapting the framework and rationality of German Idealism, and Risto Saarinen criticizes the predominantly *transcendental* notion of God among Luther scholars.[17] Not only Luther research, but German systematic theology in general, from Pannenberg to Moltmann, from Sölle to Jüngel has adapted this speculative condition for understanding the Christian *logos*—in history and at present.

"Being that can be understood, is language," writes Gadamer, and there is a clear reference to the Hegelian understanding of the Christian logos as mediation.[18] A certain moral imperative and subsequent moralization concerning the notion of God follows from this dialectical presupposition, either we consider Gadamer's philosophical or Jüngel's theological hermeneutics. According to this dialectical *logos*, the Word of God is given and understood completely and without reserve in the revelation.[19] Hence, there cannot be any hiddenness which escapes this *logos*, except for the mystery of God self, which is clarified in the logic of cross and resurrection—the paradigmatic example of *Aufhebung*. There is no space left for the hidden God in his majesty, which is questioning the basic presuppositions for this *logos* and the dialectical understanding.

There is a trace of this radical hiddenness in Luther's theology which seems to question the basic premises for hermeneutic interpretation. Moreover, it seems to jeopardize the moral imperative for understanding and indicate that the decisive questions ought to be looked for elsewhere. This is the trace I follow through the controversy between Erasmus and Luther, where questions of interpretation, of truth, and of morality are at stake. I will emphasize the question of *logos* within the *Heidelberg Disputation*, where Luther argues for a *destruction* of metaphysics—and a subversion of our moral intuitions concerning the difference between good and evil. The arguments are puzzling, and they demonstrate some basic paradoxes that run counter to the presuppositions of hermeneutic theology and philosophy.

Changing Perspectives: Scripture Interpreting Scripture

Luther's assessment of the complex set of scriptures collected in the Christian canon takes into account that the scriptures are historically conditioned and sometimes appear to be obscure. First, he hints at the praxis of expounding obscure places in the scriptures through less obscure ones, allowing scripture to illuminate the reader with more profound knowledge. The clarity is there, "shining" within the texts, he claims. His intention is not to harmonize the Bible text as a message without contradictions, though. On the contrary, he gives special attention to the contradictions in order to specify and thus *clarify* them. This exegesis begins with a detailed grammatical analysis of their plain "historical" sense. Within this analysis, however, he describes how their meaning suddenly breaks open, like a gate that is opened up or a clearing in the deep forest. The reader is invited to study the text most carefully, in every little detail and with particular emphasis on the grammar of the text. Yet in the final analysis, the understanding of this text is beyond his or her control, beyond the *spirit* and the reason of the reader, of any reader.

The most learned reader could therefore misunderstand the text just as easily as the naive or simpleminded reader. The learned scholar has the advantages of his knowledge, but also the disadvantages of his knowledge. And the latter are normally greater than the former. Hence, *every* reader, whether wise or foolish, will have to go through the humiliating destruction of wisdom described by Paul: "For the message about the cross is foolishness to those who are perishing, but to us who are being saved it is the power of God. For it is written, 'I will destroy the wisdom of the wise, and the discernment of the discerning I will thwart'" (1 Corinthians 1:18–19). Paul's point, which is once more emphasized by Luther, is that the same text is read in radically diverging ways: for the one to downfall and decay, for the other to new insight. Wisdom is thereby destroyed, not by an intellectual rejection, but by the cross.[20]

The surprising turn by Luther, however, is that the power of *decision* is thereby ascribed to scripture and not to the wise or the fool. Hence, if we follow his logic of interpretation, scripture itself draws the line of distinction and separation between one reading and the other. The border line goes through the text itself, disclosing it in two directions: one in the direction of wisdom, another in the direction of foolishness. And this movement, this division of its sense, proceeds *from within the text*. Hence, it indicates that a *double reading* is not only possible, but required in order to let *scripture* become the interpreter ("probing, judging, illuminating").[21]

Luther's counterintuitive usage of the term "scripture" may need some further clarification. A number of critics and adversaries, including Erasmus and Pope Leo, are afraid that Luther undermines the moral authority of scripture when everyone is supposed to read it on their own, and in their vernacular language. Luther turns the argument around and maintains that everyone who reads the scripture with emphasis on *saving* its moral authority is *judged by the text*.[22] From Luther's perspective, a reading of the text according to its moral authority means understanding it at one level, yet basically misunderstanding it at another. Instead of a double reading, which keeps the judgment about its meaning *open—in suspenso*—the text would then be simplified and its meaning would be stabilized within a moral framework where nothing decisive is at stake. A clarification of its meaning is important for Luther, but not a clarification according to the meanings or expectations, not even the interpretation, of the reader.

Generally, Luther suspects that all readers look for *confirmation* of their opinions when reading scripture. One of his favorite examples, which is mentioned in the *Heidelberg Disputation*, then condemned by Pope Leo X, defended by Luther in *Assertio,* and later to become the main topic of his controversy with Erasmus, is the question of free will. He argues that the notion (or "illusion") of free will, "blinds" the reader and makes her unable to see anything other than her own perspective.[23] This interpretive dilemma is the reason why the question of *liberum arbitrium* becomes so important for Luther. And when the discussion gets going, he does not hesitate to discuss metaphysics and philosophical anthropology, as well.

A similar objection applies when it comes to morality. The reader who seeks moral guidance will easily find it in scripture, but tends to overlook the *different* perspectives on moral perfection expressed by Paul. Hence, Luther suspects that moral desires for perfection take control over the process of interpretation, whatever the text has to say about the issue, rather than taking the reader by surprise, allowing the usual categories of understanding to be interrupted. In case of a 'double reading,' however, a demarcation line is drawn through the text: Depending on the topic of the text, the first reading will follow the rule of morality, of metaphysics or economics—in other words, a reading according to the law—and this is indeed one option of understanding it, although it tends to confirm the expectations of the reader. Therefore, only when the *second* circle of understanding is drawn—with emphasis on the difference separating the two circles, which destructs and destructures that rule—will the text be exposed to a *double* reading.[24] Accordingly, this space in between the two readings suspends the first conclusion and allows the text to reveal its *inherent* difference, according to its grammatical structure. Even when this second reading establishes a completely different perspective, it is related to the first one through their common source in the text passage. The second reading therefore interrupts and displaces the former.

This is only a first outline of the way I read Luther's deliberations on text and interpretation, based on his contested and circular claim that scripture ought to interpret scripture. How literally his critique of "interpretations" should be taken is itself a matter of interpretation. If it would be taken literally in the sense that philological, grammatical, and even contextual deliberations are superfluous, the interpreter would lose all credibility. On the contrary: These deliberations are all necessary in order to avoid simple misunderstandings of the text. Still, the critique of interpretations should be taken strictly literally in the sense that the *letter* of the text is to be studied carefully according to its grammatical and temporal structures.

Hence, there is a minor displacement and shift of emphasis from the first "scripture" to the second "scripture"; between the scripture which is to be interpreted and the scripture *interpreting* scripture itself (*sua ipse*), or rather, the *scriptural* way of interpreting. This displacement is sufficient to open up the space of interpretation *within* the text. If the first reading is circular and draws a conclusion, then the second reading may draw another conclusion, not in order to close the question of its sense but in order to open it. Hence, the tension between two different readings allows the text to open up rather than to remain closed. In *De servo arbitrio* Luther defines revelation as "a kind of door, or an opening, which is plain for all to see and even illuminates the simple."[25] The procedure thus outlined as a double reading gives a first impression of the space opening up within scripture, indeed *between* scripture and scripture. The tension between two readings allows new insight to break open from within the text. This movement *within* the text, in the scriptural space between two readings, may indicate a rejection, destruction, or subversion of beliefs and metaphysical convictions about the truth. A telling example of such double reading, based on a difference identified within the grammar of the text, is found in Luther's detailed exposition of the term *'iustitia Dei.'*

Justification by Grammar Alone

It has been called the key passage to the entire Reformation: Luther's famous rediscovery of justification by faith according to Paul's Letter to the Romans. The term under discussion is the *'iustitia Dei'* (Romans 1:17; 3:21–22), the justice of God, a grammatical construction Luther struggled with during his lectures on Paul's Letter to the Romans in 1515[26] and later returns to in *De servo arbitrio* (1525):

> Then there is the statement [by Paul] that they lack the glory of God. You can take "the glory of God" here in two senses, active and passive. This is an example of Paul's habit of using Hebraisms. Actively, the glory of God is that by which God glories in us; passively it is that by which we glory in God. It seems to me, however, that it ought to be taken passively here [. . .] Similarly, the righteousness of God in Latin means the righteousness that God possesses, but a Hebrew would understand it as the righteousness that we have from God and in the sight of God.[27]

Toward the end of the quoted passage, Luther points at two possible readings of the genitive construction *'iustitia Dei.'* In Latin, this construction opens up for two grammatical options—as it does in Greek—the one is *objective* genitive, the other *subjective* genitive. The former had been the dominant reading of the Latin text; hence "God's justice" is more or less automatically understood in the *active* sense, serving as the highest criterion for moral perfection. This is the justice that is God's own property, whereas the latter, the *passive* sense, has gone out of common usage in Latin; it has been marginalized or completely overlooked. Although Luther in *De servo arbitrio* argues in favor of the latter reading ("it seems to me . . ."), the result of his discussion and his hesitation is that both readings are sustained, whereas priority is given to the latter (*subjective* genitive); the justice by which God justifies the unjust human being by grace alone. This latter reading, emphasizing the passive or *received* justice, cannot simply replace the other reading since both are *possible,* but it is explicitly emphasized and therefore it contributes to a proper understanding of the former.

Since Luther's grammatical reading of the term *'iustitia Dei,'* these passages by Paul have been studied, analyzed and described in all thinkable manners and should hardly be able to contain any further secrets. It is still a fascinating construction, however, insofar as this is considered to be the basic term within the entire letter—a point which is supported by rhetorical analysis. We therefore end up with a *double* reading of this term, and of Paul's letter as a whole, without having final criteria for deciding in favor of one reading or the other. They are both written into the original text, and Luther explicitly argues that the duplicity is based on Paul's understanding of the *Hebrew* language, expressing one active and one passive sense within one and the same construction.[28]

The Hebrew grammar can with a certain right be said to express the *original* sense of the expression, not to forget the status of Hebrew as God's own language, but within common Greek or Latin usage, that sense has been forgotten. When it is reintroduced in Luther's text, it represents a supplement to the common reading but a supplement that destructs, overcomes, and inverts the "common" sense from within. Hence, the *Hebrew* sense of the expression *'iustitia Dei'* is, according to Luther, literally "the justice one has [received] from [*ex*] God and has in front of [*coram*] God."[29] This analysis of the term is strictly grammatical but includes the different layers of the word originating from the history of different languages trying to describe a thing, a word, an event, a rationality, that is, a λόγος that repeatedly will have to be redefined and rediscovered in order to remain similar to itself, or at least recognizable, and let the readers unveil the paradoxical duplicity of the term.

The duplicity of Luther's reading of the text demonstrates one of the dilemmas connected to his approach: The grammatical reading makes both readings possible, but emphasizes the latter, which makes the justice of God (in the passive sense) public and accessible for all. Still, the meaning of this text nevertheless *remains* secret due to the impossibility of giving it a single signification. As soon as this grammatical construction is stabilized and given a particular meaning, for instance, *either* active *or* passive, it is emptied of its linguistic power to provoke change. As soon as its significance is fixed within a particular system, be it moral or metaphysical, theological, political, or ideological, the *surplus* of meaning gets lost, or, rather, remains hidden within the text. What thereby gets lost is the possibility of *transcending* a particular horizon of interpretation and of destabilizing a system of thought from within.

What makes such a transgression possible, however, is basically the discovery of that distinction, that difference between justice and justice, already present in the history of scripture. It is even possible to argue that the difference between two readings, active and passive, *institutes* that history *as* a history of justice and responsibility. Scripture thus reveals the duplicity of what has become stabilized, standardized, and controlled within a particular system of meaning, and subsumed to the authority of the magistrate and the moral, sacramental, and hierarchic order of the church. The very *scripturality* or writtenness points at a meaning of the word "justice" which absolutely differs from the moral order, escaping the political and pious control of worldly and ecclesiastic authorities. Scripture understood as scripture, and not simply preaching, praying, or professing the word(s), gives access to a space of *freedom* within language, and thus within human reality. In that sense, scripture becomes the condition of possibility for *conceiving* the world according to this gift of grace *qua* gift of justice (*ex Deo*) and at the same time it redefines the conditions for that conception.

This is only one example of how the double reading of a text destructures and therefore redefines the conditions of understanding, not necessarily as a confrontation with other readings, but simply as a rediscovery of another meaning which was already there, within the text, yet according to Luther it had slumbered there for centuries. It is hidden, undiscovered, and then suddenly it lightens up the text from within and destabilizes the entire biblical corpus. For Luther, at least, it seems clear that all the scriptures ought to be read otherwise after this discovery, with due respect to this distinction between justice and justice, possibly redefining the meaning of the texts, or even destroying the first reading from within the text. Luther obviously sees it as a rediscovery of revelation, which displays the very structure of revelation in scripture; it comes up as a repetition of an earlier revelation which opens up the text for a differing sense, according to the second reading. The tension between the two readings, and the movement initiated by the text, makes this passivity of reading possible: the passive reception of a gift.

So far I have emphasized the formal and grammatical aspects of this procedure. Luther's argument is profoundly theological, but the formal structure is not bound to this text. It has a generic scope and could any time be repeated with another text. The entire process *may* be repeated in merely theological terms, and then it is perceived as the gift of God, and the revelation of the Holy Spirit through the grace in Jesus Christ. However, there is nothing in the previous analysis prescribing such formulations. The formal analysis and reduction to the question of grammar makes it *possible* to study the actual procedure ending up with this conclusion, but in the moment such a conclusion is fixed, there is always a danger that the conclusion consumes the actual point here: the rediscovery of a revelation. Hence, our focus on grammatical details and formal procedures is a reminder of the necessity of keeping the text open. The movement of the text may cross out Luther's conclusion as soon as it solidifies in another dogma.

My point is not to reject the formulation of dogma. On the contrary: Few linguistic expressions are more worthwhile studying in every detail than the condensation of dogma. But the dogmas, like all other linguistic expressions, fall into forgetfulness as soon as they are taken for granted and lose their provocative force, which falls into obscurity, be it the obscurity of history, of metaphysics, of dogma itself, or of scripture. Luther suggests another approach to dogma and to scripture, and even to the hard substance of metaphysics, and that is to study their grammar in every detail in order to rediscover the mystery of the linguistic expression and bring it to the fore. What thereby becomes visible in the given example is exactly what Luther also reformulates in theological terms: It is the *sacrifice* of Christ, the *justice* which is offered, the *secrecy* of the cross.

The grammatical reading of Paul's Letter to the Romans is therefore directly linked to revelation, to the principle *sola scriptura*, and the clarity of scripture; but is it also connected to the hiddenness of God, or the *obscurity* of scripture? Is there a hiddenness which is presupposed and even *preserved* by revelation? Or would such hiddenness have to be *excluded* in order to achieve clarity? The question of clarity and obscurity is significant for a discussion of its relevance to contemporary textual theory.

Exterior versus Interior Clarity

The double reading of scripture outlined here suggests a dynamic between hiddenness and disclosure of textual meaning, indicating that it is hardly possible to prescribe a single meaning to this particular text passage, even when we are bound to the *grammar* of the text as the law of its exegesis. It is exactly the grammatical rigor that paves the way to a different reading. The *otherness* thus situated within the text makes it necessary to read it all the more carefully, as long as we suspect that it still has secrets in reserve. It is the secrecy *underneath* the two readings that may destabilize or even subvert the interpretations we have received from earlier generations or achieved by the first reading of the text. Although Luther's theory of scripture is thus reformulated in a different theoretical context, I think this theory of a double reading gives a precise description of the procedure. Still, objections may always be raised, for example, with reference to Luther's firm affirmation, namely, that scripture is clear, or even *clarissima* (most clear), and persists in a clarity much higher than any light of reason. This was presented as a principle and presupposition of text exegesis in *Assertio* and later confirmed as the single principle of theological reasoning in *De servo arbitrio*.[30]

The double clarity of the text outlined by Luther in the introduction to *De servo arbitrio* seems to confirm our reading. Luther introduces a *double* line of distinction between two kinds of clarity and two kinds of obscurity in order to identify the reasons for confusion and misunderstanding: "To put it briefly, there are two kinds of clarity in Scripture, just as there are also two kinds of obscurity: one external and pertaining to the ministry of the Word, the other pertaining to the understanding of the heart."[31] The double clarity has thus been defined as, respectively, a *claritas externa* and a *claritas interna.*

The distinction is introduced as response to Erasmus's assumption that the scriptures are often unclear.[32] Luther claims that he confuses the two perspectives, expecting to find an immediate understanding of the heart rather than the *external* sense which is independent of the reader's convictions and state of mind. According to Luther, Erasmus blames the text of being obscure when he is unable to understand it rationally, but the actual problem may be localized elsewhere: not in the texts but in the *mind* of the interpreter who is confused about their *sense.* The external clarity is later described as a general expectation of meaningfulness, in other words, that it is possible to analyze the texts grammatically and semantically in order to make the text accessible as public statement.[33] Luther insists on such an explication of the plain grammatical meaning of the texts, which is not based on any metaphorical or tropological interpretation. The plain meaning of the text is defined by its exteriority.[34] In this respect, he seems to differ not only from Erasmus but also from the modern hermeneutics of Schleiermacher, Dilthey, or Gadamer: There is no further condition connected to interior factors like the "subjectivity" or intention of the author, the interior appropriation of meaning, a fusion of horizons, and so forth.

The analysis of the texts is not based on intention or meaning as an *interior* presupposition in the mind of the author or the mind of the reader. In that respect, Luther's theory is both anti-idealistic and anti-hermeneutic, corresponding to his critical view of speculative scholastic philosophy and theology. The distinction between exterior and interior clarity as such—in particular with Luther's emphasis on the former—introduces a critical distance to the interiorization (*Verinnerlichung*) of sense as the "heart" of philosophical or theological hermeneutics.[35]

The theory of external clarity is polemically directed against Erasmus's statement that scripture in many respects seems to be obscure and therefore difficult to understand.[36] According to Luther, the problem is not that scripture as such is obscure, even though he admits that there might be some sentences that are difficult to translate for grammatical or historical reasons. His main concern is that Erasmus, like the spiritualists, interprets the text according to his own rationality, thus closing his mind to the otherness of the text.[37] If that was the case, he would reject the different rationality of the biblical texts, simply because they (according to Luther, at least) literally (according to the letter and the grammar of the text) contradict his own view. Luther concludes that while seeking a meaning in the text, Erasmus remains blind, and while trying to read, he is only imposing his own opinions on the text material.[38]

Luther generally sees the Bible texts as offensive, even scandalous, and that raises challenges for an adequate interpretation: If the texts are divergent from *doxa* or common sense, they represent a different and often provocative *logos*. Hence, it is only possible to retain and explicate this difference when the texts are studied carefully according to their formal structures—in grammar, semantics, and rhetoric. This is not only a problem which applies to the challenge of the *skandalon*, though. When a text is similar to your own rationality, it may be even more difficult to discover the difference rather than subsuming it to your own prejudgment as corresponding to your expectations. Thereby the difference may also be more crucial in order to disclose the text. In any case, the *revealability* of the text, its capacity to reveal an insight and a point of view which seems strange and different to the reader, is bound to its exteriority—its *claritas* (respectively, *obscuritas*) *externa*.[39]

The question of *claritas interna*, conversely, addresses the problem of applying the text as a basis for understanding the meaning of this text *for me* (*pro me*). This second step is for Luther intrinsically connected to faith, to revelation, and to the work of the Holy Spirit as mediator of the true meaning of scripture.[40] Hence, the work of the spirit is in this case the spirit of understanding. Understanding according to this model of external and internal clarity implies both reading and *appropriating* a text, but the emphasis lies on the appropriation of a *difference* between interiority and exteriority: the difference between the reader's point of view and the disturbing grammar of the text. By the *internal* construction of sense, this difference is leveled in favor of a coherent interpretation. The *externality* of writing disturbs that immediate or mediated unity and interferes with the reader's point of view. The text remains foreign and its rationality differs from "common" sense and the natural expectations of the reader. Owing to this difference, every appropriation is at the same time a *de-* or *expropriation*, that is, the effort to read the text according to its own rationality, without leveling or domesticating its truth claims. To respect the "holiness" of the text will under these conditions imply a reverence of its otherness, which again is the presupposition for revelation as well as illumination—in fact, for any kind of reorientation in the philosophical or religious sense of *metabolē*, a "turning around" or conversion.[41]

Counterexamples: Certainty, Clarity, and Doubt

With Luther's emphasis on the clarity of scripture for the key issues of the Reformation, such as grace, freedom, and justification, there is no wonder that this has become a crucial point in the confessional apologetics of Protestants against Roman Catholics, often with a rationalist tendency of self-justification. In insisting on the *clarity* and the unambiguousness of scripture, there has been a tendency in the theology of the twentieth century, often called "dialectical" or "hermeneutic," to recur to a simple repetition of truth claims according to the Bible (or according to Luther, which is *almost* as good as canonical). The German theologian Friedrich Beisser published a treatise on this topic, the *Claritas scripturae bei Martin Luther* (1966), focusing on this aspect of his apology in order to clarify and testify the "absolute clarity" of the Word of God. According to Beisser, the Word is proclaimed as self-evident and thus beyond any need of questioning. In a passage where he discusses the expression *'claritas scripturae,'* he explains its importance:

> Thus we heard above that scripture is clear insofar as it preaches Christ. The Word is indeed clear by itself, but it also depends on this clarity because it has to be clear as the saving Word of God. This clarity is therefore not to be separated from the content of the Word of God. Thereby, all at once, one further thing is said: If that is the case, then clarity is not to be separated from the faith which is the purpose of the Word.[42]

This is admittedly a circular argumentation, although I am not sure if it is crystal clear. The rhetorical and dialectical strategy has one purpose, and that is to *eliminate* difference and unite all propositions in a monolithic proclamation of the evident clarity of the Word, to which everyone should agree. Although the example slightly exaggerates this tendency, it is characteristic not only of this book by Friedrich Beisser, but also for a whole generation of theologians who were convinced of the self-evidence of the biblical text and thus saw few reasons for further analyzing the nuances of clarity, the differences thereby coming to the fore, or even the doubts raised from within the text. And why should they? Beisser argues that this claim must be either true or false, and since Luther says it is clear, it is not only clear but very, very clear (*clarissima*), almost self-evident.[43] One can hardly deny that there is a certain *rhetoric* within Luther's texts which has a similar character; the confessor, the assertor, the apologist who according to the legend once stood in front of the tribunal in Worms, confessing: "Here I stand. I can do no other. God help me! Amen." However, are we speaking of the "same" clarity if the situation and the context are diametrically opposed?

A recurrence to mere tautologies is a well-known strategy in order to confirm an expected consensus or preserve traditional limits of disagreement. A number of theologians from this period were good at imitating the rhetoric of clarity and certainty, thus sounding *almost* like Luther. The risk may be that the simple *repetition* of this rhetoric in a different context sometimes achieves an unintended hilarious effect, but is any further *clarity* thereby achieved? Is there any strength of evidence, any persuasive effect? I am not convinced. It seems to me as if this insistence on the evidence of evidence and the clarity of clarity only leads back to a self-centered argument where someone seeks to protect and defend one's own position against all threatening attacks from outside. But what is defended?

If we look at the same topic as discussed in *De servo arbitrio,* Luther's line of argument is a bit more complex and there is more space for doubt, even a development of increasing doubt concerning the first presuppositions for thought. He describes a procedure of persistent doubt of authorities, not entirely different from the style of argument we find a century later in Descartes's *Meditations on First Philosophy.* There is no scientific method of doubt corresponding to mathematical principles, but there is a process of *disillusioning* of illusions, in German *Enttäuschung,* through doubt. Based on Erasmus's argument, Luther accepts that there is a general doubt concerning the truth and clarity of the scriptures and that this doubt is not only a question of details but a doubt on the very basis for thought, that is, the metaphysical and theological framework. Hence, not even tradition can give certainty and good answers to the new questions that are raised. The framework for understanding is drawn into doubt, including the confidence in one's own senses and rationality.[44] Yet the pivotal point is the doubt that pertains to the concept of God, that is, whether God is actually good and trustworthy or not. What if God is evil, or *indifferent* in the sense that he is working good as well as evil?[45] Hence, Luther deliberates on topics that are well known from the subsequent history of philosophy: Is he mad, is he dreaming, or is he possibly deceived by an evil spirit?

When the most stable foundation for thought and praxis is undermined, when the ultimate point of reference for metaphysics, ethics, and society is drawn into doubt, then we approach the real *scandal* of *De servo arbitrio,* as Erasmus correctly observes. When the authority of tradition is questioned together with the authority of reason, then the system of beliefs to which he belongs is already trembling. Moreover, the established institutional authority (for example, the magisterium, the tradition) is jeopardized and suspended. Through this rejection, the place normally occupied by the magisterium within the system of interpretation is opened up for discussion and doubt. The space of certainty and decision is left open.

Such a procedure of increasing doubt is outlined already in the first paragraphs of the *Assertio* but treated more extensively in *De servo arbitrio,* where Luther discusses all the objections raised by Erasmus of Rotterdam. He accuses Luther of heresy, and at the same time he is skeptically questioning any final authority outside the church.[46] When Luther responds to this skepticism, however, it is not in terms of a rejection, but actually an *amplification* of his own doubts, followed by a hyperbolic enhancement of the doubts that are raised by his adversary.[47] Where Erasmus, a Dutch humanist, is a moderate skeptic, Luther is a radical skeptic concerning the authorities of interpretation. Hence, he also breaks through the web of mutually balanced authorities. This includes a radical doubt of the traditional philosophy that Erasmus *defends,* albeit hesitantly. They both doubt the school philosophy, but in Luther this doubt is driven to the extreme, which seems to be an essential aspect of his rhetorical and argumentative strategy.

In *De servo arbitrio,* this doubt is first mentioned in the introduction and later elaborated. Luther agrees with Erasmus that there are several difficulties when it comes to the definition of the true church, which is hidden, when it comes to the saints, since they are unknown or dead, and finally, when it comes to the power of reason. After proceeding gradually through all these stages of doubt, Luther arrives at the insight establishing a certainty beyond reason itself, a truth beyond truth, clearer than the sun, which is mediated through scripture:

> Because we have for long been persuaded by the opposite by that pestilential saying of the Sophists that the scriptures are obscure and ambiguous, we are first forced to prove that scripture is our first principle, through which all other things may be proved, what seemed to be absurd and impossible among the other philosophers.[48]

Scripture is established as first principle, thus probing, judging, and illuminating. What anticipates the Cartesian doubt by more than a century is the claim that all other consequences may be deduced from this certainty, albeit the deduction follows the logic of scripture rather than the cogito. However, in Descartes, this insight also *constitutes* the new rationality of the Cartesian self, relying on its own authority and power of judgment. Comparing Luther and Descartes is a complex issue, given the significant differences in scope and presuppositions, but whereas the latter subscribes to a rationalism which *excludes* the sources of ambiguity and obscurity from rational procedures, the former seems to *presuppose* such ambiguity and obscurity—even when it comes to the first cause (*prima causa*). Hence, it becomes all the more decisive to rely on the clarity of scripture. Similarly, where Foucault accuses Descartes of *excluding* madness from the procedures of reason[49] in the same period as the insane were excluded from the civil society and shut up in asylums, Luther *presupposes* such madness and suggests that being foolish is the condition for doing good philosophy.[50]

The difference between Descartes's and Luther's references to God is even more remarkable: Descartes needs the ontological argument for God's existence in order to secure the evident certainty of his rationalism and the stringency of his philosophical system. Hence, God becomes the ultimate ontological guarantee of rationalist philosophy and later for the early Enlightenment and German Idealism. In Luther, the distinction is drawn prior to reason and the human power of definition, between the clarity of God as revealed *in* scripture and the obscurity of God *outside* of scripture, which therefore remains a tremendous (and trembling) challenge to the implicit *hubris* of rationalism. This elementary destabilization of the notion of God represents Luther's final rejection of its instrumentalization for the purpose of metaphysics, morality, or political theology.

A Theory of Scriptural Space

I have argued that it is possible to follow a double approach in the analysis of Luther's texts. The same applies for his procedures of reading scripture. The notion of scripture has this double sense in Latin: First it refers to writing and second to this particular set of writings referred to as scripture, often with a capital *S*. The former comes without the latter, but not the latter without the former. Hence, every time scripture is analyzed or interpreted in the second sense, it includes the former. This double movement of interpretation is the entrance to a scriptural space, where antitheses are played out against each other, although they are bound together in the *letter* of the text.

Since the polemical style of scholars like Jüngel and Ebeling invites controversy, it is time to reject three of their hermeneutic presuppositions, which have direct parallels in hermeneutic and idealistic philosophy: the univocal authority of the text (the single reading), their emphasis on the true *sense* of the text (and rejection of non-sense), and the *dialectical* exclusion of hiddenness, including the most *problematic* topos of the text. Admittedly, Ebeling does not exclude the hidden God from his theology. On the contrary: He urges the reader to "flee" "from God to God"—but the result is more or less the same. The hidden God is construed as an alien, a monster, whom we should fear and consequently avoid by returning to the safe sphere of scriptural interpretations.

My deliberations on a few aspects of Luther's text theory run counter to each of the three hermeneutic presuppositions, which are shared by philosophical and theological hermeneutics. Whether Luther's praxis of text interpretation is a good point of departure for text interpretation in the twenty-first century is another issue. I instead emphasize some of his philosophical and theological arguments and recommend them for further discussion. As long as the hermeneutical paradigm defines the conditions for reading and interpreting texts, these arguments will not be considered. The time has come to leave this framework behind and study Luther from other perspectives, including the less apparent ones.

Sometimes a minor grammatical difference is sufficient in order to open up the space of the text, as a problem, a topos of antitheses without resolution. This is the fact Luther exploits, shamelessly, in order to overturn the notions of truth, of selfhood, of morality that dominate the academic, public, and religious life of his own times. It even applies to the notion of God, which, according to Luther's argument, is consumed by economic calculation, as in the controversy on indulgences.

This is one of the topical issues of his theology, an issue that is often referred to as the triggering reason for the Reformation. His polemical formulation of justification by faith, as formulated by Paul in Romans 1:17, is an example of such a crucial topic. When we read his argument carefully, though, Luther is concerned with a *double* reading of the text, where the second reading displaces the first, or, rather, makes the reader aware of a division within the text. The tension is not resolved or reduced to a proclamation of the message, or kerygma, as the theologians of dialectical and hermeneutic theology often referred to. Although controversies are helpful for clarification, the quest for revelation introduces a different kind of movement within the textual space. Luther insists on this breaking point as a gift: a new discovery of the *clarity* of the text. It is not difficult to see its validity for certain passages in scripture, but the reading suggested here indicates that a *promise* of clarification is given within literary texts as well, within the temporal structures of writing.

There is no method or procedure indicated here that could assure the reader against uncertainty: neither the uncertainties of life nor the uncertainties of death. Even in Luther's polemical readings, his assertions, such uncertainty and doubt is trembling below the text, as an expression of the contingency of reading. The uncertainty follows his approach up to the first principle of understanding and follows his assertions as an expression of their implicit nihilism, their non-sense. This non-sense cannot be rejected, though: It is inscribed in Luther's theory of texts as the difference between hiddenness and revelation, of God outside and inside scripture. Hence, although the polemical situation may force us to choose between two readings, or two sides—and few things are more clarifying than the sharp definition of antithetical opposites—both readings remain pretexts for a theory of scriptural space.

SEVEN

The Quest for Sovereignty

Toward the end of his life, Luther warned against the danger of a collapse, of speculations, of mystifications, and of political violence inherent to this concept which is hardly a concept at all, the *deus absconditus.*[1] Luther had introduced the term for at least three different reasons: first, in accordance with the mystical theology of Dionysius Areopagita in his *Lectures on the Psalms* (1513/15); second, as a destruction of speculative theology in the *Heidelberg Disputation* (1518); and third, with reference to God's majesty in *De servo arbitrio* (1525). There are, more precisely, two different notions of divine hiddenness in *De servo arbitrio:* on the one hand, God's hiddenness on the cross, which Eberhard Jüngel has called the "precise" hiddenness; on the other hand, less specific, the absolute hiddenness of God's majesty, the Almighty, whose will is absolutely sovereign and free, but whose ways and reasons are unsearchable.[2]

The latter is perhaps the single notion that has caused most confusion around Luther's theology. The notion is indeed rather puzzling, but the many interpretations, rejections, and misunderstandings of the term are even more puzzling. Such confusion can only be the result of an inscrutable notion or a stunning stroke of genius—or perhaps both? Its obscurity may not come as a big surprise when the absolutely *hidden* God, *deus absconditus,* is addressed, but as far as I can see, Luther is not invoking this term as an expression of speculation, of threat, of mystification or collapse. On the contrary, his purpose seems to be exactly the opposite: to address this ambiguous topos in order to put it in its place, rather than allowing it to undermine any rational discourse in metaphysics, anthropology, theology, and text interpretation. Given the almost unanimous resistance and widespread confusion it provoked, Luther presumably had good reasons for proclaiming it indispensable.

The question of metaphysics and modalities is basic for the problem of free will, and still, something more is at stake in *De servo arbitrio.* It is connected to this complex relationship between metaphysics and scripture, which points in the direction of the hidden God beyond knowing, on the one hand, and the *thunderbolt* of revelation, on the other. The theological significance of this distinction has been thoroughly discussed, to such a degree that for a period it was considered *the* theological issue of the twentieth century. A similar problem is discussed in philosophy, though, as one of the ultimate problems in Kant's first *Critique* and a basic issue in

Hegel's phenomenology, namely, whether God in some respects remains hidden and inaccessible or has revealed himself completely without reservation. My hypothesis is that the most significant and influential philosophical insights in Luther are situated at this limit between the *hidden* power of *necessity* and the *freedom* proclaimed in the name of a phenomenon called *revelation*.

Kant and Luther on the Critique of Metaphysics

Over the centuries, numerous theories have emerged that try to explain what the term *deus absconditus* actually means, what it refers to, how to *understand* it, and so forth. Many interpreters have pointed at the background in divine voluntarism, namely, the mighty and awe-inspiring will of God according to medieval scholars like Scotus and Ockham.[3] This is not entirely far-fetched insofar as Luther discusses the almighty will of God in *De servo arbitrio* and even surpasses the nominalists in emphasizing God's freedom and almighty power. He argues in favor of the absolute necessity of causal determination. This is a discussion on metaphysics, however, and Luther's argument concerning the hidden God in his majesty directly addresses the metaphysical discourse on causality and free will.

The big difference between the *Heidelberg Disputation* and *De servo arbitrio* is that Luther in the latter enters the metaphysical debate with full force. He discusses the notion of God in relation to causality and insists on divine voluntarism, that is to say, the causal *necessity* of all events. Then he comes back to the theological argument on the hiddenness of God at the cross, which is also the crux of revelation. A big gap emerges between the two lines of explanation, which reaches a climax in Luther's declaration of the absolute hiddenness of God "in his majesty."[4]

The many debates on this text have either focused on metaphysics or the theology of revelation, but the significant point is the problematic and controversial *distinction*, and thus the mutual interference, between these two forms of rationality. Luther does not necessarily leave metaphysics behind; on the contrary, he seeks to rediscover the significant *question* behind these technical scholastic terms, regulating the meaning of the notion of God as well as the conditions for human existence. In order to uncover the most decisive philosophical questions in Luther's text, we have to distinguish as clearly as possible between the one and the other, in order to identify the questions of divine sovereignty, on the one hand, and human subjectivity, on the other.

In the controversy with Erasmus, Luther argues that the *Diatribe* "deludes itself [*se illudit*] in its ignorance" because it lacks the crucial distinction between a predicated and a hidden god.[5] A similar critique could be addressed to the majority of the critics: They make a major effort to reformulate or understand the precise *reference* of either a predicated or a hidden god, whereas they overlook the decisive distinction. A detailed analysis of this difference will therefore keep our attention in this chapter, not by excluding but rather *including* both metaphysics and the problem of revelation. Consequently, I examine the metaphysical notion of the hidden god, on the one hand, and Luther's notion of revelation, on the other, but emphasize the difference. Moreover, both discussions raise some political aspects of the controversy between Erasmus and Luther that are taken into brief consideration.

Kant's critique of metaphysics and its rational foundation in *Critique of Pure Reason* represents a pivotal point in the history of Western thought. The first *Critique* includes a long discussion of the notion of God, which is relevant to the distinctions we draw here. A more detailed analysis of Kant's argument will have to be postponed to my second volume, though; but another significant distinction from the transcendental analytic to be applied here is the difference between *noumena* and *phenomena*. Kant argues that the noumenon is merely a *limit-concept*, one that delimits the possibility of knowledge and thus marks the difference between the thing in itself (*das Ding an sich*) and the thing as it *appears* to us.[6] It cannot be given any positive content, and yet it remains indispensable as a concept drawing the limit (*Schranke*) of sensible knowledge. In this respect, the thing in itself is called a noumenon. Although void of (positive) content, it makes sense to underscore this border from a theoretical point of view.

Kant continues with a discussion of the *amphiboly* or ambiguity of all concepts of reflection (*Reflexionsbegriffe*), which is relevant to Luther's reflections on the revealed and the hidden God: According to Kant, the empirical and transcendental analyses are *mutually dependent*, and yet the *difference of perspective* is decisive. Kant argues that the difference is a topical one, and he thereby refers to Aristotle's *Topics* as predecessor of his own *transcendental* topics.[7] The transcendental analysis ought to be *topologically* distinguished from the empirical analysis of knowledge, he argues, and the reason for this distinction is that the transcendental *apperception* precedes all operations of reason and perception—indeed it organizes every experience of the world.[8] Hence, he also arrives at the *place* for the "highest distinction" within a transcendental analytic: the distinction between the possible and the impossible.[9]

Luther's distinction between a metaphysical discourse of God's *essence* (based on metaphysical reflection) as opposed to the phenomenal God appearing in scripture is marked by a similarly puzzling *amphiboly*. He focuses on the primary distinction between the possible and the impossible, and in my opinion this is an ultimate distinction in his topology. When Luther arrives at this "highest distinction" in his discussion of the hidden God, a corresponding antinomy seems to be unavoidable between the absolute *necessity* of divine will and the radical *possibility* of human existence, which is only achievable from the perspective of scripture, that is, the phenomenal God.

The critical potential of this notion has hardly been valued in the centuries that have passed since then. Philosophers have criticized the terrifying image of God, whereas theologians have questioned its relevance. I think the argument in *De servo arbitrio* amounts to a critique of philosophy *and* theology: As long as God is *beyond* understanding, the critique of mythology and idols proceeds from the *difference* between the hidden and the revealed, a difference that *precedes* the properties of God and the linguistic system of thoughts and values ascribed to God in either discipline.

Two ways of reading this argument are more common than others, namely, that *deus absconditus* is a frightening god *behind* the revealed or that the "precise" hiddenness is dialectically leveled by a *deus revelatus.* Luther himself is not crystal clear in distinguishing the various levels of discourse, but a reconsideration of his argument profits from a topological analysis where we emphasize the difference between the possible and the impossible as *highest* distinction of his argument. Hence, I begin with the distinction between necessity and freedom, which is one of the key issues of his controversy with Erasmus on free will. I then proceed to the metaphysical argument against free will.

The distinction was not well understood in Luther's own times, and up to the end of the twentieth century the result of Luther's attempt at a critical distinction again and again ended with more speculations, anxiety, and despair. Hence Luther's statement from the *Lectures on Genesis* (1537) is confirmed in other texts from this period: "Omit speculations concerning the hidden God!"[10]

The Violence of the Question: Necessity and the Problem of Evil

The heart of the controversy is concerned with the nature and identity of God: If there is no freedom of will, who could then be blamed for the suffering and injustice of this world? The problem often referred to as the problem of evil, or the problem of suffering, thus lurks behind the controversies and occasionally comes to the fore. Erasmus concludes toward the end of the *Diatribe* that if Luther subscribes to the doctrine of divine voluntarism, he will be unable to distinguish between the good and the evil works of God, and hence it will also be difficult to discern the saving God behind the despotic notion of the almighty ruler.[11] The entire problem of free will thus points toward the notion of God and the *place* of God's hiddenness, not only under the cross (*sub contrario*) but in majesty.

Both adversaries agree that there is a connection between the definition of free will and the notion of God, but Erasmus argues that the scriptures are unclear at this point. Hence, the responsibility for evil must be ascribed to humans, since God per definition is ultimately good. The good can safely be ascribed to God's effective grace, but *some* responsibility ought to be ascribed to human beings in order to explain evil. Erasmus is careful to avoid too emphatic conclusions, though, and argues that the scriptures are "unsearchable" at this point. Luther could not have disagreed more fundamentally. He argues that the pivotal point (and the *first* part) of the entire discussion on free will is concerned with exactly this question of drawing distinctions:

> It therefore behooves us to be very certain about the distinction between God's power and our own, God's work and our own, if we want to live a good [*pious*] life. So you see that this problem is one half of the whole sum of Christian knowledge, since both the knowledge of oneself and the knowledge of God vitally depend on this question. That is why we cannot permit you, my dear Erasmus, to call such knowledge irreverent, inquisitive, and vain.[12]

Which understanding of *liberum arbitrium* is thus rejected by Luther? Although he does not discuss the philosophical details, it is clear that Erasmus presupposes the Scotist definition of free will, namely, that the agent has an actual choice between synchronic possibilities.[13] His functional definition of free will runs as follows: "By 'free will' here we understand a power of the human will by which man may be able to direct himself toward, or turn away from, what leads to eternal salvation."[14] The definition is rather general, and it is worth noticing the words power (*vis*) and ability—and for the debate with Luther—the word "salvation." Making salvation a question of choice or "directing oneself" in one way or the other is the absolute contradiction to Luther's understanding of the issue, namely, that salvation depends on grace alone and does not depend on any human choice, power, or works. When Erasmus sees salvation as a result of human choice, it does not exclude the need for grace which "cooperates" with human efforts, though. But Luther fiercely rejects the threefold understanding of grace thus presupposed.[15] He can only see an overestimation of human powers in this definition of free will, and thus his suspicion concerning the delusion of *liberum arbitrium* is confirmed.

For our purpose, the theological issue of salvation is not decisive. Toward the end of the *Diatribe,* Erasmus also refers to philosophical debates on necessity and contingency, arguing that "[. . .] those who say that there is no such thing as free will, but that everything happens by absolute necessity, are saying that God works not only good deeds, but bad ones too."[16] Erasmus refers to the doctrine of divine voluntarism, normally ascribed to the nominalists Scotus, Ockham, and Biel.[17] However, it is the paradoxical form of this necessity as presented in Luther's disputations which gives him the occasion of accusing Luther of attributing cruelty and injustice to God.[18]

The argument hits the point of disagreement, insofar as Luther positively confirms that he believes that all events occur with necessity and from the ultimate perspective follow as a consequence of God's will, whether or not this seems rational to the human observer. Luther does not attempt concealing that he follows the metaphysical approach of scholastic philosophy, which he otherwise criticizes of sophistry on innumerable occasions. On the contrary: He believes that he is the *better* philosopher, since he rejects all moral reservations and sophisticated distinctions intended to soften the *violence* of the question.

Only God's will may be qualified as free in the absolute sense, Luther argues, and thus by far exceeding the limits of human reason. All other wills are dependent, contingent, and yet bound by the rule of necessity. At this point Luther is even more radical than his scholastic predecessors. Whereas the nominalists Scotus and Ockham emphasize *liberum arbitrium* as a significant *counterpart* to God's will, thus mediating some of the problems connected to the *absolutism* of divine majesty, this argument is not accepted by Luther. He simply denies that human beings have the "power" of free will.

His final argument against *liberum arbitrium* runs as follows: "The other part of the Christian *summa* is concerned with knowing whether God foreknows anything contingently, and whether we do everything of necessity."[19] Without further ado, Luther denies the first option and confirms the latter. He concludes that God "foresees and purposes and does all things by his immutable, eternal, and infallible will."[20] This affirmation is for Luther the definitive argument against the *liberum arbitrium*, the thunderbolt that annihilates the so-called free will. Hence, whoever wants to claim the freedom of will must "either deny or explain away this thunderbolt."[21]

Let me make it clear that Luther adopts a radical position, given the logical and ontological premises in medieval philosophy. He argues for a strong necessity in God's will; hence, not only is God asserted to be the first cause behind all things, he is also perceived as the *effective* cause in every causal relation, ordering the world according to his sovereign will. This is a topic of much debate among the scholastics. Even though omnipotence and omniscience belong to God's properties according to Thomas Aquinas, he still gives priority to reason over will.[22] In order to avoid a potential conflict, he argues for the rational character and unchangeable goodness of God's will. Ockham, conversely, emphasizes God's omnipotent will to the extent that God is withdrawn *beyond* human concepts of good and evil. Hence, God may be the absolute cause of every event and state of affairs without his goodness or divinity being questioned.[23] Luther goes even further than Ockham. In a disputation from 1517, Luther criticizes Ockham, Scotus, and Gabriel on this point.[24] Luther confirms this position in *De servo arbitrio* and emphasizes God's sovereign freedom to an extent which surpasses the nominalists, arguing that God works "all in all."[25] He explicitly claims that God is the *effective* cause in every event, and in all human acts, since both absolute power and omniscience belong to his *nature*.[26] This massive assertion immediately raises further questions: Does Luther distinguish between omnipotence (potential power) and executed power at all, or does he infer directly from the former to the latter? Does he make a clear difference between *logical* and *causal* necessity?[27]

The first question can be answered in the negative: Luther seems to *define* omnipotence in terms of executed power. Wherever there is action or change, Luther sees God at work, as the very *power to be* in all that is.[28] When it comes to the second question, he formally distinguishes between the necessity assigned to God's action and the contingency of all other beings and their actions.[29] Since God is the only necessary cause, all other causes and all other effects are contingent and therefore dependent on God in every moment of existence. God's will is not seen as necessary in the sense that it restricts the freedom of God self. God is the only sovereign, who may always will otherwise, but his reasons proceed far beyond human access and understanding. However, for humans and all other contingent beings, Luther claims that God's will is the absolute and necessary cause, not only with respect to the *conditional* consequences (*necessitas consequentiae*) but also with respect to the *actual* consequent (*necessitas consequentis*). He taunts the sophists for introducing such distinctions in order to avoid the provocative force of the problem:

> The Sophists have labored for years over this point, but in the end they have been beaten and forced to admit that everything happens necessarily, though by the necessity of consequence (as they say) and not by the necessity of the consequent [*consequentis*]. They have thus eluded the violence of this question [*violentiam istius quaestionis*], or indeed it might rather be said that they have deluded themselves. For how meaningless this is I shall have no difficulty in showing. What they call the necessity of consequence [*consequentiae*] means broadly this: If God wills anything, it is necessary for that thing to come to pass, but it is not necessary that the thing which comes to pass should exist, for God alone exists necessarily, and it is possible for everything else not to exist if God so wills. So they say that an action of God is necessary if he wills it, but that the thing done is not itself necessary. But what do they achieve with this playing with words? This, of course, that the thing done is not necessary, in the sense that it has not a necessary existence.[30]

Luther presents it as an argument solely concerning the difference between the necessity of God and the contingency of the world, but the level of distinctions is not quite sufficient compared to the scholastic debates on the issue. When Thomas introduces this distinction, it is not only in order to distinguish between necessity and contingency but also in order to enable a *temporal* qualification of existence and causation, hence, to distinguish between the *logical* inference from reason to consequence (even in God's thought) and the *causal* relationship between cause and effect.[31] This distinction is useful, in philosophy as well as theology, but when Luther deliberately blurs the distinction in favor of the *necessitas consequentis*, existence is emphasized over essence, causation over logic, and will over reason. Is this an attempt to weaken or delimit the impact of metaphysical discourse? Or is it, on the contrary, an effort to unveil the inherent *violence* of metaphysics?

Erasmus accuses Luther of presenting a cruel and ruthless God, and this impression seems to be confirmed by the collapse of the distinction. Are we thus witnessing another Lutheran hyperbole, whereby God's sovereign power is emphasized to the extent that God appears as cruel and unjust whereas Luther insists that God is nevertheless "entirely good and glorious," simply because he is God?[32] When Luther uses the word "violence" in the expression "violence of the question," it may be intentional or simply a slip of the pen, but the expression reveals the inherent violence of his metaphysical rationale which is not exactly softened by the collapse of this distinction between the two forms of necessity. If we may assume that political issues are at stake in theological and metaphysical arguments, either because theology reflects politics or vice versa, this justification of the ruler's sovereign decision throws a less flattering light on Luther's intervention against the peasants only a few months earlier, arguing that the princes ought to "stab, beat, and kill" the disobedient rioters.[33]

Luther can hardly be accused of *eluding* the violence of the question. But there is also a paradoxical protest against the entire metaphysical framework which is raised from *within* this discourse, and this questioning of the framework is situated at the heart of the problem. The modal logic of absolute necessity raises the *question of violence* (that is, whether violence happens with necessity) inherent in any metaphysical system, from within that system. This point of view requires a more subtle analysis of the different discourses interfering in the controversy between Erasmus and Luther. There are at least three such discourses converging in the question of free will, and none of them are unaffected by the paradoxical structure of the problem.

Luther's main argument is that the doctrine of *liberum arbitrium* is delusive, although it appears to be rational as long as you accept it as the condition for anthropology, theology, and metaphysics. Hence, at the same time as Luther insists on the absolute causal necessity of divine will, he establishes a distance from the premises for this discourse. In my analysis I argue for a repetition of this movement, thus drawing a *conclusion* to the metaphysical circle of necessity while at the same time opening another circle of possibility, based on a second reading of the text.

This question of possibility is one of the key issues of the debate; in fact, it is called the *heart* of the controversy.[34] The question raised by Luther is the following: Is *liberum arbitrium* an apt definition of this possibility which is lingering under the entire discourse? Or is there some other, more radical possibility? And where is the place for this possibility within the text?

The Cruelty of God

Toward the end of the *Diatribe,* Erasmus discusses the political side of the argument on free will, and he points at two aspects of Luther's concept of freedom with immediate political relevance. The first is connected to what he sees as an ambiguous and incalculable notion of God in Luther's theology, when God is portrayed as a "wrathful tyrant," on the one hand, only to appear all the more mild and full of grace in forgiving sins, on the other. Thus he writes:

> For a start they make God almost cruel, venting his wrath on the whole of mankind for someone else's sin, especially since the people who committed it amended their ways and were punished most severely for the rest of their lives. Then when they say that those who have been justified by faith do nothing but sin, so that by loving and trusting God we become worthy of his hatred, are they not making God's grace extremely misery? [. . .] Moreover, in saying that God burdens man with so many commandments which have no other purpose than to cause him to hate God more, and so be utterly condemned, are they not making him even more merciless than Dionysius, the tyrant of Sicily, who deliberately promulgated many laws which he suspected most people would break if no one were to enforce them? At first he turned a blind eye, but soon, when he saw that nearly everyone had offended in some respect, he began to prosecute them, and so brought everyone under his domination [. . .].[35]

Although this critique is directed against Luther's soteriology, it is not irrelevant for the political impact of Luther's theology. The Dionysian caricature is actually characteristic, not despite but because it represents a travesty of the original. If God is presented as a merciless ruler and this wrathful king is the one who rules the world with necessity, can the expected consequences of divine intervention in history remain unaffected? What kind of *justice* is then to be expected? Which criteria for the execution of power and use of violence are thereby validated and justified? The events of the revolution and the counterrevolution of 1525 reveal some of the implicit consequences of this notion of absolutistic political power in Luther's theology.

Erasmus's second political argument is that the ambivalent notion of divine power was already influencing the political climate in Western Europe in the early 1520s with a violent and poisonous rhetoric. He thinks that Luther seems to "delight in hyperboles of this kind in order to drive out the hyperboles of others."[36] Erasmus neatly draws himself out of the conflict, since he neither supports the papists nor the protesting movement around Luther. He criticizes the papists for believing in "confession and satisfaction," whereas Luther calls this "an invention of Satan." When it comes to the position and authority of the pope, the papists exalt "the pontiff's power most hyperbolically," whereas Luther calls all papal and conciliar institutions "heretical and anti-Christian." Erasmus worries about the increasing level of rhetorical violence, which also includes curses, condemnations, and mutual demonization of the enemy. He sees himself as a peaceful proponent of political freedom from the papal rule, but he is anxious about the consequences of this increasingly violent rhetoric: "The clash of such hyperboles produces the thunder and lightning which is now battering the world. If both sides continue to defend their overstatements so savagely, I foresee a battle between them such as there was between Achilles and Hector, who, being equally fierce, could only be parted by death."[37]

This description of the situation is precise, and it is difficult to disagree with Erasmus, the peaceful humanist from Rotterdam, that these consequences are disastrous. Whereas Luther's rhetoric of freedom from Babylonian captivity and papal bondage has proved to be effective and disruptive, Erasmus is worried about the consequences of demonizing your enemies. He locates the doctrine of free will exactly at the heart of this conflict, underscoring that every agent in the conflict ought to be responsible not only for his actions, but also for his words, and have to answer for the consequences.

In 1524 Erasmus foresees a battle which is dangerous and leads deeper into fundamentalism, with killings and excessive violence. It is already approaching, although not as a direct result of confessional controversies. He seeks to avoid a radicalization of the conflict but predicts a political warfare in the name of God, and *concerning* the name of God. Is such a conflict thus unavoidable for the sake of liberation, for the sake of real *change* in history? Is the violence of destruction, is *bloodshed,* literally a precondition for political freedom? And is there some connection between the rhetorical violence of the reformers and the political violence following during the revolution? Erasmus points at a significant and problematic point in Luther's struggle for freedom of faith, freedom of confession, freedom of speech, and against the freedom of will: The result may be exactly the opposite of what the Reformer had expected, namely, suspicion and hatred rather than confidence and faith—and chaos in the name of freedom.

The Grammar of Freedom and Necessity

Luther has no good response to the accusations of political violence. The reason is probably that he rejects discussing the questions of political power as relevant for metaphysical distinctions. In his rejection of the papal power and authority he needs the claim to God's sovereignty, though, but he consequently argues with reference to God's revelation in scripture, and not with reference to the almighty will working life, death, and all in all. There are good reasons for doing so, and I elaborate them briefly on the basis of Kant's distinction between the noumenal and the phenomenal.

As opposed to the school philosophy, Luther seems to adopt a rational scheme for understanding God's activity which basically conforms to the arguments of the nominalists. He argues that this rational scheme conforms to scripture, but I think it is more appropriate to say that Luther cultivates a few significant properties of God and neglects others. Most characteristic is the way he underscores and emphasizes the *paradoxes* inherent to the scholastic debates rather than the many efforts at resolving these opposites with a model of human / divine cooperation, ascribing *something* to free will and *something* to God. Luther argues that these are causes of completely different orders. Hence, there is no concordance between the one and the other, no sovereignty of human will in relation to divine freedom and power. The necessity is absolute and unconditional. But the same applies to the freedom which is *given* by God: It is absolute and unconditional.

Hence, we can finally disclose why it is important for Luther to take in the full scale of metaphysical questions connected to the question of *liberum arbitrium*, such as, "[. . .] what it is, what it does, how it is related to contraries, affinities, similarity, etc."[38] The point is not merely to answer these questions *within* the scholastic framework, but rather to question the framework itself by repeating the questions as precisely as possible within a *new* framework, namely, according to the grammar of scripture. Even the modal logic of necessity and freedom is based on this grammar. Luther thereby directs the axis of inquiry in another direction by destroying the metaphysics of *liberum arbitrium* and *recovering* the problem of modalities in relation to God. From a systematic point of view this looks like a simple solution: God is the absolute source of necessity as well as freedom. Still, that is no solution at all, insofar as solutions dissolve contradictions. This is the point where the problem begins: How could this metaphysical theory (*sub specie aeternitatis*) be adapted to human reality and experience?

This is where the distinction between noumena and phenomena becomes important. Whereas Luther considers this metaphysical notion to be true for nature, it appears to be in conflict with the human experience of freedom and responsibility. Hence the *difference* between necessity and possibility will have to be regulated differently, according to a grammar including human reality. And this is the point where scripture comes in and achieves a singular authority: Because of the word of scripture, humans may understand the way this paradox of necessity and freedom is structuring their reality, including actions and passions, law and grace, bondage and freedom. The phenomenology thus introduced is in all respects a *scriptural* phenomenology, which is made accessible through writing.

As a system of coordinates it structures reality *otherwise,* though, at significant points diverging from the grammar of metaphysics. When scripture so clearly is separated from the dominant system of explaining reality, the system as a whole is questioned and drawn into doubt. The challenge is to recover the question *in its most detailed and rigorous form* within this other grammar, since the *questions* are as urgent as ever, although the answers have become unsatisfactory. This is the huge task of this *destruction* of metaphysics, namely, to reformulate the questions within a new context. Luther does so by explicitly looking at the *grammatical* structure of language. Hence, the grammatical form of the verb, the *tempora* of the promise, and so forth, contribute to a *recovery* of metaphysics within the world re-formed and reconstructed according to scripture. The phenomenal reconstruction thus adapts the letter of scripture as the form of explanations, and it even applies to the phenomenal reconstruction of the notion of God, in terms of a theology of the cross (thus the transition from death to resurrection, from despair to hope, from guilt to grace, and so forth).

Still, Luther would not be a philosophical thinker if metaphysics was thereby *reduced* to the grammar of scripture. A similar problem would soon emerge the other way around: Since there are so many diverging interpretations of scripture, someone would simply argue that it could be *interpreted* otherwise. The whole quest for truth, theological as well as philosophical truth, would be handed over to a question of more or less arbitrary reconstructions and interpretations. This is where the most difficult of all questions in Luther's analysis of the relationship between the noumenal and the phenomenal world comes up: how to identify and describe the ultimate point of reference between *scripture* in its most general sense, as the written words structuring the reality we perceive in experience, with the categories outlined by metaphysics?

This is the rupture running through the entire book called *De servo arbitrio,* and it remains an *open* question insofar as it is a question without an appropriate answer. It is the question concerning the most questionable, and thus the highest level of reflection within the text. It concerns the relationship between necessity and freedom, between noumena and phenomena, between the 'thing' as such (*quod res est*) and the thing as it appears to me. It also raises the question of the difference between hiddenness and revelation and the *transition* from the one to the other, but it is primarily a metaphysical distinction, or, rather, a distinction which becomes crucial in the moment when metaphysics is destroyed and transformed into another grammar, with other criteria for distinguishing between necessity and freedom, between the impossible and the possible.

This is a question of transition from one way of understanding the world, according to nature or "things," to another, according to scripture and phenomena. Kant ascribes this transition to the *transcendental apperception,* which implies a new understanding of subjectivity, wherein phenomena are accompanied by consciousness and thereby constituted *for me.* "Being" in the Kantian sense thus means to be for consciousness. Could we say the same about Luther? The discussion so far cannot justify such a claim, but the reference to scripture indicates that phenomena in any case are reconstructed differently. I come back to this problem and discuss it in further detail below.

If scripture, or even scripture *alone,* is significant for the reconstruction of phenomena, then the condition for understanding is given independently of the *spontaneous* freedom of Kantian subjectivity. The subject is structured according to the grammar of scripture, with emphasis on the Pauline distinction between law and grace, which in this case implies the absolute necessity and the absolute possibility of human subjectivity. The self which is proscribed according to the law cannot fulfill the imperative, and so it is forced into the paradoxes of necessity. Normative necessity (the moral law) and causal necessity (the natural law) are two very different things, but in both cases the human being is confronted with its absolute limit (*peras*). With the assurance and promise of grace, the limit of necessity is suspended and an unconditional freedom is given in the form of a promise, a future where *everything* is possible. A different world is revealed through faith, a world of infinite possibility, hence *without* limit, or, as Luther emphasizes with reference to scripture, "without the law."

I will not discuss the theological consequences of this reversal of the conditions for understanding, but merely point out that the reversal implies a redefinition of the modal categories, necessity and possibility, due to the conversion (*metabolē*) experienced by the subject. Even the word "subject" should be taken literally here, in the sense that the self is *subjected* to the law, and thereby subjected to the grammar of scripture. Even when the promise of grace is accepted in faith, the *subject* remains the place for this reorganization of the modal categories, and thus the passive, receptive *site* of reorganizing the world in terms of absolute necessity and the freedom thus ascribed to the self.

Finally: Is this also the pattern for a reconstruction of the political self in Luther? In the immediate political situation it seems to be. The freedom of a Christian is inscribed in this double structure, a free lord, free from all rules and human regulations and yet the servant of every other. This is the freedom and responsibility ascribed to each individual, a call to serve your neighbor to the limit of the possible, and yet remain absolutely free and independent of the masses, an almost anarchic freedom. Yet on the political level we see a different tendency, due to the chaotic situation with upheavals and revolutions threatening the societal structure with collapse. In this situation Luther suddenly calls upon the princes and ascribes to them the unrestricted power of sovereignty—a power derived from God himself, in his dark majesty. Is this the structure of thought that comes to dominate Luther's political theology? Is it an example of the *state of exception,* where someone has to make decisions in order to avoid political chaos? This is indeed a terrifying scenario, where the princes are called upon in the name of God, the hidden God in his majesty, who works life, death, and all in all.

EIGHT

The Quest for Subjectivity

Luther's ambivalent distance to the entire framework of metaphysical discourse was polemically presented in *Heidelberg Disputation*. What Luther formulated there as a program of the *destruction* of metaphysics (regarding the "wisdom of the wise") is now unfolded as a questioning of the metaphysical tradition to which Luther belongs, not only in order to leave it behind, but also to reformulate and thus *recover* the basic philosophical problems raised within that tradition. In this sense the problem of free will, which Luther rejects as illusory, is significant because it *conceals* a number of other questions, such as the question of necessity and possibility, and thus the metaphysical problem of causality. The problem of free will, which is confusing as long as it is taken for granted, can become significant when it is formulated as a *question* of the whole medieval system of modalities and modal logic. But Luther is, as indicated previously, not just discussing metaphysical problems from *within* the tradition. He takes a step outside and raises questions concerning the *violence* of metaphysics respectively concerning the relative value and limitations of metaphysical discourse.[1]

Free Will and the Empty Site of the Self

When the meaning of the term *liberum arbitrium* is jeopardized, then the veil which used to cover these questions in a specific structure regulating actions, events, and causes is drawn aside, if only for a moment, but long enough to get a glimpse of a different structuring of reality. In order to elaborate this alternative structure of causality and modal categories, it is necessary to analyze the conditions for traditional metaphysical discourse as precisely as possible, in order to clarify the questions it raises and the problems the philosophers are trying to come to terms with. Only then will it be possible to step *beyond* tradition, in order to question its foundation or, when possible, to uncover, reveal, and reformulate the basic conditions of understanding.[2] Luther's rhetorical strategy in his critical contention with the authority of tradition is worth a closer analysis, though.

The first step is taken a few years earlier, when Luther argues that *liberum arbitrium* is an empty term, *solo titulo:* It makes no sense at all within the approach he finds required.[3] Erasmus, by contrast, has defined the *liberum arbitrium* as the place *from where* he is looking: the heart of the discourse, the place where decisions are made and the only guarantee of responsibility. From this place the person may define a space of relative freedom for action, although it is regulated by the law of nature, the law of actions, and the law of faith.[4] Moreover, Erasmus points out that it is possible to *withdraw* from this place into a space of skeptical reflection, a space for carefully deliberating on the alternatives before you decide whether you turn to one direction or the other.

While confirming that *liberum arbitrium* is the cornerstone of this building of thought, the place where the metaphysical system is intimately connected with the human sphere, with experience, choices, and responsibility, with fall and grace, with the law and the promise, Luther rejects exactly this cornerstone and crushes it in order to let the whole system collapse, in a gesture of destruction. He describes how this destruction follows after a long period of doubts and despair, and after endless attacks at the "fortress of tradition," represented by the impressive number of ancient and modern authorities. At the very end, however, this technical term *liberum arbitrium* becomes the enemy par excellence, what he labels the "Troy of reason," and thus the target of his decisive attack:

> I confess, my dear Erasmus, that you have good reason to be moved by all these [authorities of the tradition]. I myself was so impressed by them for more than ten years that I think no one else has ever been so disturbed by them. I, too, found it incredible that this Troy of ours, which for so long a time and through so many wars had proved invincible, could ever be taken. And I call God to witness on my soul, I should have continued so, I should be just as moved today, but for the pressure of my conscience and the evidence of facts that compel me to a different view. You can well imagine that my heart is not of stone; and even if it were, it could well have melted in the great waves and storms with which it had to struggle and the buffeting it received, when I dared to do what I saw would bring down all the authority of those whom you have listed, like a flood upon my head.[5]

Whereas Luther identifies *liberum arbitrium* as the invincible fortress of tradition, he also apparently discovered that this very term which disturbed him for so many years could easily be transformed into a Trojan horse for the decisive attack. As an *empty* notion (*solo titulo*) and yet located at the front of the war between two very different views, *liberum arbitrium* should be well suited for the task.[6] Still, what happens when this Trojan horse has arrived inside the city walls? We would have to turn to Homer for a clue: As soon as the horse is inside, the warriors break out in an ambush and start the work of destruction.

Although the place that was occupied by *liberum arbitrium* is now declared to be empty, the controversy lingers on. What function does it then obtain in Luther's thought? This empty site of the self is now open for a new description, not like a tabulą rasa but in the sense that it receives a new significance and a different function. The authority that was reserved to *liberum arbitrium* according to the tradition is now subjected to scripture and the rule of scripture. What happens more exactly to the site called *liberum arbitrium* within this other view? The place it used to occupy is now qualified and circumscribed by the scriptural definition of law and gospel. The law identifies the entire person, including reason and will, as "sin," and thus it is bound to death.[7] It is subjected to the grammar of scripture.

A Battlefield Called Subjectivity

In the passage where Luther describes the siege and victory over the "Troy of tradition," he identifies the place for a passionate change of view first in the *conscience* and then in the heart (*cor*). This question is also discussed by Wilfried Joest in his detailed study, *Ontologie der Person bei Luther,* where the heart and the conscience are identified as the "sphere of decision" within a person.[8] According to Joest, this site may also be called *voluntas* and sometimes simply the "spirit" in Luther's texts, due to a lack of terminological stringency. Since the decision implies a *rejection* of free will, however, the transition from one view to another is consequently described in passive terms. This passivity hardly excludes the possibility of being an active person with a strong will, but the *transition* is not the result of a choice or an act of will. Still, the redefinition of the human self that follows from the new point of view is accomplished by the person who is formed by its social relations, its flesh, its memories, expectations, and abilities. Thus, in social and political respects she remains the same person, although the conditions for being a person are reversed. The total change takes place in her heart and conscience, thus only indirectly will the changes be perceivable by the social and political surroundings. In this reversed topology of becoming, *passivity* becomes the condition for acting and thinking.[9]

The only work that remains is to hand oneself over, to capitulate and let it happen; it is simply perceived (or received) as Event. Basically, the human person is thence characterized (that is, acquires her new character) by her passions and emotions, and this clearly differs from the anthropology outlined by Erasmus. The heart is not defined according to its will, and definitely not as a *free* will, but in terms of its affective hanging. In this "hanging" Luther's definition of "God" from the Great Catechism resounds: "Whatever you hang your heart upon and confide in, that is really your God."[10]

The notion of scriptural space plays a crucial role here. After all, it is with reference to scripture that the self is circumscribed and achieves a new signification: The distinction between flesh and spirit, between the closure of sin and the passive reception of grace, is received passively by reading the scripture, by listening to the word (*ex auditu*), or by reception of the sacrament, and in each case the *passivity* of this procedure is emphasized.[11] Thereby it proceeds from an affective revolution of the personal self that goes to the root (*radix*) rather than simply being reproduced within the cognitive faculty (hence, rather different from the Cartesian cogito as self-constitution of the self).

Luther identifies scripture as the place where humans encounter the divine and Heaven comes down to the earth, and thus it is becomes the *locus* of revelation.[12] He carefully describes how this site is occupied and thus taken over by the cross, disclosing a secret which otherwise remains *concealed* to reason. The place that used to be occupied by the *liberum arbitrium* is circumscribed when the cross "crosses out" the old self (the traditional notion of subjectivity) in a gesture of destruction.[13] Luther describes the scriptural correlation to this topos as the revelation of God's most profound hiddenness:

> In order that there may be a place [*locus*] for faith it is necessary that everything which is believed should be hidden. It cannot be more remotely hidden [*remotius absconduntur*] than under an object, perception, or experience which is contrary to it [*sub contrario obiectu*]. Thus when God makes alive he does it by killing, when he justifies he does it by making men guilty, when he exalts to heaven, he does it by bringing them down to hell, as Scripture says: "The Lord kills and brings to life; he brings down to Scheol and raises up." (I Samuel 2:6)[14]

Hence, according to the logic followed here, there is at least one place, one *locus,* where hiddenness becomes the condition of possibility for disclosure: the hiddenness under an object, perception, or experience which is contrary to it. The ultimate opposites of the new self are the double qualification of life and death, of natality and mortality. Even these ultimate notions are inverted by the circumscription, though. The *apparent* life signifies death, whereas the death by the cross reverses death into life.

Even when Luther argues for a reconsideration of the philosophical framework of the tradition, he has not presented a clear-cut alternative that may serve as alternative foundation, except for the numerous references to scripture as authority. Hence, scripture becomes the condition for restructuring thought, but scripture is encountered at the battlefield, the field of controversies and polemics. At this point Luther seems to be much more radical than Joest has discovered in his analysis, which remains caught up in an *existential* ontology of human "existence" or being-in-time.[15] When Luther emphasizes *liberum arbitrium* as an empty notion, this *site* has now become an open place, ready for new descriptions and definitions, but also a site which symbolizes this ambiguity between the old and the new, between the tradition and scripture, between death and new life. The place thus identified, attacked, and redefined as battlefield is the first place to be analyzed according to Luther's scriptural analytic. It is the battlefield later called subjectivity.

PART III

The Hidden God

Spent into the ground with the unmistakable trace: grass, written asunder. The stones, white, with the shadows of the stalks: Stop reading: look! Stop looking: go!

Verbracht ins Gelände mit der untrüglichen Spur: Gras, auseinandergeschrieben. Die Steine, weiß, mit den Schatten der Halme: Lies nicht mehr—schau! Schau nicht mehr—geh!

—Paul Celan[1]

NINE

Deus Absconditus

On one point Erasmus of Rotterdam and Martin Luther perfectly agree: There are too many myths circulating in society, church, and academia, and too much superstition, ignorance, and mysticism surrounding the notion of God. Malicious tongues would probably comment that things haven't changed a lot over the five centuries that have passed. For the discussion on the hidden and mysterious god, *deus absconditus,* this general estimation of beliefs and superstitions turns out to be significant. Erasmus claims that the very notion of *'deus absconditus'* contributes to the confusion and the speculations concerning the nature of God and distracts from the central question, namely, how to lead a good and virtuous life and enjoy the pleasures of serious intellectual debates. Hence, he accuses his opponents (not only Luther but also Müntzer and Karlstadt) of obscurantism and obfuscation, and warns with reference to an old Greek myth against trying to penetrate into the secrets of God, while fumbling in the dark.[2] Indeed, not many concepts are more liable to abuse and confusion than the concept of God, and in particular the *hidden* God. Hence, Luther agrees with his opponent on this point, with solemn assertion, before he concludes with an old adage from the Greeks: *Quae supra nos, nihil ad nos.*[3]

The problem is not unknown to the biblical authors. In the writings from the Old Testament, we find traces of a prolific and manifold religious life, with fertility cults, a number of deities, mythologies, and various ritual practices. Baal is often mentioned as a deity competing with JHWH (Yahweh) in terms of loyalty and worship. It is all superstition, Luther would say, in perfect agreement with the biblical prophets. These beliefs are simply constructions and projections of human wishes and have no connection with reality. His reference to *'deus absconditus'* is not an invitation to further speculations, though. It is exactly the opposite: a critical notion aiming at demystification of the difficulties and contradictions which unavoidably come up when power, benevolence, and omniscience are discussed in relation to the concept of God. Luther repeatedly underscores that this is a notion of ultimate concern by demonstrating that all efforts at *constructing* an image of the hidden God are in vain. The notion of *'deus absconditus'* is radically destructive, indeed *iconoclastic,* when it comes to myths and images of God. Hence, there is also an infamous irony which meets Erasmus's disinterest and indifference with the adage: *Quae supra nos, nihil ad nos.*[4] A similar irony would not be entirely misplaced in discussions with contemporary academics who avoid the very *question* concerning the hidden God, in its most general form.[5]

It is precisely as a question we meet this term in Luther's texts: a question of the place, the topos, where the distinction is drawn between necessity and possibility, between presence and absence, between action and passion, between good and evil, between God and idol, between oneself and the other. Our reading of the *Heidelberg Disputation* and *De servo arbitrio* indicates that the text is organized around such basic differences, but the logic organizing them still needs a more detailed topological analysis. Moreover, given our textual approach to the question, we ask whether this could be the place for linguistic distinctions between mythos and logos, between the 'sign' and the 'thing' (or the signifier and the signified), and indeed for the 'inside' and 'outside' of scripture? The generic scope of the question also includes the most basic forms of perception, like time and space, to which I briefly return later in this chapter.

In the light of these extensive questions, it is perhaps less evident that the notion should be no concern of ours (*nihil ad nos*) and completely irrelevant for an inquiry into philosophical and theological issues. Even if we restricted our scope to the question of mythology and speculation, which is a recurring issue in the controversy between Erasmus and Luther, this notion soon becomes critical for the decisive difference between God and idol, mythos and logos; in Luther's writings, a question of never-ceasing interest, disturbance, and despair.

Abscondity and Incomprehensibility

"Thus God is hidden and incomprehensible," Luther writes as early as 1513, commenting on the passage "Darkness is his hiding-place" (Psalms 18:12). His model of thought is formed by the negative theology of Dionysius Areopagita, to whom he explicitly refers.[6] The passage is all about the place of the divine: on the one hand, that God is hiding in *darkness,* on the other, that an inaccessible *light* has become God's hiding place, to which a human being may ascend only by following the way of negations. God is not bound to either darkness or light; hence, the place of God is beyond this distinction. These examples follow the Dionysian pattern of exceeding *beyond* the common limits of reason, beyond the visible as well as the invisible, beyond being as well as non-being: "There the simple, absolved and unchanged mysteries of theology lie hidden in the darkness beyond light of the hidden mystical silence, there, in the greatest darkness, that beyond all that is most evident exceedingly illuminates the sightless intellects." (*Mystical Theology* 998A-B)[7]

Dionysius is a common reference for philosophers and theologians in medieval Europe, an authority who comes close to the biblical authors. It is nevertheless worth noticing the way Luther adopts Dionysius in his commentaries, indicating that the query [*quaerare*] for God advances through negations and negations of negations; hence, God "is" neither light nor darkness, neither being nor non-being. Luther's negation of the Scholastic definitions of God is the philosophical and linguistic precondition for everything he will say and write about *deus absconditus* later on. Toward the end of the short text known as *The Mystical Theology,* this way of negations brings Dionysius into linguistic difficulties when describing the unknown cause of all, which transcends and thus logically precedes philosophical distinctions, including the Aristotelian rules of logic, stating that things should either be classified as being or non-being and propositions should either be true or false: "It is not non-being nor being, not known as it is by beings, not a knower of beings as they are. There is neither logos, name, or knowledge of it. It is not dark nor light, not error and not truth." (*Mystical Theology* 1048 A)[8]

How do these contradictory statements influence the rationality of Dionysius's text? Instead of taking the meaning of the name "God" for granted, it is drawn into a reflection upon the difficulties of defining its referent. Hence, intellectually *grasping* the ultimate referent of the linguistic and philosophical system is rendered impossible. Instead of being the answer to all questions, the name of God has itself become a question, and a way of questioning the foundations of Scholastic theology and metaphysics.[9] These radical negations introduce a general doubt about the linguistic system and the Aristotelian Law of the Excluded Middle as well as the Principle of Non-Contradiction. Luther becomes increasingly skeptical of Aristotelian scholasticism in this period, and Dionysius's apophatic theology is helpful in order to open up a space for a different logic and thereby question the *place* of God. This place cannot be rationally identified, he concludes; it brings reason to rest in silent reverence of the Hidden One.

In Suffering

In the *Heidelberg Disputation* (1518), the abscondity of God is confirmed once more, but the point of view is different: Luther describes the sovereign God who is hidden in suffering (*absconditus in passionibus*). The cross is identified as the specific *place* of hiddenness. The denials that pointed *beyond* the world are now drawn into the human world; the "visible" things of God are thus placed "in direct opposition to the invisible, namely, his human nature, weakness, foolishness."[10] When I analyzed the *Heidelberg Disputation* above, I underscored the paradox, thus crossing out and subverting the principles of Scholastic metaphysics in a *destruction* of man and of human constructions of God. Dionysius's way of negations, referred to in the *Lectures on the Psalms* (1513/15), never rejected the power and superiority of the Almighty. On the contrary: This double negation of the possibility of grasping God is indirectly a confirmation of divine power. With the *Heidelberg Disputation,* negative theology suddenly takes a *political* and *bodily* turn, subversive in its criticism of human power, strength, and wisdom. The body is the visible *site* of this suffering, at once concrete and tangible, although the suffering of Christ is historically linked to a singular event of the past. Hence, the perception of anything divine in this body depends on belief; on seeing this body as a sign of the invisible (*invisibilia*) within the visible (*visibilia*), as a broken sign. Luther argues with Paul (1 Corinthians 1) that such insight into the wisdom of God presupposes a certain folly, or counterintuitive wisdom. Hence, the question is whether this text represents a new way of reasoning: Is the destruction of human wisdom an implicit criticism or even an explicit rejection of the negative theology he endorsed only a few years earlier?

The decisive difference is linked to the passivity of perception, to suffering, to the subversive understanding of power. A new anthropology emerges, which emphasizes the vulnerability of the human body: The suffering of Christ is experienced in the flesh, and the cross becomes the symbol of humanity suffering in Christ, and of God who is experienced and recognized in suffering, in passion, in passivity, rather than in superiority and perfection. This *logos* of reasoning is explicitly based on Pauline Christology but proceeds differently compared to negative theology. Moreover, it is of immediate political and social relevance. It is clearly based in Luther's grammatical discovery of a double (or triple) *iustitia Dei*, and thus of grace understood as a gift of unconditional absolution.

With the *Heidelberg Disputation*, we see a change of conditions and a change of perspective, from essence to existence, from power to suffering, from the invisible *supra nos* to the invisible within the visible. This conversion or subversion of the categories is identified as an event, indeed a *repetition* of the events of the cross, that is, of death and resurrection, of destruction and creation, of annihilation and new existence: "The Law brings the wrath of God, kills, reviles, accuses, judges, and condemns everything which is not in Christ. (. . .) Yet that wisdom is not of itself evil, nor is the law to be evaded; but without the theology of the cross man misuses the best in the worst manner."[11]

The confrontation with philosophy is open and direct: Philosophical authorities are rejected in favor of Christology, apparently an inner-theological discourse, and yet Heidegger has shown how Luther's destruction of metaphysics exceeds the limits of theology. His rejection of philosophy is one of the reasons for a permanent ambivalence between philosophy and theology in the centuries to come. But is theology of the cross therefore completely irrelevant to philosophy? This is a question of much debate, of whether the conditions of the two fields from here on follow diverging paths or remain in critical dialogue, even within Protestantism. However, it is at least possible to argue that Luther's excessive doubt of the premises for thought becomes a paradigm for critique in terms of (existential) doubt and despair. Hence, I have suggested a reading of the text which includes and reformulates the metaphysical questions within a process of destruction, rather than simply excluding them and leaving them behind. The *Heidelberg Disputation* would not only be read as a theological statement rejecting philosophy, but also as a more sophisticated critique of the premises for philosophical reasoning, just as indicated by the division into 28 theological and 12 philosophical theses.

Two entirely different understandings of *deus absconditus* emerge, though: a hidden god beyond reason versus God hidden in suffering and weakness at the cross. The former applies the negative theology of Dionysius, pointing beyond the logic of reason. The latter draws the beyond back into the world, to the suffering and the cross. Whereas both transcend the limits of reason alone, the latter locates this transcendence within the experience of suffering in Christ. This *immanent* transcendence interrupts the process of rational reflection at its weakest point; interrupts and destructs the carefully constructed concept of God with respect to omnipotence, being, glory, and perfection. The paradox of Christology is located in the wounds, in the suffering which takes the reader by surprise, not in the light of her perfection but in the darkness of her passion.[12] And outside of this suffering, Luther asserts that there is no gift of selfless love, no grace, no forgiveness of sins, and so forth.

Beware of the Numinous Majesty

The discussion between Erasmus and Luther in *Diatribe de libero arbitrio* (1524) and *De servo arbitrio* (1525) is more complex when it comes to the logic and structure of thought, much due to the objections from Erasmus. He brings in new aspects to this debate: first, the critical objection of whether it is important to delve deeper into these questions at all, since every discourse on these obscure issues seems to produce further speculations and end up with frightening myths rather than knowledge;[13] and second, the insinuation that Luther's position may imply a threatening and dark image of God, which leaves all believers and non-believers in doubt when it comes to the most decisive questions of Christian faith, namely, whether God is good beyond goodness or also the ultimate cause of evil.[14] Is God ambivalent when it comes to the distinction of good and evil? Is God partial and unpredictable when some people are elected whereas others are rejected? May anyone then trust God, or should everyone fear God as the ultimate cause of terror and confusion, of fear and trembling?

The objections go to the core of Christian faith, but also to the general philosophical question of sense and coherence: Is the ultimate source of being reasonable and at least to a certain extent predictable? Is the world in which we live governed by a higher principle of reason and goodness, or do we have to cope with arbitrariness and injustice as the basic conditions of life? When Luther denies that there is any such "thing" or faculty called free will (*liberum arbitrium*), Erasmus accuses him of ascribing both good and evil to God. And he does not exactly find Luther's reference to a hidden God helpful or comforting. On the contrary: This leaves us with an inhuman, threatening, and unsettling deity, he argues.

Such unsettling ambivalence of the divine has its own dark fascination and is well known from Manichaeism, mystery cults, and Gnostic systems of beliefs, mostly rejected as heretic by the defenders of Christian doctrine, and in particular when such notions are ascribed to the biblical scriptures. Hence, Erasmus warns his opponent against this danger lurking within the text. Scripture promises some secret knowledge and insight, he writes, yet he fears that the promise will be delusive and thus disappointing—or even worse: that the mysteries of the text possess an incredible fascination, owing to their site in the depth of secrecy. Humans have always been attracted by secrets and mysteries, although such secrets in the long run tend to drive them to despair. Erasmus warns against disseminating such mysteries among the common people, since they are apt to spread confusion and irreligiosity.[15] He even insinuates that fantasies about the hidden God may lead to political turmoil and riots, probably hinting at the secret teachings of Andreas Karlstadt and Thomas Müntzer, both charismatic preachers. With his references to Karlstadt as an opponent of *liberum arbitrium,* he insinuates that there is a connection between radical theological doctrines and radical political doctrines that would disaffirm Luther in the public debate.[16]

As a leading academic and humanist, Erasmus is not a supporter of mysteries. He prefers to leave the authority in questions of faith and doctrine to the church. However, he is aware that the textual references to the hidden God are still there within scripture, and therefore he can only appeal to the responsibility of the interpreter and warn against the consequences of delving deeper into the potential *meaning* of these passages, which may be disruptive in political as well as religious respects, and a threat to the unity of the church. An image from Greek mythology gives an apt circumscription of the ambiguity he sees lurking beneath the surface of the text:

> For there are some secret places in the divine letters into which God did not intend us to penetrate more deeply and, if we try to do so, then the deeper we go, the darker and darker it becomes [*hoc magis ac magis caligamus*]. This is presumably in order to make us recognize the unsearchable majesty of divine wisdom, and the frailty of the human mind. It is like that cave [*de specu*] near Corycos of which Pomponius Mela tells, which begins by attracting and drawing the visitors to itself by its natural beauty, but then as one goes deeper, a certain horror and numinous majesty of the divine presence that inhabits the place makes one draw back.[17]

The myth of the Corycian cave becomes an allegory of text interpretation, illustrating but also mystifying the study of Holy Scripture. This is an explicit warning and prohibition against entering the *secret places* in the divine letters. Moreover, it is a warning against the *speculative* dangers of text interpretation, not only because of the weakness of the mind and the potential narcissism of the mirror (*speculum*), but also the confusing darkness of the cave (*specu*).[18] Although such places seem attractive at first sight, they will soon reveal their true horror, he assumes, connected to the numinous majesty of divine *presence*—thus Erasmus draws back into safe distance, an escape into the protective shelter of interpretation. Separation is the first response to this uneasy suspicion, raised by the obscurity *within* scripture, alas, not "everywhere" but on "certain places" (*adyta quaedam*) where the text becomes less transparent and difficult to understand.

The myth of the Corycian cave is identified by Erasmus as the *limit* of reason, a limit which should not be crossed unless one is willing to accept a mythical discourse. Old myths like the story of the Corycian cave, or the creation myths, or the fall, do not follow the logic of non-contradiction to which philosophers have subscribed since Aristotle. Hence, the distinction between good and evil, true and false, God and humans may be suspended by reference to a third *place* or a third genus, as described in Plato's *Timaeus.*[19] A similar evasion of the Principle of Non-Contradiction is developed in negative theology, but according to Erasmus, philosophical explanations are thereby confused and it gets darker and darker until the *logos* of reason collapses altogether in the depth of the cave, confronted with the ultimate divine mystery. By rejecting such irrational distinctions, Erasmus tries to save scripture from speculative theories and from all the religious enthusiasts flourishing at the time of the Reformation.

Against Obscurantism

Quae supra nos, nihil ad nos: What is above us is no concern of ours.[20] This is Luther's ambivalent commentary to Erasmus's retraction from the problematic places of scripture. On the one hand, he sees the dangers and agrees; yet on the other hand, he thinks that Erasmus is undiscriminatingly afraid of the controversy that might *clarify* the issue and more precisely define the difficult issues at stake, just as he thinks that the Dutchman is afraid of conflict, afraid of assertions, afraid of the truth. It can hardly be denied that Erasmus adapts a strategy of avoidance in questions that are often considered essential to theology, like the question of the Trinity, of the Incarnation, of grace and justice—and the problem of free will.[21] This is the first reason why Luther rejects the allegory and ridicules the myth of the Corycian cave. The other reason is connected to the notion of a text which results from Erasmus's warnings: a dark but fascinating cave that after drawing the visitors into its depth by its "natural beauty" suddenly demonstrates its true danger by terrifying and confusing the reader with mysticism and secrecy. Such allegories are everything but helpful, Luther argues; they merely contribute to further confusion and obfuscation of the questions discussed. Claiming the clarity of scripture even on the most obscure places, he argues against all kinds of obscurantism, even the intellectual form presented by the humanists.

Although they may seem hard to penetrate with reason, these secrets are not to be kept at a distance, Luther maintains: This is exactly the place where the exegete ought to study the scriptures in every detail, and thus venture into the danger zone of the text. Life itself is at stake, according to Luther, and there is no safe place *outside* the text, no place of withdrawal or detachment. The *place* of scripture is not limited by Erasmus's proscriptions or the magisterial efforts at control; its purview might in principle be everywhere. Thus, Luther is not surprised when readers of scripture, including his opponent, are struck by anxiety and unease, since the space that opens up within scripture ceaselessly draws the reader into questions concerning the conditions of life and death, of hope and despair. This is not the time for retraction, though; it is the time for discoveries in the light of scripture, of discerning the decisive differences within the text in order to disclose the distinctions between the world which remains obscure and hidden and the world which proceeds in a different light.

Even if the myth of the Corycian cave were an apt allegory of the text, venturing into the cave would thus be unavoidable. But Luther rejects the image. Scripture, he argues, is entirely clear; much clearer than any light of reason that might enlighten the human being from within. He therefore introduces the metaphor of the fountain as a direct contrast to the Corycian cave: "Who will say that a public fountain is not in the light because those who are in the alleys don't see it?"[22]

Martin Luther can hardly be called a proponent of mysticism and esoteric interpretations. On the contrary: Thanks to the printing revolution and the tedious work of the Bible translators—most notably Luther himself—the text is now available to anyone, including simple people on the street, insofar as they are able to read or listen to someone who knows the noble art of reading. This gesture of freedom and enlightenment is as dangerous as it is audacious, but he is willing to accept the consequences, even when they may include political tumults and riots. There is no reason to mystify the text or keep it secret from common people in order to protect them, he argues. If scripture is a public matter and *exoteric* rather than *esoteric;* if it is situated in the light and made accessible to anyone, it must be possible to draw *distinctions* based on the text, or, rather, *in the light of the text,* in order to understand its message properly.

Paradoxically, he sees the common belief in *liberum arbitrium* as one of the major dangers to such clarifications; for Luther it becomes the epitome of the all too human tendency to look for confirmation of oneself and of personal opinions within the text. According to Luther, this is a permanent source of obscurity and confusion. Hence, the distinction between internal and external clarity becomes all the more decisive: "To put it briefly, there are two kinds of clarity in Scripture, just as there are also two kinds of obscurity: one external and pertaining to the ministry of the Word, the other pertaining to the understanding of the heart."[23] Luther distinguishes one kind of obscurity from the other, the interior from the exterior, just as there are two kinds of clarity: the external clarity based on grammar and writing, and the internal clarity which seeks understanding, consensus, and coherence. These distinctions are significant, since every proper understanding of scripture emerges from writing, from grammar, from external differences—and not the perspicuity of reason. Thus, if we take a look at ourselves through introspection, he argues, we will soon be confused and deluded by illusions and unclear presuppositions; but as soon as we try to spell out the differences and the principles of understanding elaborated within scripture, we will slowly be able to distinguish between light and darkness, between life and death, between God and idol. Within the limits of scripture, everything is clear, Luther claims, like a shining torch.

But is God then delimited by the scriptural definition of God? Or is God also more than what scripture may capture? May God perhaps be completely otherwise than presented in the scriptures? This is the crucial question. And there is no hesitation in Luther's response. With a certain impatience, he explains the most obvious knowledge concerning the relationship between God and scripture: "The distinction I make—in order that I, too, may display a little rhetoric or dialectic—is this: God and the Scripture of God are two things, no less than the Creator and the creature are two things."[24] Whereas Luther affirms that the scriptures are crystal clear when it comes to grammar and external structure, he points out that God remains hidden in many respects, and many things remain hidden in God. This reference to God *outside* scripture is thus delimited and excluded from the notion of God *within* scripture.

This difference is decisive; it is the necessary condition for the clarity of discourse. Drawing a clear distinction between the notion of God *outside* scripture and the way God is understood *according* to scripture appears to be necessary in order to avoid complete confusion. Hence, the former *ought* to be circumscribed. Such circumscription presupposes some definition, though, and this is exactly what is lacking. Erasmus's parable is appropriate in describing the experience of losing one's way, of approaching the impassable, where every explanation, in the proper sense at least, remains impossible. Luther more than agrees with this analysis, arguing that the hidden God remains more secret than a *multitude* of Corycian caves.[25] Paradoxically, the name of God is therefore applied to *both* secrecy and clarity, to the clearest distinctions and the most absconded obscurity, where all distinctions collapse in a space prior to reason, logic, and faith. Hence, albeit the distinction is declared to be most decisive, is it not already contested by the notions involved? Is the scholar who endeavors to distinguish between the two entitled to draw such distinctions at all? How could this distinction possibly be a clear distinction when it seems to be jeopardized, and even necessarily *ought to be* jeopardized, from the moment it is drawn?

This 'outside' is thus excluded from scripture, but scripture still refers to the same name. Does it not mean that the name is destabilized, even desertified, like *the waste land?* That it covers a lot more than the scriptures divulge, indeed a surplus of which we remain ignorant? If this assumption is confirmed, then there is, and must be, secrecy, even *within* the scriptures, due to this *beyond* which is inscribed in the name of God. But is it then still possible, as Luther tries here, to draw a clear line of distinction between God as encountered outside and inside scripture? And whether it is possible or not, according to what kind of logic? Either/or? Both/and? Exclusion or inclusion? The limits between the outside and the inside seem to get *blurred* by the God who is absconding. Where are, then, the limits of scripture? How to define its 'outside' as opposed to its 'inside'?

If we focus on logical distinctions first, before we proceed to the "dialectics and rhetoric" Luther displays, the distinction is an effort at establishing an either/or, and thus God *outside* of scripture is initially excluded from the discourse between the two adversaries. The logical distinctions are significant at this point and they will become even more significant in the following. The argument first pursues a logic of exclusion, and the limit between the inside and the outside continues to be decisive, yet a number of questions are raised from *outside* scripture, where the notion of *deus absconditus* basically remains a question. Yet still, as soon as this question is raised, even within the limits of scriptural discourse, is not the limit already transgressed? Or is it necessary to prohibit, ban, or simply *outlaw* every problematic question in order to preserve clarity? To me it seems like the God outside scripture has already become a topic of the discourse, and will not so easily be excluded or outlawed, and definitely not as long as Luther explicitly allows and occasionally supports, indeed also raises such questions. Even the difficult questions of violence and destruction are raised from *outside* scripture, before they reoccur within scriptural discourse.

The disturbing effect is that this *outside* scripture keeps on *displacing* the distinctions frequently applied to clarifying the concept of God, such as light and darkness, good and evil, being and non-being. Every time the name of God is mentioned, the negative theology of Dionysius recurs, as a destabilization of the distinctions drawn within the text. The potential confusion and despair introduced by the *abscondity* is excluded again and again, with the most decisive and categorical rhetoric. Still, the need for repeated assurances does not exactly contribute to an ending of the suspicions of something more, of a secret which is and remains concealed. Conversely, these rejected indications of abscondity also remain a possibility of understanding *otherwise,* like a luring promise of disclosures to come *within* the text, like a surplus of sense, a gift of what was not to be expected.

A logic of *separation* is therefore at stake here, of separation and difference, which Luther regards as endangered if the text is perceived as obscure and unclear. At the same time, his own textual theory is nourished by the ambiguity of a surplus and abscondity presupposed but not included within the text. Thus, there is also a *participation* which circumvents these efforts at separation. Although the immediate categorial separation of the one from the other, the outside from the inside, is absolute and indisputable, maintaining such absolute separation in the length of time appears to be difficult, if not impossible. It is undermined by the temporal gap between the question and the response, as soon as someone hesitates and doubts the distinction for more than a moment. Luther's point is to demonstrate—by way of dialectics and rhetoric—that what human beings may see or understand of God is very limited, indeed almost nothing compared to the tremendous cosmic force of creation and destruction. Even this very little is enough to introduce a difference, though, and a decisive difference. That is why it gets all the more important to begin where there is some clarity and basic distinctions which make a difference to human life and self-perception, to a general understanding of human experience, to the perception of phenomena in the world, to ethics and politics. All these differences are obscured if the text is perceived as dark and enigmatic.

Luther repeatedly returns to this problem of textual obscurity and lack of differentiation throughout the argument. Such mystification of the text lets the *logos* fall down into *mythos,* he argues, and even the interpretation of the biblical scriptures is left to speculation and tropological reading. This is his repeated argument against "interpretation," which in his vocabulary means using the text as a stepping stone before leaving it behind in order to speculate about the invisible things of God (*invisibilia*); the essence, the power, the will. This is a further reason for *excluding* the question of the hidden God from the scriptures: *Quae supra nos, nihil ad nos.* Alas, the *deus absconditus* is excluded, then, but still presupposed, and exactly thereby included as the *space of possibility* for speaking of God at all. If it was not presupposed, as possibility, as actuality, even as necessity, it would not be a discourse on God (as Luther exclaims with reference to Paul: "God cannot be mocked!"[26]), hence the result of merely excluding this vast space *outside* scripture would be the smooth protection and conservation of religious truths and images *in the name of scripture;* in dialectical theology explicitly understood as the friendly flip side of nihilism. In my opinion, this is what happens in Jüngel's texts on the issue.[27] Conversely, if the hidden God would be indiscriminately *included* in theological, literary, or philosophical discourse, the result is an endless production of new monsters and myths.[28] These are the less fortunate prospects unless the limit of scripture remains a contested limit and an issue of controversy, in words and politics.

In the controversy with Erasmus, the allegory of the Corycian cave is therefore given in return, as an illustration of his method of interpretation: *Liberum arbitrium est merum mendacium,* Luther writes—free will is merely mendacious, or "pure fiction" as the English translators prefer.[29] Moreover, this fiction of free will is accused of *producing* its own myths, continuously, and therefore contributing to the obfuscation of human understanding. The notion of God is no exception; on the contrary, it seems to be particularly susceptible to human wishes and projections. At the same time, *'liberum arbitrium'* is according to Luther an empty word, an empty gap, and every notion attached to free will or free choice is just another product of illusion. Hence, within this approach adopted by Erasmus, he sees illusions upon illusions and words, words, words. Consequently, the myth of the Corycian cave is abruptly rejected with reference to Christ who brings the secrets of divine power into public, and makes the most profound *mysteries* accessible to everyone, regardless of social or religious status and insight.[30]

Divine power and profound mysteries made accessible to *everybody:* This is politically explosive. The statement is followed by a peculiar debate about places, dignity, and power. Erasmus sees academic dignity and religious aesthetics under threat in discussions about *where* God could be and where not, for example, in a cavern or in the sewer. Luther responds according to his anti-aesthetics of destruction, indicating that ugly and inconvenient circumstances are more apt to reveal God: for instance, the belly of a woman, of which Christ was born in flesh and blood. Erasmus's thoughts about God, he claims, are not only human but "all too human."[31] Elsewhere Luther argues that *any* creature and every phenomenon may turn out to be a mask of God—*larva Dei*—not as mystification but rather as disenchantment and clarification of the world. The world in its complexity is not excluded by this understanding of scripture; rather, it is observed and perceived in its otherness, as a stranger, in a world made different. Yet within this masquerade of images, the most unlikely and despicable places are considered more likely to reveal the decisive difference between God and idol than any image of power or perfection: "What is fouler than death? What more horrifying than hell? Yet the prophet praises God who is present with him in death and hell."[32]

Time of War—War on Time

At this point politics and theology intersect, in the questions of power, death, concealment, destruction, and revelation. Luther sees the violent conflicts coming up in the 1520s as a sign that the Word of God is dangerous and efficient. With a number of references to the prophets and the apostles, he argues that this is a war between those who read the scriptures as beautiful fables and those who read them literally, as decisive for questions of life and death, and consequently understand the fight for the freedom of the word as a life-and-death-struggle, a war between God and idols:

> The world and its god cannot and will not endure the word of the true god, and the true god neither will nor can keep silence; so when these two gods are at war with one another, what can there be but turmoil in the whole world? To wish to stop this turmoil, therefore is nothing else but to suppress and prohibit the word of God. For the word of God comes, whenever it comes, to change and renew the world. Even the heathen writers testify that changes of things cannot take place without commotion and tumult, nor indeed without bloodshed. [. . .] For myself, if I did not see these tumults I should say that the word of God was not in the world; but now, when I do see them, I heartily rejoice and have no fear, because I am quite certain that the kingdom of the pope, with all his followers, is going to collapse [. . .].[33]

What Luther refers to as a war of gods, we could add, is also a war of interpretations. Both sides are convinced that their god is the true God, and that the others are apostates, heretics, or infidels. The scene is apocalyptic, but Luther leaves one question open, for a moment: Who is who? Which of these masks belongs to the world, hence is an empty mask, and which mask belongs to the true God, the *larva Dei?* Luther sees the war as a sign of God's presence; that is, the presence of the true God.

Without this war, Luther complains, God is absent; there is, at least, no clear sign of his presence, unless the tumults result in blood and violence. This is a dramatic turn in his theological approach, and it comes up with reference to the *temporality* of the words mediated in scripture. Although scripture becomes available to everyone, even in vernacular language and thus is readable for literate members of the population, this is not sufficient to see it as present. On the contrary: It is kept away from ordinary people by the "interpretations" given by the church. It is softened, leveled, and thus *absent* and without effect as long as it is read as an explanation of how the world *is,* namely, some kind of scriptural ontology.

The temporal mode of the word is entirely different, Luther argues: "the word of God comes, whenever it comes, to change and renew the world." The truth of the word thus belongs to the future; this is the implicit *promise* of the word, and whenever it comes, it comes from the future in order to initiate *change.*[34] This change appears, politically as well as philosophically, as an interruption and disturbance of authority and powers; indeed, an interruption of the framework defining "things" and beings as they "are." The perception of things, of powers and structures of understanding, is apparently thrown into chaos because of these conflicting gods at war. It is definitely *not* the case that as soon as the "god of scripture" is recognized, then the whole world is enlightened and adopts a unified understanding of the world. On the contrary: Between these two gods "at war with one another," a vast space of indefinite questions opens up, questions of signification, of power, of identity, and of violence. Luther is not interested in closing off this space or excluding these disturbing questions; rather, he sees them as signs of promise, of a world made different.

The basic problem here is God's absence, not in general but in scripture. Proclaiming the universal presence of God makes no immediate difference; the world would be more or less the same. But scripture makes a difference in the announcement of a promise. In the grammatical form of pledging or promising (mostly in *indicative future* or *conjunctive present*), scripture infers a difference in the perception of the world: The current authorities and structures of understanding are suspended and thrown into an indefinite future. Hence, when taken literally and read according to its grammatical structure, scripture temporalizes the words, the events, the wars. Scripture as absent conceals a promise which is there in writing but not in speech, which is there as a condition of possibility for temporalization.

The war thus described is therefore a war of two temporalities: the regular time, which is exterior and ontologically bound to *things* and inherited structures of human power, such as the princes, the church, and the pope. And then there is this other temporality breaking in with the promise, a promise of change: a disruption and destruction of the current order. In the collision between two temporal structures, there are not only tensions but also disunity and fragmentation; there is inner turmoil. By uncovering the *absence* of God exactly at the sites where divine *presence* would be expected, Luther argues, the promise of scripture becomes a threat to established structures of power and understanding, even to established structures of time and space. The society, indeed the whole world, is allegedly out of balance, due to this word breaking in, shattering its metaphysical foundations if and when and wherever it comes.

Luther literally *rejoices* when he observes such turmoils, considering them a sign of the word breaking in and making the world new. Like a true revolutionary, he argues that no real change can take place without turmoil, indeed without bloodshed. The world is "shaken and shattered" by the word, he observes, that is, by the *power of scripture* which is released by a detailed, zealous, and audacious reading of the text. He questions institutionalized power in terms of the power of interpretation; or, rather, of disclosure, of "truth," although the *fulfillment* of truth remains a promise for the future: Again and again it is deferred, and thus opens up another scriptural space. What is thereby extremely difficult, if not impossible, is to draw a clear distinction between the warriors of God and the warriors of this world—between the truth worth dying for and the "empty mask" which uses the words of scripture as pretense for securing one's own interests and power.

Given the paradoxical structure Luther detects within the text, he tries to thwart every attempt at taking personal or patriotic benefit from the words. But isn't there yet another danger in this argument, namely, that the cry for conflict may trigger bloodthirsty identity politics? Luther's appeal to the conscience and the freedom of the text is first and foremost directed against the suppression of *scripture* and its inconveniences for any strategic or personal reasons. Yet the danger is there.

Original Difference

Interpretations can always be functionalized for one reason or another. In the face of suffering and death, they may serve the function of calming the reader and curbing conflicts—in most cases a strategy with the best intentions. The interpretation thus functions as protection against the problems raised by the text, for example, as protection against the thought of death and political conflict. Karl Marx's characterization of religion as "opium of the people" points at this tendency to sugarcoat poverty by promising eternal salvation rather than trying to change the material conditions here and now. Incidentally or not, the rhetoric and aesthetics of Marx follow the same pattern as Luther, namely, to give a realistic impression of the problems and difficulties rather than softening them and playing them down for the sake of harmony.

'*Deus absconditus*' is a critical notion in this respect, not only when it comes to rhetoric and dialectics, as Luther notes, but also when it comes to grammar, logic, and ordinary language (*usus loquendi*). Luther is occasionally accused of projecting all difficulties inherent to theology onto the shadowy figure of a hidden God, thus avoiding all the difficulties related to evil and suffering, to omnipotence, to the questions of salvation and predestination, and to the nature of God. Reading *De servo arbitrio* according to a strategy of avoidance is therefore indeed possible and has lately become the rule rather than the exception, owing to a strong Barthian influence in Protestant theology.[35] However, if we take a closer look at the problems Luther raises and the logic he applies, this strategy is not entirely convincing. Let me mention one example, the death of a sinner, which is discussed in relation to two passages from Ezekiel 18 and 33, where the prophet gives voice to the following message from God: "As I live, says the Lord, I desire not the death of a sinner, but rather that he should turn and live." (Ezekiel 33:11)[36]

Absurd, mocks Erasmus, if the good God would "lament the death of his people which he himself works in them."[37] What kind of goodness is that? The cruelest goodness the world has ever seen? A dubious double game intended to gloss over the brutal reality?

Giving a good answer to these disturbing questions seems difficult if not impossible. It appears that Luther turns the question around and takes these difficulties as a point of departure. Where Erasmus expects divine *identity* and unity of will, Luther rejects it as illusive. We have to presuppose an original *difference*, he argues, within God: "One will have to argue *otherwise* [*aliter*] about God and the will of God as preached, offered, revealed, and worshiped, and otherwise [*aliter*] of God as not preached, not offered, not revealed, not worshiped."[38] The difference thus presupposed is significant but remains inscrutable nonetheless. Although the difference is established rhetorically as well as dialectically, the limit between the one and the other remains problematic: As soon as the limit is drawn, it is also questioned, if not erased, by the questions raised concerning the death of a sinner, by the doubts and despairs of everyone who interrogates into the questions of intentions, of power, of deploration, of mourning. Is there any line of distinction that could circumscribe the absconding? Or will every question raised with reference to the *'deus absconditus'* also be silenced in reverence of the name? In the final analysis, secrecy seems to prevail *within the name*. Luther writes:

> This will is not to be inquired into, but reverently adored, as by far the most awe-inspiring secret of the divine majesty, reserved for himself alone and forbidden to us much more reverently than an infinite number of Corycian caverns.[39]

Many interpreters of this text are blinded by the religious language with mythical connotations, but the theoretical consequence of this original difference within God is exactly the opposite—a critical destruction of myths and speculations concerning the hidden God, but also a destruction of ideals and wishes projected at the invisible. A radical abstraction draws the conflicting interpretations down to an open question, an interrogation of God, while facing the unfathomable abyss of not knowing, indeed, not even knowing how to ask. Hence, the repeated prohibition against interrogating into the intentions of the divine force: *Quae supra nos, nihil ad nos.* However, whereas the warning targets asking for reasons and grounds, it is not directed against the *difference* as such, between being hidden and visible. On the contrary: This difference is crucial for establishing a space of understanding at all, in particular when it comes to the most simple and basic conditions for human life, suffering, and action.

The readers of *De servo arbitrio* have frequently been blinded by the notion of a hidden god, allegedly situated somewhere out there in the universe. However, the theoretical significance of this term concerns the *conditions for speaking, or writing, about God.* Hence, this is the most decisive place for opening a textual space, in order to reflect upon the conditions for naming and defining God, including the conditions for interpreting scripture. If such space is lacking, scripture and the interpretation of scripture are prone to producing a static symbol, bound to particular rules of understanding, including such definitions of God as *x*, given a particular understanding of *x* (e.g., goodness, being, etc.). However, the possibilities of conceptual language, and of scripture, in describing this reality and possibility referred to as "God" turn out to be extremely limited.

Every effort at understanding God therefore has to be cautious in order to avoid inventing new rules of understanding, new categories, new human laws, or, oppositely, simply *reproducing* the old and enclosing the concept within clearly defined limits and gates, to which the interpreter himself has the key, such as, a "key of interpretation." Luther therefore recalls the insight from negative theology: When it comes to the most basic questions concerning God, a space has been *reserved* (*soli sibi reservatum*) above and prior to all other questions and distinctions, that is, a space of possibility and of otherness, a space which makes it possible to read and understand the world otherwise (*aliter*), a space of difference and of change. The paradox is that the argument for a strict division between abscondity and revelation leaves the reader with profound and unavoidable ambivalence.

An Otherness Void of Protection

The space thus opened up within the text breaks the concept of God open, in fact radically open, even as far as it belongs to scripture and is called upon as authority of the law, as witness, as creator, as judge, or as speaker of a promise. The discussion is concerned with life and death, the merciless law of life and death, which pertains to every living creature and regulates nature according to the inherent laws of necessity. Now, can God *deplore* the death of his people, or of any human being, if the law of life and death, of creation and destruction, in the final analysis is regulated by the will of God? The contradictions inherent in this question seem to be invincible; moreover, they suggest a cruelty of divine calculation which would not inspire confidence. However, the objection thus raised is not presented as an open question. It is an objection which reduces all properties of God to a single, problematic, contradictive, identity: In the *Diatribe* the argument is pressed toward a reductio ad absurdum.

Surprisingly, this reduction is not merely rejected by Luther. On the contrary: He seems to agree that this is exactly where the problem lies. The reduction is linked to the experience of suffering and death. Hence, the reader has to follow Luther into a phenomenological reduction of the conditions for understanding and naming God: It is indeed impossible to define God as far as "God himself" is concerned, he argues. Confronting the reader with *deus absconditus* means emptying the fixed meaning of the name 'god,' a bit like walking into the desert or wasteland, hence what Heidegger calls a "desertification"(*Verwüstung*) of language, and thus forcing the reader into a desert of not knowing, incessantly reminding us of an ancient biblical topos.

Deus absconditus is the name for such a desert, for such a wasteland within scripture, or without scripture, and the other experiences to be expected or even not to be expected out there; an otherness void of all the protections established by wishful thinking and projections, by allegories and metaphysical constructions, by illusions and interpretations of the invisible. There are further examples of phenomenological reduction in scripture, such as Moses's encounter with the backside of God (Exodus 33) and Isaiah exclaiming: *Vere absconditus tu es Deus* (Isaiah 45:15), to which Luther explicitly referred in *Heidelberg Disputation*. Whatever the historical background for these narratives, in *De servo arbitrio* they indicate a radical reduction of phenomena, properties, and concepts describing God. We are left with the absconding, with the dark night of absolute unknowing and concealment, as premise for everything we might wish to say about the revealed, about scripture, about metaphysics, about doctrine or tradition, about experiences of God, and so forth. God is thus absconding, absent, concealed, beyond knowledge, beyond knowing, not even accessible by prayer or by mystical vision or intuition, and the *reverence* mentioned here is simply the reverence of such a dissociation between what is said, heard, seen, or sensed and what remains unsaid, unseen, and unheard of.

Metaphysically, one may still speculate about power and causation, about prescience, presence, and necessity, as Luther does in the following sections; but strictly speaking, the secret of abscondity is not accessible for temporal categories. There is neither memory nor hope nor expectation; with this absolute abscondity, there is neither time nor space.

The reduction thus described is the condition for thinking according to the *difference* that opens up between the *absconditus* and its other (*praedicatus, revelatus, oblatus, cultus*) like an abyss or chasm within God—itself not temporal but rather a *condition* for the temporality Luther seeks to define, which he finds preconfigured in scripture, namely, the difference between past and future, between memory and promise, between the tradition which has given the premises and preconditions for thought, and the repetition which in every instance depends on the unpredictable, the absolute possibility—in short, on the gift of grace.

The difference emphasized, as the secret of the *absconditus,* is not to be confused with the majesty, with the absolute will and power of the divine, or with the "nature of God" referred to in the following passage. Indeed, this fine distinction is significant to emphasize, since it tends to be overlooked: The difference is not to be identified with the hidden God,[40] and not to be identified with the revealed,[41] but the abscondity preceding both; this is not another concept defining the presence or absence of God, but rather the gap, the trace, the chasm separating the one from the other. An *identification* of the difference with the majesty of the divine will would therefore be fatal; as a matter of fact, it would also lead to fatalism.[42] Hence, this "deus in maiestate et natura sua" (God in his majesty and nature) is no concern of ours, not here, at least, and not now.

What *is* of our concern is the difference between *'deus absconditus'* and *'deus revelatus'*; that is, the line of distinction, and the temporal, spatial, linguistic distinctions that are at stake. My theory, which admittedly is nothing more than a theory, but nevertheless a thought with far-reaching consequences, is that this distinction *as such* has been overlooked by the innumerable authors who have written about Luther over the last five centuries, and the situation is not very different today. Instead of discussing the relevance of *deus absconditus* "after" metaphysics, or "after" modernity, or all the difficulties connected to omnipotence, to omniscience, to theism, to atheism, and so forth, it is time to take a look at this minute distinction, which grammatically, at least, draws the line of distinction and makes us aware of the difference. If we look carefully at the text, we can see the difference which concerns the author of *De servo arbitrio* at this point of the book, almost exactly in the middle of the book. But why?

It is a question of perspective, hence of theory, of *how* you look at things, how you approach the text, in order to find solutions and certitude or the opposite, to identify and scrutinize the problems raised—even if they are not solved, and thus simply preserved as problems, as quandaries that may trigger the reader to read otherwise. Readers of Luther continue to look for descriptions of God, for clarifications, for definitions, and for interpretations. Whether they intend to criticize his work or look for an authority to follow, they are looking for answers. I have been looking for the questions raised by this text, and a number of the most basic questions take this distinction as their point of departure. This original difference is in one respect theological, but then again it is *pre*-theological, since it precedes the *logos* of theology. It forces us to take into account the concealment of the divine, and the *conditions* for speaking or not speaking about God, whenever we offer critique or defense of religion, whenever we look for revelation, experience, or interpretation, whenever we discuss theism or atheism, the dead or the living God.

This pre-theological difference is not merely a question of theology, though. It is also connected to *logos* or reason in general. As the previous analysis indicates, this distinction is *grammatical* as far as scripture is concerned. As a grammatical distinction it is primarily a question of linguistics, of how language constructs, defines, and destructs reality; and of course it is a question of scripture. This grammatical difference is the condition for a number of other linguistic distinctions, including the various tenses and forms of the verbs. It makes us aware of the need for careful grammatical analysis, which Luther repeatedly underscores in his discussions of internal versus external clarity of scripture.

The difference between God as hidden and revealed is the most generic difference we can detect in the controversy between Erasmus and Luther, and that is probably the reason why it can hardly be separated from other issues, normally regarded as metaphysical, political, ethical, and anthropological. In all these respects, we find distinctions that are influenced by the original difference between abscondity and revelation.

PART IV

Modernity in the Making

The greatest hazard of all, losing one's self, can occur very quietly in the world, as if it were nothing at all . . . any other loss—an arm, a leg, five dollars, a wife, etc.—is sure to be noticed.

—Søren Kierkegaard

TEN

Topology of the Self in Luther

The hidden God is to a certain extent a neglected *topos* of modernity, either in the form of a passive forgetfulness or an active exclusion of this topic due to its inconvenient, problematic—indeed, rather *unmodern*—connotations. In particular Protestant theology seems to be dominated by a rationalistic tendency up to the Enlightenment, which is strictly opposed to this crucial distinction in Luther's thought and therefore tends to exclude it from the scope of theological inquiry.[1] The major philosophers are more apt to raise the basic questions concerning the conditions for thought, including the limits of reason and the distinction between hiddenness and revelation, and thus they also inquire into the questions raised by the Reformation. A careful analysis of each philosopher would by far transgress the limits of the present volume, but in a planned second volume I will outline some trajectories of thought running from Luther up to the present, based on a topological approach.

That the perception of this topos has changed with the course of time is not exactly a controversial claim. But what is the criterion for *measuring* these changes? What is the ultimate point of reference for modern philosophy? Reiner Schürmann sees the question of the self as the ultimate point of reference in modernity, its "ultimate differend." In his topology of the modern era, not only historical but also systematic issues are at stake. David Kangas has pointed out that a genealogy of modernity most commonly begins with Descartes, in particular if we follow the assessment of Continental philosophers adopting a historical perspective in order to better understand the conditions for thought.[2] That is the case if we read Hegel as well as Heidegger or Husserl and most of the contemporary histories of Western philosophy.

Central to this discussion is the redefinition of subjectivity: How and why was self-consciousness established as condition for valid and certain knowledge in the sixteenth and seventeenth centuries? The Cartesian doubt questions the very basis of late-medieval rationality. The conclusion reached by the cogito introduces a double principle of epistemology and method, which since then has influenced not only the humanities, but also the rules of perception and certainty within the natural and social sciences: (i) self-consciousness became the decisive criterion for true and evident cognition; and (ii) infinite mathematics delivers the ideal for clear and rigorous deductive thinking. Moreover, it forms the way we organize, reflect upon, and represent sense impressions.

In *Crisis* (*Die Krisis der europäischen Wissenschaften,* 1936), Husserl points out that the theoretical principle of infinite mathematics had been introduced already by Galileo but there was still need for a framework *in consciousness,* not established until the cogito and even then in terms of a problematic dualism.[3] Moreover, he argues that the latent crisis of the European sciences in the twentieth century was due to deficient reflection of the mutual dependence of subjectivity and infinite mathematics in order to *constitute* a life-world and thus the modern view on any phenomena.[4] Although Kant is criticized for being too abstract in his theoretical philosophy, Husserl argues that self-consciousness remains the transcendental condition for sense impression as well as theoretical reflection; for ethical, aesthetic, and "pure" reason.[5]

Reiner Schürmann offers an alternative to Husserl's and Heidegger's reading of the history of modern philosophy, based on the opposition between natality and mortality. He analyzes these thinkers in terms of a topology, thus challenging the idea of *progressive truth* which dominates not only the disciplines of history of ideas and political science, but also systematic disciplines like philosophy and theology. Schürmann argues that the turn to self-consciousness was established already with Luther.

In Schürmann's argument for self-consciousness as the *ultimate condition* for the entire philosophical discourse developing throughout the modern era, Kant comes to play a central role. But he points at Martin Luther rather than René Descartes as the thinker who prefigures the Copernican turn in Kant, thus establishing self-consciousness as hegemonic principle and ultimate condition for thought, action, and representation.[6] This is, however, an argument which demands careful consideration, in particular of what the question of *transcendental conditions* concerns. Luther could hardly be credited with the introduction of infinite mathematics as the scientific basis of human perception. In that sense, he is a medieval thinker, referring to a finite Ptolemaic view of the universe and basing his view of history on biblical sources. Hence, God who created the world is also seen as the almighty creator of whatever happens in nature and in history (*creatio continua*). Still, the reference to divine hiddenness is more ambivalent when it comes to the ancient/modern division. Luther is influenced by late-medieval voluntarism (Scotus, Ockham) in attributing every single event to the will of God. This could actually be seen as a *modern* trait of his thought, which he has in common with Descartes and the majority of early modern science. Even his argument concerning the hidden God is not merely an echo from an ancient past, since it breaks up the medieval framework from within and makes possible this transition beyond the limited universe of medieval cosmology and the sociopolitical economy of medieval society.

Luther's decisive contribution to transcendental thinking is not scientific in the technical sense, though; it rather must be characterized as phenomenological. Schürmann thus argues that the key concepts of Luther's theology, including the concept of God, are not discussed under the perspective of how things "are" but rather how they *appear* for consciousness. According to this line of reasoning, we may read the famous distinction in *De servo arbitrio* between God hidden and God revealed.[7] This is also a significant point in Schürmann's argument for a genealogy of the modern self, going back to Luther.[8] His approach implies a rereading of Luther on conditions which are less common in Luther research. He argues that Luther's turn toward consciousness *de facto* and *de jure* institutes a new hegemony, the *modern* hegemony. The Latin hegemony is thus left behind, which according to Schürmann based its thinking on 'nature' as ultimate reference, whereas the new hegemony refers to self-consciousness as the ultimate condition and justification.[9]

If Schürmann is right, a few books on the history of modern philosophy ought to be rewritten. Still, there are some weak or at least unclear points in his hypothesis, and the theory as a whole deserves a critical examination, including a more detailed discussion of Kant's transcendental turn in its relation to Luther. We begin with a few preliminary remarks on Schürmann's theory of broken hegemonies and his topological approach.

Schürmann on Luther's Topology

Schürmann's analytics of the ultimate conditions for Western philosophy are clearly influenced by Heidegger and Hannah Arendt and reach all the way back to Parmenides and the other pre-Socratic philosophers. Parmenides instituted what he sees as the first hegemony in Western philosophy: The One, *to hen,* is perceived as the ultimate but internally divided condition which holds together the contradictions as well as the contraries. Focusing on the institution and destitution of *hegemonies,* Schürmann then moves on via Plato and Aristotle to an analysis of Plotinus, where he sees *henology* as being "turned against itself" before it dissolves.[10] The second hegemony is instituted by Roman political and rhetorical thinkers and establishes *nature* as the ultimate condition of thought. From Cicero and Augustine to Meister Eckhart, Schürmann sees nature as basis for the logical organization of time, being, thought, and will. When the concept of nature as hegemonic condition fractures in the fourteenth and fifteenth centuries, with the nominalists on the one hand and the mystics on the other, he argues that there is another transition taking place, to a hegemony based on consciousness. According to Schürmann, Luther introduces this modern hegemony, but all the implications of that overturn will not be realized until the theoretical philosophy of Immanuel Kant. In Heidegger, Schürmann sees the modern hegemony as deeply questioned and dissolving.

Schürmann's topological approach is not unaffected by the differences in conceptuality between Kant and Luther, but it is a significant counterstrategy to the common illusion that the truth is always found in the *present*, or, rather, an insight to be achieved in the *near future*. Moreover, topology opens up for a comparative reading of Kant and Luther without overlooking the significant differences of their historical, political, and religious contexts. Self-consciousness as the new site of thought introduced by Luther is treated as a hegemonic *fantasm*, but nevertheless the ultimate expression of truth within this conceptual framework. The existential pessimism of Schürmann's approach presupposes a skeptical relativism. Hence, it is hardly a neutral position. Still, as an analytic approach, the tragic condition is helpful in addressing some key questions at stake in the history of Western thought, which include philosophy, politics, ethics, and theology. Like Nietzsche's genealogy, Schürmann's tragic skepticism scrutinizes some of the most influential concepts of modernity, yet avoids some of the monstrosities inherent in Nietzsche's thought.

The notion of God is, like key notions of the various hegemonies such as the self, nature, and the One, also identified as a "fantasm." This seems to be a deliberate strategic choice with significance for the overall project, an analytic of ultimates. In order to be analyzed comparatively, he assumes that any claim to ultimacy needs to be bracketed and suspended. Conversely, given Schürmann's lifelong occupation with mystics like Meister Eckhart, the notion of God remains significant within and beyond this text. Schürmann is not a critic of religion in general; his approach appears to be agnostic, as radical mysticism and modern negative theology often tend to be. Schürmann's *diremption* (*Entzweiung*) of the history of modernity seems to have left this space open behind the blindfold of ignorance:

> What comes to pass for us is not the destitution of one fantasm after the other, but a *diremption* that deprives us henceforth of any fantasmic recourse. By "diremption," I only mean secondarily the will not to want to posit, which is only another posture of the will. "Diremption" means first of all an expiration has happened, the annihilation of normative acts that cleanses the tragic condition.[11]

The secondary definition of diremption indicates a classical Stoicism, that is to say, the *will* not to want to posit, which experienced a new revival in post-modern philosophy toward the end of the twentieth century.[12] The primary definition is an expression of withdrawal from all normative acts, and in this case it implies a passivism or mystic retraction in order to resist all forms of metaphysical and normative violence. The somewhat unusual term "diremption" (*Entzweiung*) betrays an unmistakably Hegelian operator at work within Schürmann's monumental project, although he expresses the will to avoid the inherent hubris of Hegel's speculative Idealism. Therefore, the diremption as such is also recognizable in the discord between Schürmann's philosophical analytic of ultimates and the space of the hidden God which is left unarticulated and unaffected by his analysis. This space will keep our special attention when we discuss Schürmann's hypothesis, that modernity begins with Luther.

In order to confirm or reject his hypothesis, however, it is not sufficient to show whether or not Luther based his thinking on self-consciousness, since that is a mainstream feature in the tradition he belongs to—at least since Augustine. Neither will it suffice to show that he is occupied with phenomena or that he shifts focus from exteriority to interiority. Both are important topics for Luther but do not point in the direction of an ultimate condition. We have to discuss, with reference to the more detailed readings of Luther in part II, whether a major shift is introduced by the way Luther constitutes phenomena, that is, whether he thereby establishes a new site with its peculiar logic, and whether self-consciousness *structures* reflection as well as representation and thus establishes the main *topos* for an entire epoch.

Three Topoi of Self-Consciousness

During the last third of the twentieth century, a transcendental approach to Luther is elaborated by a few philosophers and theologians. Studies written by Wilfried Joest (1967) and Rudolf Malter (1980) establish, respectively, a Heideggerian and a Kantian perspective on Luther. Both Joest and Malter begin with Luther's critique of metaphysics and show how Luther exposes and then rejects the inversion of philosophy into egocentric (*ichhaftes*) understanding.[13] Their point is a more traditional version of my analysis of the *Heidelberg Disputation* in chapter 5—namely, that this naturally *egocentric* human attitude renders the direct application of philosophical truth in theology impossible.[14] Hence, Luther rejects the usage of metaphysics as basis for the interpretation of scripture and is generally skeptical about any theory of human existence or of God based on metaphysical conceptions. However, this negative point of departure does not prevent Joest and Malter from writing positively about Luther's ontology and Luther's metaphysics, given that we presuppose a modern understanding of the terms.

Joest puts particular emphasis on the "excentric character" of Luther's anthropology in contrast to earlier concepts of a person as *substance*. The latter were either based on the structure body / soul / spirit or sense / reason / spirit, and both substance-definitions are well known from medieval philosophy and mystical theology.[15] Joest argues that Luther's approach is different: He elaborates the different *places* of the ontological structure as the will (*voluntas*), the heart (*cor*), and the conscience (*conscientia*) of a person.[16] These are not identified as substantial definitions but rather three different topoi of the struggle between the logic of the flesh and the logic of the spirit. Joest's elaboration of a topography of human existence thereby conforms to Melanchton's Aristotelian definition of topos rather than the questioning of the place coming up with Luther's notion of the hidden God.[17] Still, the distinction between flesh and spirit transgresses the rational and decisional abilities of a human being. Accordingly, the transition from one logic to the other has to be passive (*mere passive*), and follows as the result of attentive *listening* to the word.

The decisive moment of justification implies such a *transition* from the logic of the self-centered *ego* (flesh) to the logic of the *excentric self* (spirit) as the organizing principle of a person with its center outside itself. Joest's analysis is not radically different from that of other theologians like Elert or Ebeling, or philosopher Erwin Metzke, but his identification of an ontological structure in Luther establishes a different framework for the analysis which comes closer to the phenomenological tradition after Husserl.[18] Following a similar pattern, Rudolf Malter emphasizes what he takes to be the basic *transcendental* thought of Luther: justification through faith alone (*sola fide*).[19] According to Malter, the discovery of this basic truth is immediate and simple, and nevertheless as complex and far-reaching in its consequences as Descartes's cogito:

> The abolition of self-centered understanding and the constitution of spiritual understanding takes place in one single process, to which reason relates passively—turned passive despite its own intentions according to the law [. . .] That human reason receives its metaphysical determination from outside and yet in terms of knowledge, is by Luther formulated as justification by faith: that is the center of the thought of the Reformation—simple and yet highly complicated, as Descartes' thought of the cogito or Kant's idea of a transcendental deduction.[20]

Malter takes the topographical analysis one step further by defining the different positions of the self in its relation to the law: The first topos of the self is *outside* the law; the second *in the face of* the law, where the human subject is judged, *subjected*, and, so to speak, *crisscrossed* by the law; and the third is *beyond* the law, in passive and receptive justification.[21] The law thus makes the transition possible, from the logic of the flesh toward the *other* logic of the spirit, but is nevertheless surpassed by the knowledge of justification by faith. Malter also emphasizes that the transition follows passively *ex auditu* (by hearing) and implies that God is accepted as the only true agent (hence a transition *mere passive*). This is what Malter calls the transcendental-practical metaphysics of Luther: Whereas the old metaphysics was concerned with substance and attributes of the invisible God, the *new* metaphysics has a practical aim, transforming not only the conceptual framework but, more significant, the ethical orientation and motivation for practical philosophy.

The perception of the world is thus transformed in the light of faith and through the grammar of scripture. Hence, the *phenomena* are reappropriated according to the logic of the spirit. At this point Malter sees Luther anticipating Kant, who also denied the option of a speculative metaphysics and established a transcendental thinking with a threefold purpose: perception, action, and judgment.[22] There are still principal differences between the two, such as, between Luther's heteronomy and Kant's autonomy, but even here, Malter sees an embryonic concept of autonomy in Luther, namely, in his emphasis on the freedom of a Christian according to the spirit and on the positive practical responsibility toward other human beings.[23]

This is the theoretical background for Reiner Schürmann's argument that Luther introduces a fundamental change in the history of thought. Following Malter, Schürmann claims that Luther introduced an epistemological shift about a hundred years before Descartes, which established new ultimate conditions for rational discourse.[24] Schürmann admits that Luther has not yet recognized the ultimate condition *as such,* but a site has nevertheless been established *from where* all knowledge is to be tested and *wherein* even a moral conscience will find its justification, and that is human self-consciousness. If this is supposed to be an ultimate condition for the discourse, however, it must be clarified to what extent this referent is normative, thus establishing a new *order* of perception, recognition, reflection, and action. According to Schürmann's phenomenological analysis, it is not only a question of defining a principle of thought or being: "Rather, consciousness makes the law; it makes the law in the manner of a condition 'determining' all phenomena, a condition which is perhaps not altogether opposable to a cause effectuating phenomena."[25]

With this shift to self-consciousness, Schürmann sees an overturning of all thinking prefiguring the Copernican turn in Kant and German Idealism, even what the sense of being concerns: "[A]fter Luther, 'to be' means 'to be for consciousness.'"[26] *Truth* is thus no longer defined by an order of essences but in an "originary act of consciousness." Schürmann's argument is not delimited to a phenomenological analysis of Luther; his work *Broken Hegemonies* is first of all a *topological* inquiry tracing the origin of modern philosophy back to Luther. Following Malter closely he emphasizes one important difference, though: The Lutheran self is *not* autonomous, even though it is seen as "nomothetic," nor is it spontaneous in its freedom.[27]

The question thus coming up is whether Luther's self should be considered a philosophical rather than a theological self if it remains heteronomous and based in divine law. Schürmann by no means denies the theological rationale in Luther, but he argues that his theory of *language* is the theoretical basis for his theology: *the word* which serves as common ground for philosophers as well as theologians in the sixteenth century.[28] Luther thereby emphasizes the *spoken* word as liberating and saving. That is a word spoken in public and defended in public, but also a word based in scripture. Through the voice, the word becomes efficacious; it justifies and gives promise. Schürmann even refers to the double work of the word, as law and promise, and argues that the *topography* of the new self is based on this distinction.[29]

This topography draws the map for the subsequent *topology* where he argues that self-consciousness organizes and structures the perception of self, God, neighbor, and world. In this analysis, Schürmann follows the key steps in Malter's reconstruction: The first topos situates the self *outside* the law, in indifferent freedom. That, however, is also the site of pre-morality and ignorance, similar to the pre-linguistic stage of infancy. Second, there is the topos of the law, including a moral judgment and consciousness of sin, based on the word of scripture with divine authority. Third, there is the word of grace which establishes the self as the *site* for evaluating and perceiving everything else, including the process of reconciliation, of reflection, of representation, of recognition, and of reappropriation. This is what Luther has defined as the *freedom* of a Christian, and according to Schürmann that is the historical moment when the modern self is established in terms of the *sola fide*.[30]

Turning the Axis of Inquiry from Things toward Phenomena

According to Schürmann's topological analysis, Luther establishes the new topos for philosophical as well as theological reflection.[31] I cannot follow his argument in every detail here, but I will discuss his general hypothesis and the consequences such a genealogy may have for a reconsideration of the modern era with respect to challenges of contemporary philosophy and theology. Since Schürmann introduces his own conditions of thought as a critique of an alleged denial of the tragic in the history of philosophy, this tragic difference dominates his reading of Luther, too.[32] In the line of Hannah Arendt's political philosophy, he defines the double principle of the tragic as natality and mortality, and he argues that this is the basic *human condition* on which all the ultimate hegemonic notions depend, even though the philosophers tend to forget it.

Natality thus produces principles and universalizations in order to organize the world—our metaphysical vein, so to speak. *Mortality*, conversely, draws us toward singularization and decision (compare with Heidegger). These are the alternative conceptualizations organizing Schürmann's genealogy: The tragic condition is supposed to outstrip and expose the ultimate differences traditionally organizing the history of philosophy as illusive "fantasms," although there is little reason to doubt that they represented an ultimate metaphysical reality to the philosophers who referred to them in their thought.

Schürmann argues that the *tragic* condition tends to become more important in the breakthrough of a new hegemony and provides what he characterizes as an appropriate analysis of human thought, power, and action. What he soon discovers in Luther, however, is that natality produces "the contrary of what it promises. It produces death."[33] Conversely, in Luther's grammar, awareness of our mortality enables us to discover ourselves *coram Deo*. Hence, because of a conversion of premises and consequences, Schürmann argues that Luther's consciousness of death "becomes the source of life."[34] Like Heidegger he sees the constitution of self as determined by the subject's relationship with its own death; what Derrida in turn describes as *spacing* the self in terms of writing.[35] This new sense of the tragic is, according to Schürmann, based on a logic which overturns all the premises of thought and being in late-medieval thinking. It initiates a rethinking of nature, action, and faith in terms of phenomena for consciousness. He further claims that

> [Luther] is reorienting an entire mode of thinking; he does so by directing the axis of inquiry elsewhere, thus rendering the old problems problematic in a different way; and he is no less explicit about the old orientation, hereafter senseless, than he is about the new, henceforth the only sensible one: to think no longer according to "things," but according to "consciousness."[36]

When Schürmann claims that Luther no longer thinks according to things or essences, it is not precisely in accordance with Luther's own terminology. Luther often refers to a thing in the world as "res," and such references become even more frequent when he later discusses the elements of the sacraments. The adequate question is, however, not only whether he refers to "things" or not, but *how* he refers to "things," as nature or as phenomena. This seems to differ, depending on the context of his discussion. The ambiguity is palpable in a significant example from the introduction to *De servo arbitrio,* where the true matter (res) of the scriptures is under discussion:

> The subject matter [*res*] of the scriptures, therefore, is all quite accessible, even though some texts are still obscure owing to our ignorance of their terms. Truly it is stupid and impious when we know that the subject matter of scripture has all been placed in the clearest light, to call it obscure [*res obscuras*] on account of a few obscure words. If the words are obscure in one place [*loco*], yet they are plain in another; and

> it is one and the same thing [*eadem vero res*], published quite openly to the whole world, which in the scriptures is sometimes expressed in plain words, and sometimes lies as yet hidden in obscure words. Now, when the thing [*res*] signified is in the light, it does not matter if this or that sign is in darkness, since many other signs of the same thing [*res*] are meanwhile in the light. Who will say that a public fountain is not in the light because those who are in a narrow side street do not see it, whereas all who are in the marketplace do see it?[37]

This passage demonstrates how the *matter* (res) of a text, of a problem, of faith or knowledge is perceived as a *phenomenon,* not according to the "light" of reason but according to the letter and grammar of the text. Luther may still speak of "things" as something we find in nature, but the axis of *inquiry* is directed elsewhere: toward the source of light, with respect to the clarity of the written text, that may *clarify* the problem under discussion. Hence, scripture is indeed *nomothetic* for the perception of phenomena and for the reconstruction of consciousness. What differs slightly from Schürmann's theory is that Luther consequently refers to scripture and its *external* clarity rather than the *internal* clarity of self-consciousness. The difference is not quite insignificant.

The Latin word used for clarity in this passage is not *perspicuitas* but *claritas,* later to be explained by reference to a shining torch. The distinction between *external* clarity, referring to the fountain which is clarified by the light of the text, and *internal* clarity of understanding is explained by the ability to see and understand the world in the light of scripture, whatever arguments and intentions reason may have to reject it. The theory of knowledge thus established is a theory of things *as* phenomena, that is, not as they are "in themselves" but *as they appear when reappropriated in the light of scripture.*

This is not the only way Luther applies the Latin word *res* or the German *Sache,* but it is a characteristic turn of thought in *De servo arbitrio.* Hence, Schürmann has a good point when he argues that there is a change of focus, although it is slightly overemphasized in his analysis. Neither phenomena nor self but the *scriptures* (*sola scriptura*) establish the different point of view, as I argue in part II. Hence, even the constitution of self-consciousness is submitted to the passive receptivity of texts, in particular the Pauline letters. These *writings* are constitutive of the divided self, according to the letter of the law and the gift of grace.

Albeit frequently focusing on the spoken word, Schürmann also sees the *linguistic* turn to the word as constitutive of the topology of the self. He points out that Luther's self-consciousness is not self-sufficient, since it always remains dependent on the other—both on the contingent speaker and on the authority of God as absolute other—in order to become itself. That is what Schürmann calls the "differend" of self-consciousness, which makes the self aporetic to itself: a self dependent on another, divided between the exterior and the interior, active and passive, hidden and revealed. The brokenness and complexity of consciousness make it capable of serving as ultimate condition for an entire epoch. Schürmann's three *sites* (topoi) of the self—(i) outside the word, (ii) in front of the law, and (iii) in the "tranquillity of received justification"—are seen as three distinct *phenomenal worlds,* all of which are possible options for the subject, even at the same time. He argues that "for the first time in history" we are made aware of *phenomena* in the critical sense, and since Luther they have become the crucial concern of epistemology.[38]

The phenomena are not simply things *an sich,* since they always depend on reflection and representation. Hence, he sees them as *desubstantialized.* Schürmann argues that this applies even to "things" like the "I" and God: "If the I boils down to the activity of consciousness accompanying the modifications in self-understanding, then, with this, every notion of the entitative I ceases."[39] He sees personal existence in Luther as depending in every moment and in toto on the gaze of God, thus being accepted or rejected.

Conversely, Schürmann argues that Luther also makes the concept of *God* dependent on consciousness. Hence, he claims that there is a mutual interdependence between the concept of God, established by faith, and the faith itself, which is seen as totally dependent on God's gaze, promise, and justification. There is some textual evidence for such an argument, for instance, Luther's commentary to the First Commandment in the *Great Catechism,* where he claims that *what* and *where* God "is" is not defined by his essence or attributes but by the right faith: If your faith is right, then you believe in the true God; if it is wrong and false, then you believe in an idol. If this is to be something more than a truism or a logical tautology, then the criterion for truth is moved from an external power to an internal certainty or evidence, that is, to consciousness: "That now, I say, upon which you set your heart and put your trust is properly your god."[40]

The Passivity of Perception

This turn of criteria is not peculiar for the catechism but runs through some of Luther's major texts, in particular the texts surrounding the break with the church, such as the *Commentary on Romans,* the *Heidelberg Disputation, Assertio,* and *De servo arbitrio.* In this period, Luther questions the truths proclaimed by the church just as deeply as he distrusts the "speculations" of late-medieval Scholasticism. He is constantly accused of trusting his own conscience more than the authority of the tradition, but his principles of interpretation are not arbitrary. He is careful to define generic principles for his procedure of thought but refers to grammar and rhetoric rather than essence and ontology for their justification. These political circumstances are decisive for his definition of another *site* for reflection and different criteria for truth.

Many questions arise with Schürmann's rereading of Luther. A typically late-modern interpretation of Luther's phenomenal God would be to see it as a mere *projection* of one's thoughts and images in the sense of Feuerbach (who explicitly referred to Luther's distinction between the hidden and the revealed God as the source of his critique of religion): that every subject *produces* its own God and that his "existence" is simply inferred (or projected) from the belief that God exists. Such a projection thesis of religion is sharply contradicted by Schürmann, though:

> But Luther says something quite different. He is concerned with the cause-being—thus with the causality—of this cause which is the word (the phenomenal God). The being of the word resides in consciousness where all words must be assessed in order to become efficient. This in no way diminishes the otherness between the human subject and the cause of its liberation. The systematic place that Luther reserves for the positive word suffices to show that he intends to safeguard this otherness more resolutely than anyone before him. It is a *non sequitur* to trace assessment back to production and, as a result, to fiction.[41]

Whereas I find Schürmann's conclusion of a *non sequitur* plausible, I basically disagree with his premises, namely, that the word according to Luther "resides" in consciousness and is assessed by consciousness. This would come true for a theologian like Schleiermacher, but for Luther the opposite is the case: The word of truth approaches us from outside, *extra nos,* and is not "assessed" by consciousness in order to become effective. On the contrary: Once such assessment is established as *criterion* for truth, it would once more suspend the authority of the other, of scripture interpreting itself, and preclude an *invention* of the other. If we stick to the letter of Luther's texts, we should at least admit that the "systematic" place of the word in this sense is prior to consciousness. Moreover, the identification of this place is rendered problematic by the ultimate difference between God hidden and revealed. Hence, such secrecy is presupposed even prior to the efficacy of the word and requires a *second* reading.

Although Schürmann in this respect ascribes *too much* to self-consciousness, his notion of subjectivity is differentiated by his subsequent analysis of the topology of the self in terms of a *pathetic* differend between self and ego: "I *suffer* the self, the principle of life." And then: "The ego is what I *make* of myself and, because of impotence, the principle of death." Schürmann here finds a unique opportunity to apply the double principle of natality and mortality and argues that the "[. . .] pathos of all transcendental dualism is indeed born in the gap between self and ego."[42] He defines this gap between self and ego as the origin of "spirit," with reference to Luther's *Commentary on the Romans:* not a pious harmony or high spirituality but the continuous conflict between self and ego, between the principle of life and the principle of death. In a narrow sense, spirit has its opposite in the flesh (compare with Romans 7), but in a wider definition of Luther's anthropology, 'spirit' covers the entire person, including its relationship to God as the ultimate other.

Schürmann elaborates further on the temporality of the ego, closing itself up, and the temporality of the self, initiated by the promise and open to radical possibility, wide beyond the horizon of the ego. The temporal difference is connected to a more general difference in the perception of the world and of the neighbor as *other.* The basic disposition of the ego is to *posit* the other and define the other in terms of understanding. The structuring disposition of the self, in contrast, is that of *letting be;* the sobriety (*Gelassenheit*) which echoes a key thought of Meister Eckhart.[43] Whereas the former belongs to the illusory representation of things, the latter is based on receptive appropriation of the other within the gaze of God. The former implies obscurity to oneself and one's reasons, whereas the latter implies transparency—not in the sense of "understanding" oneself but in the sense of accepting the gaze of the other as gift and grace.

Even though the structural analysis is outlined by way of an either-or, he sees no such disjunction in the spirit that may exclude the self or the ego from self-consciousness. Only where the perspective of the spirit is totally lacking will the identity of the person be organized from the perspective of the ego. The world, the other, and God himself will then be defined and understood according to the logic of *things.* However, as soon as there is deeper receptivity, a self, a pathetic *differend,* these perspectives are continuously rivalling in self-consciousness. The deceptive view of the ego will time and again dominate perception, self-perception, and action, but the view of radical possibility, of received self, may interfere and even "bring to death" the powers of sin and death. That is the lesson learned from a phenomenological paraphrase of Luther's *simul iustus et peccator:*

> What is being? [. . .] The being of the ego is a fiction, for, by taking a stance in the face of the law, I usurp it. The being of the self is an effect, for, placed in the fulfilled law, I let my self be granted it. The light of this granting alone is true [. . .] Its clarity reveals that I posit and I let be simultaneously. What is being? The categorical *simul* of these two acts. Can we conceive of a sharper conflict than that between being as fiction, thus as false, and being as election, which alone is true?[44]

Even this *simul* is rephrased by Schürmann in transcendental terms. The "both-and" is a priori, the "either-or" is a posteriori, and they are intrinsically bound to each other in a double bind, determining the aporia of self in modernity. Even though this Kantian terminology applied on Luther suggests a specific *interpretation* of his thought, his topology of modernity raises a perspective on the texts which is basically convincing.

ELEVEN

Kant versus Luther on Self-Consciousness

Whereas Heidegger draws a more or less direct line of modernity from the foundation of modern subjectivity in Descartes up to its fulfillment in Nietzsche's will to power, Schürmann argues for a more complex analysis of the period, for instance, by including Luther as a key thinker of modernity. Within this period, there are significant changes connected to subjectivity as the *site* of thought, but he argues that the new site allows for different perspectives and approaches—and that the basic shift comes up already with Luther. Hence, the historical narrative of modernity as continuous *progress* is rejected in favor of the tragic thought circling around two principles, natality and mortality. Where Heidegger argues in favor of a *destruction* or *Abbau* of metaphysics that may continue for decades or even centuries, Schürmann chooses a strategy of passive opposition, analysis, and translation by letting metaphysical thought be opposed and analyzed in terms of tragic thought.[1] The most urgent task of thinking, he argues, is "[. . .] to better know the tragic condition. To learn to love it."[2] The analytic of ultimates allows him to *display* the operations at work in the history of Western philosophy from a tragic point of view, and thereby demonstrate the conditions of evil.

Schürmann does not discuss the political thought of Luther or the complex relationship between metaphysics, politics, and theology in his thought. However, from my reading of Luther's texts, I cannot find that he is an exception to the political violence often inscribed in metaphysical conceptions. On the contrary: There seems to be an inherent tendency toward violent excesses in his metaphysical theory of divine sovereignty. Conversely, it is also a key concern of his theology to uncover the causes of evil. His efforts at naming, understanding, and analyzing the conditions of evil are intimately connected with his topology of the self and of the hidden God. Luther identifies the radical evil of original sin as an *interior* enemy of each individual with disastrous consequences for society. As long as original sin remains unacknowledged, it will continuously produce illusions or images (*facies*) which distract and confuse human beings and keep them away from the sources of *life*. This illusory life "which is death" is bound to notions and narratives that ought to be overcome, but the consequences thereof remain utterly tragic. Breaking through these appearances means discovering the world as it really is, and what really matters (*quod res est*).

In order to make this topological transition possible, Luther develops an analytic of human beings that according to Schürmann anticipates Kant's transcendental deduction and his theory of pure apperception. These concepts are undoubtedly far away from Luther's own terminology, but that can hardly be a decisive argument against the validity of his argument. Schürmann's claim of a passive transcendentalism in Luther ought to be justified or rejected in terms of a *structural* comparison between Luther's phenomenology of the word and Kant's transcendental analysis in the *Critique of Pure Reason*. If his hypothesis is to be considered as more than a coincidental analogy, we must be able to demonstrate that there is a *methodological* correspondence between the way phenomena are restructured by the "new" self in Luther (constituted *passively* by the word) and the way the absolute 'I' constitutes any experience according to Kant's analysis. Such a more detailed textual analysis is wanting in Schürmann's study, but nothing prevents us from going back to the sources, in this case Kant's transcendental analytic in the *Critique of Pure Reason*.

Kant's Original Apperception of Self-Consciousness Revisited

Let me briefly recall the transcendental analytic in the first *Critique*, in particular paragraphs 15–19 where Kant elaborates on the pure apperception. Considering the conditions of any experience, he writes:

> All the manifold of intuition has, therefore, a necessary relation to the 'I think' in the same subject in which this manifold is found. But this representation is an act of *spontaneity*, that is, it cannot be regarded as belonging to sensibility. I call it *pure apperception*, to distinguish it from empirical apperception, or, again, *original apperception*, because it is that self-consciousness which, while generating the representation *'I think'* (a representation which must be capable of accompanying all other representations, and which in all consciousness is one and the same), cannot itself be accompanied by any further representation. The unity of this apperception I likewise entitle the *transcendental* unity of self-consciousness, in order to indicate the possibility of *a priori* knowledge arising from it. For the manifold representations, which are given in an intuition, would not be one and all *my* representations, if they did not all belong to one self-consciousness.[3]

Kant underscores three aspects of the transcendental analysis: (i) the original act of the *I think* which initiates the apperception; (ii) the difference between pure and empirical apperception; and (iii) the original apperception as the transcendental unity of self-consciousness. If we can demonstrate that there are three corresponding aspects of Luther's constitution of phenomena and an inherent logic uniting them, the argument for an implicit transcendentalism in Luther will be considerably strengthened, whatever differences there might be apart from this.

The Original Act

It is clear from the outset that Luther does not think of the 'I' as an autonomous subject which is free to act as it wishes or to constitute itself. The *freedom* of the self is not established until a liberation has taken place: the liberation of oneself from oneself—that is, from the basically egoistic structure of being in the world and from the tendency to organize the world according to "things." Hence, the liberated I is established in terms of an event of liberation, where the subject passively receives the *condition* for representing phenomena according to the "rule" of faith. Schürmann recognizes this passive constitution of the self as instituted through the justification of a sinner, which is first elaborated in the *Commentary on Romans* and further developed in the *Heidelberg Disputation* and *Assertio.* Contrary to Schürmann, I emphasize that an obvious difference is indicated by the fact that this change is initiated *from the outside* (*extra nos*), namely, by the reading of scripture or by listening to the word. The dependence on exteriority and exterior sources, on *contingent experience,* implies a break with Platonic reflection and idealism in general.

Although he does not emphasize the exteriority of Luther's theory of perception, Schürmann is aware of the *ex auditu* and the basic passivity of Luther's notion of subjectivity. Hence he argues that Luther must *presuppose* a subjectivity which is given anterior to experience and structures it. That is above all a *receptive* structure including the capacity to listen.

Despite some significant differences between the two models, the latter argument is convincing. Whereas Fichte's self-constitution of the self is avoided, the argument in favor of a *created* structure which is given anterior to experience and structuring it (although itself being unfolded and established as the *site* of perception by the experience of faith) corresponds to the topology developed by Luther. Schürmann bases his argument on the famous insight from *De servo arbitrio* (prepared by the *Lecture on Romans*), underlining the double direction of justification as subjective and objective genitive: When God *makes* just, that complies with the reception of oneself in anticipation of the *given,* but still unacknowledged, possibility of a freedom *to come.* When God "is" just, however, it means that God *becomes* just by justifying sinners, that is, appears for consciousness as being just—and not until then will it be clear what is implied in God's justice.

Schürmann rephrases this piece of classical Reformation theology in terms of phenomenology. The most astonishing point is perhaps the wide range of consequences he draws from this basic change (*metabolē*) in self-consciousness: Not only the God relationship has changed, but the entire rule for (nomothetically) structuring the representation of any phenomenon, including God, the world, the neighbor, and oneself is given with the reception of oneself in faith. The "re-" of the reconciliation betrays the re-structuring of the self which takes place, facilitating a re-presentation of self-consciousness and of God.

Hence, Schürmann may argue that Luther anticipates the distinction between an *a priori* structure and an *a posteriori* content of cognition.[4] The analysis opens up astonishing perspectives on Luther, but the considerable differences between the two thinkers makes it necessary to exercise a bit more caution. One example is the principal difference between reason and revelation. Even if we accept the structural similarities and apply the Kantian vocabulary to Luther, it is the event itself ("revelation") which discloses this (revealable) structure inherent to subjectivity and thus makes possible what seemed impossible to the person whose topos is "the world" and the person situated before the law. Revelation (*a posteriori*) and revealability (*a priori*) are equally original in the analysis of this event, which henceforth will restructure any phenomenon as it is perceived in faith. This point of view puts even the rationalism of Descartes and the transcendentalism of Kant in a different light: The self-evident character of the cogito and of the *transcendental apperception* look very similar to a *revelation* in Luther's sense of the term.[5]

This is the first aspect of what Schürmann has labeled the *passive* transcendentalism in Luther. Transcendental analysis is commonly based on the spontaneous self as origin and free agent. The foundation of self in faith alone, however, presupposes subjective *passivity* anterior to any active choice, reflection, or representation. Schürmann nevertheless sees the synthetic unification of consciousness by Luther in analogy to Descartes's cogito. Given the total receptivity of the third topos (faith), Schürmann argues that it must include the *audio,* "I hear," and the *credo,* "I confess," in one single response. It should also confirm the single causality of God and the heteronomy of the act producing self-consciousness. Schürmann finds a synthetic solution in the passive-active verb *to obey* (*gehorchen*): "In Luther, the subjective modification—the place where his critical transcendentalism takes shape—is *the act 'I obey.'*"[6]

This is actually a creative effort at establishing a parallel between the *I think* and the *I believe,* which topologically integrates the first and the second topos in the third. Moreover, it is an effort that points in the direction of practical philosophy of obedience before the law. And still it does not make justice to the *exteriority* of this procedure in Luther's writings. This exteriority pertains to the medium of writing, the external clarity of scripture, but also to the hearing of the word. Moreover, it is the exteriority of God (*extra nos*), who remains different, remains separated from this interiority, even in the moment of reconciliation. Hence, in order to avoid a theory which is based on mere reconstruction from Kant to Luther, whereby Kant's thesis is projected back into the works of the Reformer, I emphasize that this passivity has basically one expression, namely, the gift, and one verbal form: *I accept.*

The pure and *original* apperception is thus perceived, conceived, and received as a gift, the pure and originary gift of grace, which makes possible not only the new self but also the reconciliation and reappropriation of the world as given, hence the *transcendental* unity of self-consciousness. This representation is actually capable of "accompanying all other representations," and *qua* self-consciousness it is universally accessible, although it remains bound to the topological transference from ego to self—*mere passive.*

The difference is significant, since the world thereby achieves the character of a gift (corresponding to Heidegger's "es gibt . . ."), a point which is deeply rooted in Luther's phenomenology. Moreover, the same gift is communicated in the sacraments, which are constitutive for Luther's perception of phenomena—as it was in the medieval controversy on universals. And finally, it indicates that the topos of selfhood, even according to a transcendental analytic, remains dependent on the topos of the hidden God, not only in his majesty, but more precisely in the sacrifice of Christ, as a revelation *sub contrario.* The two topoi remain in communication and spatialize this discourse on selfhood rather than reducing it to a merely temporal procedure.

The Difference between Pure and Empirical Apperception

The difference between an original, pure apperception and an experienced apperception is important to Luther, but for other reasons than to Kant. Let me illustrate this difference with the topological distinction between conscience and consciousness, which Schürmann adopts from Malter. Conscience is the site of moral judgment, of the practical distinction between good and evil, and is thus necessarily analyzed with reference to its content. Luther repeatedly denies the option of a "neutral" conscience which is independent of good and evil—hence he opposes the philosophical possibility of a *liberum arbitrium.*[7]

Schürmann also concludes that there is no neutrality in Luther's conscience, but consciousness is different: "Self-consciousness, on the other hand, remains neutral toward its contents, its function amounts to accompanying all subjective modifications. [. . .] Whether or not the word binds us or frees us, consciousness produces nothing, above all not an order of good and evil."[8] The argument is evident: Only when the identity of the 'I' is defined prior to and beyond any moral category can it possibly *become* a liberated identity. It is confirmed by my analysis of the controversy on morality and immorality between Erasmus and Luther in chapter 4, where I conclude that Luther argues in favor of an immoral or *amoral* receptivity to scripture, that is, a site of self-consciousness *beyond* good and evil. This site is not identified as free will (*liberum arbitrium*), but as the 'I' constituted by justification through faith.

Even when the self is formally given prior to its content (*a priori*), Schürmann argues that it also will have to appropriate itself by referring all phenomena to the new perspective, thus responding to and reproducing the received in a way corresponding to the pure apperception in Kant. This is a point where Schürmann sees an irreducibly modern trait in Luther:

> Far from 'remaining a medieval at heart' because he attributes all spontaneity to God, Luther opens wide the gulf between *subjective, formal, quasi-spontaneity* and *divine, efficient spontaneity.* The first connotes neither causality nor autonomy. It emphasizes nothing more than the faculty for again getting hold of that which is to be understood (a faculty rendered autonomous only by Kant, precisely in the name of the understanding). It institutes the I, referring all phenomena to it as a formal act. It opens the modern era, the era of reflection through estimation. But it also divides the estimating subject into receptive-passive and receptive-spontaneous subjects. It divides subjectivity into a suffering and a doing, a duality which we will see breaks the new hegemony.[9]

The distinction here between formal spontaneity ascribed to the *a priori* apperception of subjectivity and efficient spontaneity ascribed to the phenomenal God confirms the paradoxical double direction characterizing the institution of the 'I.' This does not imply a mixture of reception and construction but a total passivity, *mere passive,* in the reception of faith and of self-consciousness in faith. It is nevertheless an act; it is at least followed and accompanied by an act, namely, a foundational *act* of understanding oneself, one's neighbor, and God (*pro me*) differently. The distinction between a formal condition which is given prior to the gift, and the gift as such, which is *a posteriori*, corresponds to a sound analysis of a key problem in *De servo arbitrio.*

Schürmann thus has a good point, but the argument as a whole is not entirely convincing. The disturbing point about God's absolute causality in Luther's *De servo arbitrio* is that it evades phenomenality altogether. He claims that the will of the hidden God "[. . .] is not to be inquired into, but reverently adored, as by far the most awe-inspiring secret of the Divine Majesty [. . .]."[10] Hence, whereas Luther's reconstruction of the revealed God in terms of a phenomenology can be said to introduce the modern era, the hidden God does *not* belong to modernity, and neither to pre-modernity. The impact of this notion of the *unthought* can hardly be fixed in a particular era at all. This particular problem questions the possibility of defining ultimate epochal or hegemonic conditions in the first place. The *deus absconditus* remains the indefinable condition for phenomenality by resisting the grasp of human reason. And hence, paradoxically, the ultimate reason why the new hegemony remains broken and aporetic from its very institution.

The Transcendental Unity of Self-Consciousness

In Kant's transcendental analysis, the original apperception secures the transcendental unity of self-consciousness, hence the manifold representations become unified as *my* representations. The pure apperception of the 'I' is given in the original act, the *I think,* which on the one hand makes the representation possible but on the other hand simply *accompanies* the perception when it is observed by self-consciousness. Its transcendental unity must, according to Kant, be given *a priori* but is nevertheless a *synthetic* unity given the synthetic character of the perception, including the so-called "pure" or original apperception.

Schürmann sees the *I obey* as a constitutive act of the transcendental 'I' in Luther's work. It is not strictly speaking spontaneous, since it is a *response* to the word coming from outside. It is nonetheless spontaneous in the sense of an *unconditional* (*unwillkürlich*) resignation, response, and return to the absolute beginning in the *other.* Could this act of unconditional resignation and obedience be called an original act of self-consciousness? If we take a look at the synthesis, it consists of the interior and the exterior perspectives, it includes law and grace, it is temporally stretched out between the actual present (indicative) and the possible (future; promise), and finally it is represented as the split 'I,' the justified sinner, *simul iustus et peccator.* All these aspects are separated and fall apart when self-consciousness is wanting.

Hence, there is in fact a rigorously methodological sense in which we may talk about a transcendental apperception in Luther's work, given that we focus on the *formal* conditions for self-consciousness. In Luther, this is way beyond the capacity of the subject, though. It is ascribed to the gaze of God and the work of the Holy Spirit. Still, all three points confirm that we may speak of a passive transcendentalism in Luther. Moreover, this analysis confirms, by way of a topology of the modern self, that Luther belongs to modernity in the sense that he institutes the modern self. This is not a rejection of his dependence on medieval models of thought, though. It is a confirmation of such dependence, unless we are speaking of a mere phantom or *mendacium.*

Although we may thus speak of a modern self in Luther, I still cannot avoid the impression that Schürmann overemphasizes the modern traits in these texts. When we take a closer look at *De servo arbitrio,* which is his most important textual evidence in these questions, we soon discover that Luther is still arguing according to Aristotelian metaphysics, in particular when it comes to the question of causality.[11] The hidden God, Luther claims, effectuates every event through his almighty will, and there is no exception, neither when it comes to good nor evil acts, nor injustice or suffering.[12] The will of God remains far beyond human comprehension, it is even beyond scripture, and in this respect, as causal explanation, it is "no concern of ours" (*nihil ad nos*).[13] Christ on the cross introduces (that is, reveals) a different notion of God, however, and God in Christ could, according to Luther, never *will* the death and suffering of the sinner. This latter revelation of God's *proper* will has the primary scope of saving humankind, that is, of turning despair into joy and death into life. The causality thus instituted is a causality of the word, working through faith and opening the future for *promise* and hope, hence for unexpected possibilities. The inherent antinomy between causal necessity and freedom discussed in chapter 7 ought to be examined more carefully, with reference to Kant's first and second *Critique.* It belongs to the questions Kant is unable to solve within the limits of reason alone.

Schürmann thus basically succeeds in identifying the origin of modernity and of the modern *differend* in Luther, but the other topos which is equally determinant but not always acknowledged by modern philosophers is the *deus absconditus.* Schürmann's reference to self-consciousness as the ultimate referend makes Luther fit too easily into the transcendental scheme. Hence, for a genealogy of modernity which not only confirms but also questions the conditions for modern philosophy, we need to imply the topos of the hidden God, or, more precisely, of the difference between hiddenness and revelation.

TWELVE

Spacing the Hidden God

The Temporal/Spatial Divide

If this *topos* of a difference between the hidden and revealed god, as discussed by Luther in *De servo arbitrio,* is situated prior to temporal distinctions, it remains *anachronistic* in its relation to the *chronology* of history. It is, insofar as it "is," *older* than beings and prior to their coming into existence. This anachronism or, rather, anachrony of the place would then be the premise for understanding its history and its genealogy. It remains non-contemporary with us and with itself.[1] It will continuously escape our efforts at a temporal identification of it as belonging to a particular era or period. It cannot remain *identical* with itself in periods of shifting worldviews and changing conceptualities. When the concepts are changing, however, these concepts of change are *measured* by the difference rather than measuring this difference. Since this basic difference tends to be overlooked, and in particular by an era which identifies itself as "modern" or even "post-modern" as opposed to the ancient and medieval worlds, the effort to think this difference will take the form of a recollection, a rediscovery, in order to reverse the forgetfulness of modern human beings with their limited memory of ancient structures of thought.[2]

For this work of remembering, scriptures are more or less indispensable. Inscriptions in various forms are witnesses of human understanding, of human presence and search for truth, but also silent witnesses of their vanishing and absence. The scriptures of authors past and gone are apt to demonstrate this ambiguity of presence and absence, and the ambiguity is particularly significant when we read texts that have formed a tradition or even a civilization, including forms of understanding shared during the early twenty-first century. Written texts give testimony to this original but lost presence, which according to Emmanuel Levinas is only retrievable as a *trace:* The trace makes aware of an original presence, of the face, yet the trace is a sign of its absence.[3]

This ambiguity of absence and (original or re-presented) presence is characteristic of the *written* sign. Moreover, the written sign is visibly identifiable in space, with a certain extension. This notion of the trace is therefore recalled by Jacques Derrida when he discusses the ambiguity of the sign which is spatialized in writing. According to Derrida, it is the difference between the appearing and the apparent which is the origin of all other differences, including the difference between the signifier and the signified, the difference between the world and experience, and so forth, and this difference is marked by the ambiguity of the trace (that is, the temporal-spatial *différance*).[4] Following the transition from temporal to spatial categories introduced by Heidegger's *Kehre,* Derrida describes the writing of *difference,* the concrete fabric of the trace, as the origin of the experience of time and space, a trace which "permits the difference between space and time to be articulated, to appear as such, in the unity of an experience."[5]

In this vein Derrida describes *spacing* as the origin of signification: unperceived, non-present, and non-conscious, prior to the *activity* of speech. It is passive and perceptive and recalls the "dead" time which is at work within the "living" present. Hence, it is also related to subjectivity by an insistence on the passivity of *becoming* a self:

> Spacing as writing is the becoming-absent and the becoming-unconscious of the subject. [. . .] As the subject's relationship with its own death, this becoming is the constitution of subjectivity. On all levels of life's organization, that is to say, of *the economy of death*. All graphemes are of a testamentary essence. And the original absence of the subject of writing is also the absence of the thing or the referent.[6]

Derrida explicitly refers to Levinas's critique of ontology as the background for his usage of the term *trace* in order to describe the original absence which becomes visible in writing. He claims that it provokes a *desire* for presence and the origin which is unachievable, since it remains anterior to any representation. The trace thus undermines the ontological project of Heidegger insofar as the latter identifies the *meaning* of language in the *presence* of speech. Derrida introduces the term "arche-writing" in order to identify this *spacing* of writing which comes prior to speech and makes sense possible, as construction and destruction of the *logos* of metaphysics. This is also described as a *deconstruction* of the theology of rationalism, insofar as the latter destroys the play and ambiguity of difference in favor of an indifferent unity of divine presence.[7]

The significance of Derrida's grammatology for a rereading of the *deus absconditus* in Luther lies in his emphasis on writing as *difference* rather than the identity of the same. The absolute origin in the *deus* is thus already preceded by the difference between abscondity and appearance, an unheard-of difference prior to all references to the word, the *logos,* etc. And this difference is presupposed by scripture, as the "arche-scriptural" difference. Hence, we may perceive the difference between *absconditus* and *revelatus* as prior to any identification of a single *entity* or a single *identity*—in particular the "identity" of God. Even the naming of

God depends upon this distinction and presupposes it for the reading of scripture, and this is exactly the point of Luther's deliberation on the *absolute* hiddenness of God.[8] When we follow this grammatical and detailed exegesis of Luther's text, the *spacing* of the discourse remains the condition of possibility for sense in general, at least insofar as *scripture* is supposed to give sense.

The absolute abscondity referred to by Luther is, according to this argument, a *general* abscondity which is no concern of ours insofar as it destroys and creates, as it is willing and acting, but is necessarily a concern of ours insofar as it remains the condition *sine qua non* for the repetition of scripture in a new context, for the passive perception of the words, including the word of justification, and for the destruction of absolutistic and monstrous images of the living, powerful, perfect, moral, and almighty God. The topos of *abscondity* is thus inscribed and presupposed *within* the text, although it remains outside *scripture*. Moreover, the distinction between abscondity and revelation is for Luther necessary in order to avoid the conclusion that there "is" no God, since it opens up that space *outside* of scripture which temporalizes its words and differentiates its meaning in every repetition of the text.[9] Hence, this spacing of scripture makes possible the distinction between interiority and exteriority (of the subject), between the inside and the outside (of the text), although it remains an *enigmatic* relationship.

This has been a topic of much confusion among theologians of the twentieth century. Hence, Paul Althaus argues that Luther ends up with two gods or a double *essence* of God, whereas Ebeling urges every believer (and non-believer) to flee "from God to God," while human existence is described as oscillating between the two.[10] The confusion is presumably a consequence of an inherited division of rationalistic theology; dividing and organizing the world in immanence separated from transcendence, presence opposed to absence, and more recent definitions of meaning as the ultimate expression of *existence*, which requires the exclusion of nihilism and destruction of sense. If God is supposed to be present, meaningful, and good, then the absolutely "hidden" God must be excluded from every theoretical discourse on theology, as Jüngel argues with reference to Karl Barth. Still, if we study Luther's text more carefully, according to the grammar, and avoid too many speculations concerning its "meaning," the point of this distinction can hardly have been to present two "essences" of God in ultimate contradiction to each other. If it has anything to do with essence, it must be the *questioning* of this essentialization of the name of God within a particular metaphysical tradition ascribed to Thomas and Aristotle.

When Luther insists on this distinction, it is not the result of metaphysical speculations or spiritual visions; it is rather the condition of possibility for his reference to scripture, indeed for a new emphasis on scripture *qua* writing; *sola scriptura*. Only when this distinction is introduced as original difference within scripture can the question of God be raised once more, as questionable and paradoxical distinction of the space separating man from God. A huge space is opening up for a reconsideration of the notion of God, according to scripture and the grammar of the text. Still, the name thus given to *x*, in this case as a determination of "God," is *not* identical with conventional procedures of philosophy (called *theologia gloriae*), nor with a static understanding of scripture as "revelation," but proceeds from the difference between *ab-sconditus* and *re-velatus,* in a double movement of separation and repetition.

There is much at stake in this double operation. Hence, it is definitely not without risk. The space given to scripture as prior to the subject implies a suspension of other definitions of subjectivity, for example, according to works, according to social status, or according to philosophical determinations of the human being. *Spacing* the scriptures in the vein of Luther's *sola scriptura* thus means accepting the loss of control and passively handing oneself over to the *economy of death.*

Although the grammatology of Derrida is helpful in order to discern a theory of scripture in Luther, I think the former correctly points out that this relationship is disturbed by deep separation and unbridgeable difference, for example, due to the authority Luther ascribes to scripture and his *assertions* of the truth, whereas Derrida sticks to negations and theoretical analyses of every proposition. Still, do they belong to completely different filiations, as Derrida claims? Or is even this difference brought into play by the spacing of the texts? The *topos* of the hidden God is hardly a space which invites the sublation of difference into an overarching identity. When we study the modern genealogy of the hidden God from the site defined as self-consciousness, it seems to confirm the first outline based on Luther's controversy with Erasmus: It is a contested place which produces contradiction and dissent.

PART V

From Revelation to Revolution

The truly apocalyptic view of the world is that things do *not* repeat themselves. It isn't absurd, e.g., to believe that the age of science and technology is the beginning of the end for humanity; that the idea of great progress is a delusion, along with the idea that the truth will ultimately be known . . .

—Ludwig Wittgenstein

THIRTEEN

The Power of Interpretation

Controversies on the Book of Daniel

A new debate on political theology has emerged since the turn of the millennium, due to a general shift in the understanding of the relationship between religion and secularity in modern societies. After José Casanova's *Public Religions in the Modern World* (1994) and Habermas's speech on faith and knowledge (2001), where he coined the term "post-secular society," there have been a number of controversies on the issue, including debates on this specific term.[1] Hans Joas has pointed out that the term is misguiding, since there has never been such a thing as a *secular* society, not even in the modern West. Religion has been there all the time, he argues, in various forms, but its constitutive significance even for modern societies has often been neglected by sociologists, political scientists, philosophers, and scholars of religious studies.[2]

A more differentiated understanding of the secularization process has slowly emerged through major contributions from philosophers Charles Taylor and Giorgio Agamben, sociologist Hans Joas, anthropologist Talal Asad, and a number of others.[3] None of these scholars would question that secularization has taken place and still continues as a process of differentiation, but the critical role of religion in understanding global politics and modern societies has been rediscovered and has raised a number of significant controversies across the disciplines. With new genealogies of the secular—indeed, of *various* secularities—the genealogies of religion are also reconsidered, and we have observed a surprising revival of *political theology* as a field of interdisciplinary discourse on politics, sociology, philosophy, history, and theology.[4] Hence, even traditional controversies like the one between Luther, his Catholic opponents in Rome, and charismatic preachers such as the revolutionary leader Thomas Müntzer receive new interest, although they were writing in a period when the relationship between religion and politics was very different from today. Mark Lilla claims that we now have reached "the other shore" and thus are incapable of understanding, or even imagining, the tremendous problems that used to occupy political theology. He argues that political philosophy has established a totally different theoretical and practical basis for both politics and religion, and that the problems still occupying less modernized and secularized societies (on the "other bank") puzzle us because we have only a distant memory of what it was like to think as they do.[5]

Lilla points at some significant methodological problems, although his analysis of the absolute disjunction between political philosophy and political theology seems a bit too simple. Historically, there is a complex web of influence between political philosophy and theology moving in both directions and continuously being fed and challenged by the cultural framework, narratives, and models of social coexistence that is available within a society or the wider context of a civilization. Hence, Paul W. Kahn comes closer to the actual dilemma when he points out that such a massive break which Lilla assumes took place with "the Great Separation" between the seventeenth century and twentieth century actually never really occurred. He argues that the radical claim of political theology today is rather that the state "is not the secular arrangement it purports to be." In his 2011 book on *Political Theology*, Kahn defines the task of political theology:

> Political theology does not just challenge a particular configuration of legal institutions, as if the question were one of scaling down the separation between church and state. It challenges the basic assumptions of our understanding of modernity, the nature of individual identity, and the character of the relationship of the individual to the state.[6]

Kahn argues that the state still creates and maintains its own sacred space and sacred history. In doing so, it is the true heir of pre-modern political theologies. Hence, in order to better understand the development of modern societies, the secular critique of religion (and religious critique of secularism), and politico-religious revolutions, we have to reconsider the relationship between politics, metaphysics, and theology in early modernity. Luther's debates with his adversaries represent a repository for understanding controversies that formed history. Hence, the complex relationship between scripture, metaphysics, violence, and politics in this period deserves careful attention.

In the more popular public debates of the sixteenth century, the difference between God's hiddenness and revelation is more than anything else perceived as a *political* difference. The apocalyptic prophecies played a significant role in political movements during the fifteenth and sixteenth centuries, in particular among the radical Franciscans and the Hussites. This had given the biblical apocalypses, represented by the Book of Daniel in the Old Testament and the Book of Revelation in the New Testament, a dubious reputation, but according to Irena Backus, no one had seriously questioned the canonicity of the latter.[7] The message of the Apocalypse of John is historical, political, mythical, and prophetic, with its double expectation of disaster and liberation, of dystopia and utopia. In the light of its mystical prophecies of the Final Judgment including a universal battle between good and evil, preachers and theologians since Joachim of Fiore (twelfth century) had sought to interpret the history of the church from Christ up to their own era. Based on these speculations, they predicted the End of Days and the soon advent of God's kingdom. They preached repentance, suffering, and a violent struggle against the evil enemy (the Antichrist, Lucifer, the Beast), framed within prophecies of the Last Millennium. Inspired by these urgent expectations, the apocalyptic visionary or politician interpreted actual events as signs of divine intervention. Moreover, such perspectives could potentially mobilize the masses in a violent battle for the sake of the poor.[8]

Among the rulers and the nobility, these texts were seen as politically dangerous, in particular if the interpretation of the texts was detached from the moral and political authority of the church. Although the apocalyptic texts thus were perceived as theologically and philosophically problematic, their popularity was overwhelming. Even the nobility would not question their divine authority. When Martin Luther intensified his criticism of the church from 1517 onward, including its hierarchy and political aspirations, apocalyptic motives seem to have been a natural part of his rhetoric, not exactly softening the conflicts in which he was involved. The pope was repeatedly identified as the Antichrist and Rome was called the new Babylon. The former notion relies on the Letters of John, whereas the reference to Babel/Babylon is based on the Book of Daniel and the Apocalypse of John.

Historical Interpretations and the Question of Canonicity

Erasmus is the first theologian to question the place of the Book of Revelation in the canon after the third century, and he does so for strictly formal reasons.[9] Although Luther is familiar with Erasmus's work, he questions its canonicity for different reasons, namely, the obscure image of Christ presented there.[10] He is troubled by the lack of clarity and by the offensive threats of divine punishment in the book. Paradoxically, while Luther does not accept its teaching of Christ he does accept its implicit references to the *Anti*christ, as becomes clear by his Introduction to a Commentary from 1528.[11] His mind seems to be twisted on the issue, though. He has difficulties in classifying the Apocalypse and finding a proper approach to its contemporary significance in the sixteenth century. It does not fit into his three basic criteria for Bible interpretation: the clarity of scripture, its capacity to "convey Christ," and its literal (that is, non-allegorical) historical sense.

Luther therefore expresses a certain skepticism when it comes to the canonicity and thus the apostolic authority of the Book of Revelation, but he cannot escape the apocalyptical spirit of his times. Moreover, the dramatic images and the violent rhetoric of the apocalyptic genre seems to fit well with the Reformer's imagination—the richness of the texts is almost like a temptation he cannot resist, even if he wanted to. He sees the turmoil caused by the Reformation as a sign of the times. The rediscovery of the clear word of the Gospel has, according to Luther, caused the whole world to react with turmoil against God.[12]

The Book of Daniel became important for the interpretation of history in the sixteenth century. Luther never questions the canonicity of this book. Both Luther and Müntzer have presented interpretations of the Book of Daniel; Luther in a controversy with Ambrosius Catharinus Politus in 1521, and Thomas Müntzer in a sermon from 1524. The Book of Daniel connects strands of the prophetic tradition in Old Israel with the apocalyptic genre, which spread across the Middle East in the second century before Christ. Apocalypticism played a key role in Persian religion from this period and later in Islam (most typically in Shia Islam). The apocalypses generally emerge in times of acute crisis and they connect dramatic *visions,* often conveyed by an angel, with a prophetic message concerning the End of Days. Although their background is often closely linked to a specific historical situation, the message is universal and the outcome of historical events is interpreted as decisive for the future of the cosmos.

In the Book of Revelation, this is underscored by the parallel events of universal war between Christ and the Antichrist in Heaven and the terrestrial conflicts between the Christians and their adversaries. In Daniel, the image of the stone plays a central role, connected to King Nebuchadnezzar's vision of a huge statue. Daniel is the Jewish interpreter of this vision. This key role of the mythical figure of Daniel is critical for the book as a whole, and his mysterious power of interpreting the signs of the times has been perceived as both tempting and terrifying by interpreters who saw themselves in a similar role, in times of severe crisis.

Luther versus Catharinus on the Book of Daniel

In his *Apology* (1520), Ambrosius Catharinus Politus had declared that Luther deceived the common people in eleven different ways and thus suggests that he must be considered the new Antichrist.[13] In his *Response to the Book of Ambrosius Catharinus* (1521), Luther unfolds his rhetorical skills in a powerful satirical gesture. He is not satisfied with paying back in kind, though. After arguing that Catharinus as well as Pope Leo X represents the Antichrist, he insists that the entire papal hierarchy—in its claim of representing the Roman Catholic Church—qualifies for this dubious honor.[14] With reference to Daniel 8:23–25, Luther argues that they all belong to the kingdom of the fiend. Let us therefore take a look at the Book of Daniel, which is the bone of contention.

The protagonist Daniel was a noble Jew who became a servant of the Babylonian king, Nebuchadnezzar, during the Jewish exile. One night the king has a strange dream, but none of his advisers are able to interpret it. In this dream, a huge statue appears which is subsequently destroyed by a massive stone. The king is worried, but Daniel offers an interpretation of its meaning, namely, the prophecy of four subsequent kingdoms which are crushed, one by one: "And there shall be a fourth kingdom, strong as iron; just as iron crushes and smashes everything, it shall crush and shatter all these. [. . .] And in the days of those kings the God of heaven will set up a kingdom that shall never be destroyed, [. . .] and it shall stand forever" (Daniel 2:31–44).

The text introduces a powerful king and a prophet who is able to interpret the mystical dream. This situation is easily translatable to subsequent periods, and the dream has influenced endless speculations about the four ages and the coming of the eternal kingdom. The Vulgate uses the word "statue" for the figure in Nebuchadnezzar's dream, whereas Luther translates it as "image" (*Bild*), which has connotations to the idols that were destroyed by the prophets in the Old Testament. In chapters 7–12 we find reports about further visions, most of them ascribed to Daniel and all of them dealing with the Last Judgment in dramatic terms. The vision that is most thoroughly discussed is found in Daniel 8:23–25. It is dated to the third year after Nebuchadnezzar's death, under Belshazzar's rule. A wicked king is prophesied, and despite his indisputable strength, he is described as a fraud:

> At the end of their rule, when the transgressions have reached their full measure, a king of bold countenance shall arise, skilled in intrigue. He shall grow strong in power, shall cause fearful destruction, and shall succeed in what he does. He shall destroy the powerful and the people of the holy ones. By his cunning he shall make deceit prosper under his hand, and in his own mind he shall be great. Without warning he shall destroy many and shall even rise up against the Prince of princes. But he shall be broken, and not by human hands. (Daniel 8:23–25)

Whereas Luther focuses almost exclusively on the signs of this fraud in chapter 8, Catharinus argues with reference to the stone in Daniel 2.[15] Daniel has given a prophecy of the cornerstone, he argues, hinting at a common metaphor for Christ: "The stone that the builders rejected has become the cornerstone; this was the Lord's doing, and it is amazing in our eyes" (Matthew 21:42).[16] Catharinus identifies this stone with the Rock upon which the church was to be built, namely, Peter (Matthew 16:18). With the pope as Peter's successor on the Holy See, Catharinus sees the papacy as the cornerstone of the church and the substitute of Christ on earth, hence with the title *Vicarius Christi*. This is common knowledge in late-medieval theology and serves the sustenance of the papacy as head of the Roman Catholic Church, claiming authority even of the universal church.

A number of interpretations and inferences in Catharinus's text are jeopardized by Luther, including those seen as common knowledge. The stone described by Daniel must be seen as a prophecy of Christ, he argues, but it cannot be valid for Peter and not at all for the so-called successors of Peter on the Apostolic See. With reference to Paul, he argues: "Paul tells us: 'what fellowship is there between light and darkness? What agreement does Christ have with Belial?' Thus, either the rock means solely light or solely darkness, that is, it signifies solely a Saint or solely an impious man."[17] Luther will show that his adversaries are erring, and, consequently, that Catharinus's attempt to put the pope and the See in Christ's place is an indication of their confusion, darkness, and impiety. He concludes that by showing this, he has conquered their "fortress"; they have no legitimate place for exercising the authority they have captured.[18]

The topographical figure applied here is interesting and follows the same pattern as Luther's attack on the "Troy" of tradition: Luther argues that by conquering the alleged *center* of interpretation, the entire text achieves the opposite meaning. Rome is thus accused of being the new Babylon, and as such it achieves a totally different position in this war of interpretations. Finally, Luther concludes that neither the passage in Daniel 2 nor the passage in Matthew 21 has anything to do with Peter, and, hence, the "godless papacy" is accused of having used these passages in order to put itself in God's place, on the throne of Christ. His enemies are consequently accused of being impious liars.[19]

This is merely the introduction, though. As soon as the topography of reading and the roles are distributed, Luther argues that the prophecies of Daniel should be directly applied to the historical situation of his times. Still, the *inferences* from the text differ in every detail from the ones presented by Catharinus. He bases this argument on the typological parallelism of the historical context: Daniel spoke against the Babylonians of his times, Paul and John preached against the rulers in Rome, hence the Babel of *their* times. Thus the parallelism continues to Luther's times, which allegedly are suffering under the authority of the pope: "To us, then, who are submitted to the Roman Babylon, are these words directed; the words that were predicted by Daniel, Christ, Peter, Paul, Judas, and John in the Apocalypse, must be fulfilled among us."[20] The problem is not merely that they have denied the Gospel or interpreted it inaccurately, he argues; they have simply "smuggled in" their own additions and impositions next to the words of scripture. Hence, the ordinary language is abused and falsified, including the identity and reference of names like God, Christ, Spirit, church, justice, et cetera.[21]

Daniel warns about a future king who will rely on new, egregious, and powerful weapons, and the decisive feature of this "monstrous king" is, according to Luther's translation from Hebrew, that he will have visions (*facies*).[22] A key question for the kind of historical application Luther aims at is the identification of this monstrous king in the contemporary experience of a crisis. Luther has a particular king in mind, with the following features:

> [His weapons] are the visions [*facies*], i.e., external species, appearance, pomp, with another word, superstitions, rites, ceremonies, what is exposed visually in the form of gowns, food, persons, buildings, gestures, and so on. Among all visions and appearances, there is no more powerful, gracious, and therefore pernicious face than superstition and hypocrisy, which has merely a semblance of piety and superficial religion.[23]

After this harangue, Luther concludes that the prospective king must be the Antichrist, namely, the fiercest adversary of Christ and his kingdom. And it is hardly a surprise when this "Antichrist" in turn is identified with the pope, or, more precisely, not only the pope in person, but the institutionalized papacy. Luther is hardly known as a friendly and respectful opponent, but in the subsequent passages he surpasses himself in a veritable orgy of curses and allegations. Hence, the following exclamation belongs to the *mild* expressions of his anger: "Oh, you idols of this world! May the Lord Jesus annihilate the papacy, the cardinals with all your faces! Deep into the abyss of hell with it! Amen."[24] Luther is cursing in the form of a prayer and praying in the form of a curse, thus violating the limits of each form of expression in order to achieve a powerful linguistic effect. The most holy representatives of the church are identified with the idols of the Old Testament and harshly condemned, not only according to the first commandment, but also according to the annihilating logic of the Apocalypse, anticipating the coming of the Last Judgment.

Of Visions and Appearances

Luther then proceeds directly from the Book of Daniel to the Book of Revelation and interprets his own times in the light of the twelve "visions" in chapters 8–10 of the Apocalypse.[25] The connection is established by the *masked face* (*larvalem faciem*) described in Revelation 9, which allegedly refers to the same kind of *false appearance* as prophesied in Daniel 8. The twelve visions are seen as testimonies not only against Pope Leo X, but also against the very *institution,* thus revealing the true nature of this ignis fatuus. The papacy is accused of having put the potency of Satan at the site that *apparently* belongs to Christ.

This application of the Book of Revelation introduces the pattern for how divine authority and judgment are supposed to annihilate the satanic kingdom, a pattern which is full of violent and dramatic images and prophecies. Still, Luther is not prepared to accept a *literal* interpretation of these fantastic images. On the contrary: He warns against killing and bloodshed. The fine distinction emphasized here is extremely significant, but not always accepted by Luther's contemporaries: The Apocalypse is applied in order to interpret and thus better *understand* the contemporary situation of crisis, but the images are nevertheless seen as *images,* and thus they are not applied as an invitation to violence or warfare. The apocalyptic authority of judgment belongs to God—to the *hidden* God—and not to any human power, be it in Babylon, in Rome, or in Wittenberg. Hence, it is worth noticing that he is not prepared to mobilize military power for the apocalyptic war against the Antichrist. Although he apparently aims at destabilizing or even overthrowing the power of the pope, he wages war with words rather than weapons.

When Jesus according to John 21:17 tells Peter to tend the sheep, Luther sees this as a demand to Peter's alleged successor to teach the Gospel *with a living voice* (*viva vox*). Yet in Catharinus's *Apology,* he sees nothing but a defense of the ruling power of the pope *without* the Gospel and thus the exercise of "tyranny" and violence in the world.[26] This betrayal of Christ equals the work of Judas rather than Peter, he argues. Pope Leo X and the papists are accused of having abused that power and thereby "distorted" the words and "prostituted" the church.[27] This is the point where Luther brings the passage from Daniel 8 to its full bearing—literally according to the Hebrew rather than the Latin text, as he points out: "A king will stand there, powerful through visions [*facies*]."[28]

The Latin word *facies* is translated as "visions," but *visibilities* may be a better word, namely, the emergence of external *appearances* that cover up the inner devastation of the church; the wasteland. According to Luther, these *facies* are represented by the visible pomp, hypocrisy, and all the other indicators of the adversary of Christ; in other words, the mock appearance of the Antichrist.

The crucial point is the relationship between Christ and Antichrist, between being and appearance, whereby the latter is defined as a mendacious image (*mere mendacium*) and thus a mere caricature of the former. This new external image has allegedly *veiled* the image of Christ, and thus the church has been emptied of its most precious gift: It has become externally impressive but hollow and shallow inside. Thus the argument goes. Appearances such as ceremonies, superstitions, and justice by the works have *replaced* and thereby excluded the original definitions of grace, love, and justice by faith alone, and hence they cover up and distort the meaning of these words and practices. The hard currency of the word has been devalued by an economy of counterfeit money—a pattern which by now should be recognizable from Luther's critique of indulgences, morality, and metaphysics. The prophecy thus fulfilled is the prophecy of decline and devastation: "He will devastate wonderful things."[29]

Luther notes with amusement that this sentence may be read in different ways: "Daniel is ambiguous here, so that one either can understand these 'wonderful things' as *things* the king will corrupt or the *deeds* of the king are described as corruptive and as such they are characterized as amazing and incredible."[30] This ambiguity is a key point for the whole argument, since it illustrates the *double* face of the monstrous king. On the one hand, he has an impressive appearance through pomp, cathedrals, and beautiful costumes. On the other hand, he "devastates" the people from within.

Luther's decisive point is that the prophesied king of visions has submitted the Word of God to his own opinions and prescribed his interpretations for others. His power is seen as *authoritarian* and *totalitarian,* since he rejects and condemns all other voices. Hence, he demands that all people should merely listen and subject themselves to his words. Moreover, he is accused of putting his own power above all others, including God himself, so that "not even God demands with such majesty and power."[31] This boldness is, according to Luther, the final indication of his *success,* and thus of his insolence (the magnification of his heart), which in the near future will bring him to fall.

According to Patrick Preston, Ambrosius Catharinus's polemics have probably served as the "literary origin" of the Counter-Reformation.[32] Hence, the controversy plainly invites confessional polemics concerning who is right and wrong in their interpretation of the historical development. The continuation of such debates is hardly relevant today, but it gets all the more significant to understand their inner dynamic. There are pretensions, pride, and unreasonable allegations on both sides. Still, measured according to literary standards, Luther's subversive rhetoric is unmatchable, exploiting the power of humor, irony, and satire in order to uncover and thus denude the figure of the emperor in his new and holy clothes.[33] This is indeed an effective rhetoric against any abuse of power. Having recently experienced the process of excommunication and being declared an *outlaw,* Luther holds a certain legitimacy as dissident. With bitter irony he points at totalitarian traits of the system that seeks to control the public sphere and silence divergent voices. Luther challenges this authoritarian power in a language which is scornful and ironic. Could it possibly also be perceived as blasphemous? It moves far beyond the limits of conventional academic discourse, at least.

Following the ambiguity of devastation in Daniel, Luther's critique of images, myths, and idols requires a double approach. On the one hand, there is the power of the world which is growing through success and deceit, yet for Luther this power is only surpassed by the majesty of the hidden God. Hence, the *critical* potential of this notion is once more at stake. The reader is faced with the exclusive alternatives of scripture: You cannot serve two Lords; you have to serve either God or Mammon (Matthew 6:24). On the other hand, the *facies* tend to confuse and thus level the difference between God and idols. Hence, Luther turns to the images of the cornerstone and the cross; figures that target uncovering and thus *disillusioning* the masks, the monstrosity, and the power of the monstrous king.

The separation between two orders of power opens up a space of interpretation and discernment. Luther's radical critique of power thus follows the pattern of the hidden God in his majesty. However, his most effective and devastating rhetoric is formulated as the *Christological* mockery and subversion of the images of power. Christ is thus the *scandal* who has been devastated and replaced by the monstrous image of the king. Luther therefore predicts his imminent return in the form of a stone, namely, an iconoclastic destruction of *appearances* by the stumbling block.

Satire, Subversion, and Blasphemy

The apocalyptic visions belong to a contested genre, and Luther has been skeptical to the legitimacy of historical interpretations based on the Book of Revelation. Still, he applies the Book of Daniel in a devastating critique of the papacy. The "king of visions/faces" is identified with the pope, and he counts the four kingdoms as if these visions represented a detailed account of historical events. He also identifies no fewer than twelve "faces" that prove the alleged hypocrisy, including pageantry, titles of honor, gowns, waste of money, and abuse of sacraments.[34] In a key passage, he even interprets the visions from the Book of Revelation chapter 9, corresponding to highly concrete references in the history of the church.[35] This is indeed a bold undertaking, although the text betrays that even Luther becomes hesitant when he ventures into concrete interpretations.[36] Could we possibly conclude that Luther's pamphlet against Catharinus indicates a firm belief in the historical accuracy of the apocalyptic visions?

This is a tricky question, and the answer is hardly as obvious as may be assumed by Luther's direct assaults on his opponents. There is little doubt about the earnestness of his concern, yet at the same time, the exposition of these texts are kept in a humorous and satirical tone, with correspondingly ironical distance to the imagery described in the apocalyptic visions. Although he argues in favor of a simple, grammatical exegesis of the text, his own interpretation is anything but sober and literal. Hence, even if these rules are accepted, it remains an open question of *how* these images and visions ought to be read without completely misinterpreting the genre. Luther thereby transgresses a few conventional limits for academic and public discourse, to put it cautiously.

One thing is to venture into a direct historical application of the texts, thus identifying singular events as predicted in scripture. Another is to keep up these visions of the text as a mirror for the contemporary society, in order to identify certain symptoms of power abuse and hypocrisy. Although Luther comes closer to the latter, and thereby differs from both Catharinus and later from Müntzer, he also seems to have a more ambitious goal, namely, to deconstruct a particular reading of Matthew, of Daniel, and of John's Apocalypse that supports the status quo and the traditional authority of the papacy in Rome. He argues effectively for the point of view that these apocalyptic texts have less than nothing to do with ensuring secular power and the suppression of common people through religious authority. On the contrary: These texts are apt to ridicule and shatter such power in an epic rhetorical gesture.

Luther adopts a suspicious approach to the dominant *interpretations* of scripture. His suspicion is directed at the *facies,* that is, the dazzling appearance of power. This suspicion undermines its religious and political foundation by ridiculing its authority. Moreover, Luther suspects a hidden *atheism* to be the source behind all the marvelous symbols of rites and ceremonies; an atheism which is the result not only of hubris, but also of occupying the place which belongs to Christ and then justifying this occupation with a theory of substitution. A critical description of these *facies* identifies them as idolatry combined with an ideology of power and exploitation, and Luther's hermeneutics of suspicion ends up with a massive critique of this ideology which serves the mere preservation of power.

The apocalyptical text plays a specific role in this textual procedure. It is not merely applied in order to interpret history according to a millennial matrix of events but in a more general sense, unmasking the totalitarian and tyrannical tendencies of papal rule, executed by the system of canonical law. By these means, including the authority to interpret scripture, to prescribe laws, to judge perpetrators, and excommunicate political or religious enemies, the ecclesial hierarchy has been able to control and suppress the freedom of expression.[37] The economy of retribution instituted by the letters of indulgences is therefore only a symptom of a total system which penetrates everything from political decisions to the power of eternal life and death, or, as Luther points out, claims its sphere of sovereignty to apply even over the gates of Hell.[38]

The Book of Daniel and the Book of Revelation play a key role in unmasking what Luther sees as systemic abuse of power. It is exactly as *scripture* that it may achieve the role of "revelation" in this political sense, that is, revealing the ruling ideology in its most magnificently devastating form and thus exposing it to laughter. The role of these apocalypses is not primarily *historical* but rather *literary,* like a piece of fiction: With literary devices reminding one of a short story by Franz Kafka or a novel by Milan Kundera, it mirrors the structure of society and ridicules the authority of the powerful. And Luther does not shrink back from the most blasphemous exclamations. In order to provoke scandal, he leaves all scruples behind, producing a text which in its imagery demonstrates a wild masquerade of *facies,* and thereby further develops the fantastic genre of the Apocalypse rather than simply adapting it to a schematic theory of historical stages.

The Apocalypse serves as a model of political expression, and also as a model of thoughts that subverts the structure of society. Hence, Luther is faithful to the idea of destruction. If the German theologians and philosophers of the 1930s had been more aware of this fantastic and satirical side of Luther's literary production, they might have been better prepared for an effective critique of the totalitarian system emerging as a monstrous power of apocalyptic dimensions. And the apocalyptic model of mirroring society in a fantastic, even mythical, imagery will hardly be less effective when confronted with present and future systems of surveillance, seduction, and control.

What further contributes to the efficacy of the genre in this case is that both adversaries refer to the same texts, although in radically differing interpretations of it. Moreover, Luther is faithful to the authority of the text in the sense that he sees it as a form of divine intervention, indeed, an *invention,* of the other: unexpected, terrifying, and revealing the true character of hypocrisy and appearances. Hence, the authority of the powerful is haunted by its own ideological foundation. The genre of apocalypse therefore becomes a paragon of the *critical* function of the *deus absconditus* in Luther's thought. The hidden other surpasses the system of rites and rules, and thus it is able to break the system open from within, in a violent but possibly liberating gesture of destruction and grace. This is the source of the subversive power of apocalypse, literally understood as "unveiling" or "revelation": its ability to *reveal* the seductive structures and masks of power. If the description is trenchant, even though it is excessive, Christ becomes the model of massive and overwhelming system criticism from within.[39] Luther is not the first or last theologian to make that point, but it has rarely been done with similar linguistic and rhetorical force.

Luther's Rhetoric of Scandal and Satire

Martin Luther is generally acknowledged as the creator of a homogenous vernacular German language through his translation of the Bible. However, Birgit Stolt points out in her study of Luther's rhetoric that he has the habit of mixing German and Latin, high and low style, biblical references and local German idioms, and, finally, to combine blessings and curses.[40] Moreover, Antónia Szabari argues that when reading some of his polemical pamphlets "[. . .] one is struck by how artificial, hybrid and strange his language is."[41] Being a learned scholar and translator, just as familiar with the liberal arts as with the biblical scriptures he translated from the original languages, Luther was a creative and skillful user of language. At the same time he drives these languages and rhetorical conventions *to their limit,* if not way beyond their conventional limits.[42] The effect on the public sphere was astounding; nothing similar had been made accessible to the common public, and the texts became extremely popular, at least when measured according to earlier standards.[43]

Luther thus draws on a number of sources and rhetorical traditions, including satire and *pugna verborum* (rhetoric of blame), but he also insists that the biblical language is antithetical and contentious. Hence, when he blesses or curses his enemies, wishes them to Hell or bestows honor upon them, he insists on being in conformance with *scripture,* and hence with the "Word of God." He therefore denies that there is anything provocative about his brute style or infamous verbal attacks on his enemies—an assertion which presumably only adds to the provocative character of his speech. In the period around 1520, the temperature of Luther's verbal violence developed to perfection in German as well as in Latin, and the examples are legion in the letter against Ambrosius Catharinus. For instance this passage on the "blasphemy" of the thought that Christ and the pope are united at the Apostolic See:

> O blasphemy of most absurd blasphemies! This impious and immoral pederast, this usurer, sacrilegious man and bloodthirsty tyrant should mix with Christ, our God, and unite with him? O come, Lord Jesus Christ, and put an end to this horror of horrors! Amen.[44]

This is an example of how Luther mixes the harshest and most offensive denunciations with curses and then, at the end, a prayer to the Lord. The form of this final prayer is taken from the Apocalypse, more precisely from the Book of Revelation chapter 22. It is a prayer to the Lord that he will come and put an end to the suffering, and thereby save the just and condemn the impious to eternal fire or annihilation. The rhetorical point of the Apocalypse is that these are two sides of the same coin. What is heard as salvific truth by the one is heard as a word of judgment by the other. This is the crucial difference between the *inside* and the *outside* of the book, so to speak (see Revelation 5:1). Accordingly, Luther reads every word of promise as a threat or warning, too. Scripture is thus presented as a sword: It divides between the ones who are able to understand and those who are unable and thus *by their hearing* demonstrate that they are predestinated to perish. This view corresponds to his theory of scripture as its own interpreter: a judge between true and false interpretations. Hence, the pronunciation of the word *shibboleth,* which divides between life and death, is *put into context.* Luther apparently sees it as his call and his particular task to *reproduce* this divisive speech in its most hyperbolic form, hence the series of verbal excesses which virtually overflow in his polemical tracts from this period.

Antónia Szabari argues that the effect is "[. . .] not political division (or sedition, as the charge went) but the politicization of public speech. In his writing practice, Luther makes blasphemous statements that can be interpreted in opposite ways: one is either offended or converted by them."[45] This discussion of the public sphere is, for the subsequent development of political discourse, the most interesting aspect of Luther's controversy with Catharinus. The political theology displayed here is one of the first examples of addressing a wider public sphere, based on political discussions accessible for the entire literate population. It is indeed an apocalyptic and excessive discourse, but also satirical, polemical, and critical of power abuse and ideology. As an early example of *democratization*, it may be more significant than the critique of indulgences, justification by faith, and other theological doctrines of the Reformation.

This controversy further contributes to the understanding of early mass media in the public sphere with its contested use of images and icons: Is the image of the church presented by the Roman Curia true to the original image, or is it merely a simulacrum of the church? Luther effectively replaces the Greek word *doxa*—the radiance of divine sacredness and power also ascribed to the Holy See—with the Latin word *facies*, and thus he scornfully depicts the sanctimonious hypocrisy of the "king of *facies*."

Toward a Modern Public Sphere

Finally, the controversy is about scripture and the authority and power of interpretation, or, more precisely, a fight concerning the power and authority that may be exercised in the name of scripture. This question is awkward, since the theologian adopts the role of a prophet, who transfers the will of God into new political controversies. Hence, the words of a theologian can determine the life or death of thousands of people. Luther seems to be aware of this responsibility, although he cannot be aware of all the political consequences of his rhetorical inventions. His strategically smart draw is to disclaim any responsibility of the consequences, since he is not speaking on his own behalf; he is simply proclaiming the clear words of scripture—and thus scripture is the only judge between him and his opponents, since both sides agree that scripture represents the Word of God. What people read in this text is at the same time the judgment of their reading and of their way of receiving the word of promise: in offense or in confidence.

If Luther enacted what Edwards has called the first successful mass media campaign in history, at least in printed texts, he also contributed substantially to the formation of the public sphere in early modernity. Szabari goes one step further and argues that Luther thereby created the structure of the modern public sphere, although this public sphere remains chaotic and contradictory, excessive and offensive from the very beginning:

> If the Reformation—rather than the Enlightenment, as has often been assumed—can be said to create the modern structure of the public sphere, that is because it calls into question all conceptions of the public sphere as transparent: curses can be prayers and prayers curses. Enlightenment or secularist theories of the emergence of the public realm have missed the Reformation's genuine modernism,

> which consists in bringing out the potentially contentious, "excitable," character of religious and, perhaps, any speech.[46]

A number of intellectual historians, such as Jürgen Habermas and Charles Taylor, have claimed that the modern public sphere was created by the intellectuals and their newspapers in the coffee houses during the Enlightenment.[47] However, this estimation is based on an idealized image of the public sphere as these philosophers would like to have it: a bourgeois, secular conversation, not necessarily void of conflicts, insults, and caricatures, but nevertheless with a common expectation of universal rational and formal standards. This is far from the public sphere we experience today, however, with a collapse in the absolute distinction between public and private, and insulting cross-references between various styles, languages, public religions, and authorities. And it is equally far from the public sphere we discover in early modernity, with its ambiguity, its exaggerations, and its violently apocalyptical aspirations.

FOURTEEN

Political Theology of the German Revolutions

The rise of the Peasants' War in Germany 1524–1526 is intimately connected with the events of the Reformation.[1] It was not the only uproar of peasants in fifteenth- and sixteenth-century Europe but definitely the most important one, and the only upheaval deserving the name of a revolution—in the modern, political sense of the term. It also produced one of the earliest charters in favor of more general freedom rights in Europe, the so-called Twelve Articles of Memmingen (1525). There were other manifestos before and after this one, but none of them had a similar influence on political events. Its principal tenor may be traced directly back to the palpable influence from Luther's *On the Freedom of a Christian* (1520), the letter accompanying his written defense against the papal bull. The Twelve Articles open with an assertion of the right of each parish to install and depose a pastor according to their conviction. According to the first article, the pastor is obliged to preach the Gospel clearly and without any human additions, since the Word teaches "that we solely through the true faith can come to God."[2]

Luther's Fateful Ambivalence

The right to appoint and dismiss teachers and pastors was an important demand of the peasants, since it gave them an *independent* basis of power, in particular with respect to the power of interpretation. During the first years of the Reformation, they discovered a new sense of freedom which had not been accessible before. They were granted individual rights independent from the authority of the church, and the word of scripture became a source of responsibility and legitimacy versus the nobility. Hence, Luther was definitely seen as an ally when he in 1523 published the pamphlet *That a Christian Assembly Has the Right and Power to Judge All Teaching and to Call, Appoint, and Dismiss Teachers, Established and Proven by Scripture.*[3]

Luther is careful not to leave the impression that he was a supporter of rebellion and upheavals, though. He knows all too well how dangerous such a development could be for the reformation of the church. Moreover, he thinks that it contradicts the Word of God, although he is not quite clear at this point. He defends tumults as an unavoidable *consequence* of the clarification of scripture, but rejects tumults that *transgress* the word of scripture. So, what is the difference? A difference of interpretation? Luther would hardly admit that. He is possibly facing a predicament here, a double bind, between the ideal of clarity and the difficulties of finding a rule which is valid for all concrete conflicts.

While acknowledging the public right to elect pastors and teachers, Luther warns already in 1522 against insurrection, rebellion, and violent political pamphlets. Thereby, he sees the trembling heart and anxiety of the parsons and papists as an anticipation of eternal suffering: "Scripture promises such terror and fear to all God's enemies as the beginning of their damnation. Therefore it is right, and pleases me well, that such torment is beginning to appear among the papists [. . .]. Its bite will soon be sharper."[4] Luther even argues that if he had ten bodies, he would rather see them struck with the "gentle lash of bodily death" than allow them to stifle insurrection. It sounds almost like a *Menetekel* of the harsh alternatives coming up when the revolution breaks out only three years later. The tricky point is that Luther in principle thinks that the pope and his followers have abused their power and thus deserve a destiny in the "horrible yawning abyss." Still, he warns the peasants as well as the princes against taking the law into their own hands:

> [T]hese texts have convinced me that the papacy and the clerical estate will not be destroyed by the hand of men, or by insurrection. Their wickedness is so horrible that no punishment is adequate except the wrath of God itself, without any intermediary. [. . .] Even if a few should get roughed up, there will be no general resort to violence.[5]

In this pamphlet, Luther gives a number of reasons to avoid rebellion: that insurrection is just a theoretical possibility, completely superfluous, and moreover, that it lacks *discernment*. He therefore encourages people to keep their eye on the authorities, judge them with words but not with violence, and thereby avoid insurrection, which is most probably "a suggestion of the devil." The same tendency that was observed in the controversy with Catharinus is followed up here: violent and subversive rhetoric, but strong admonitions against upheavals and armed resistance.

In these years another faction comes up, disturbing the order within Wittenberg and in some cases destroying churches and monasteries. These radical reformers are often referred to as Spiritualists, Anabaptists, *Schwärmer*, or fanatics. The most famous representatives of this movement are Andreas Karlstadt, Gabriel Zwilling, and Thomas Müntzer. In *De servo arbitrio* Luther affirms that his fight for the Word of God is a double one: against the "fanatics" on the one hand and the Roman Catholic Church on the other.[6] He complains that these so-called fanatics under guidance of Karlstadt and Müntzer boast of their own spirit. Thereby they are not servants of the word, he thinks; on the contrary, they place their own spirit above the scriptures and may find in them whatever they wish.

The Roman Catholic Church, symbolized by the pope, is accused of committing exactly the same failure, albeit for different reasons. When Erasmus and the Roman theologians claim that the scriptures are obscure and ambiguous, they need the papal magisterium in order to secure a sound interpretation. As we have already seen in chapter 5, Luther sees the human spirit placing itself above the scriptures; it becomes self-sufficient and immune toward objections from the texts or from other interpretations. Thus he claims: "[T]his voice is no human invention, but a virus sent into the world by the incredible malice of the prince of all demons himself."[7]

Both tendencies are countered with reference to scripture. A number of quotations from Paul are applied in order to show that the Gospel in itself is a powerful message that necessitates a revolt of all methods, orders, and rules. It institutes an absolute and basic egalitarianism which suspends other distinctions and orders organizing the Christian civilization, although Luther explicitly confirms the political authority of the princes and the continued validity of the social organization of the late-medieval society. A crucial point for this way of reasoning is the reference to Paul as separate authority, which is not bound to the interpretive office of the church. Claiming that the sense of the scriptures is clear and accessible to anyone—in accordance with the principle *claritas scripturae*—is a precondition for his alternative approach to the text.[8] This principle of interpretation was dangerous to the political stability in late-medieval Europe, and it was instantly perceived as such. Luther must therefore have been aware of the political topicality of his theology. His understanding of the biblical text as revelation further contributes to its revolutionary potential, by justifying tumults and rebellion as soon as the word is set free from its "Babylonian captivity."[9] However, he is also highly conscious of the dangers of this politico-theological amalgam: Theology may be used for almost any purpose and interest; hence, idealists, revolutionaries, and rulers may all find justification for their aims in the scriptures. He therefore insists that a careful and suspicious analysis of the arguments according to the *external word* (rather than the inner conviction) is required.[10]

The indicative reference to the *sola fide* in the Twelve Articles is another indication of how intimately the revolution was connected with the Reformation and its proclamation of equality for all human beings in relation to God. Although Luther had not intended a political but rather a strictly spiritual reading of *On the Freedom of a Christian,* it is not difficult to recognize its political relevance. In fact, hardly any political issue would be treated independently of religious order and belief at the time, be it in terms of oppression or liberation, of regulation or uproar. Among the peasants and miners, the uprising was thus interpreted as a divine intervention. It was perceived as an apocalyptic sign of the coming of the End of Days, when God was expected to reinstall justice on earth, although under increasing conflict and bloodshed. The most central figure in developing this radical political theology, connecting reformation to revolution and biblical Apocalypse to justice and liberation, was the preacher Thomas Müntzer.

Thomas Müntzer: From Visions to Violence

Thomas Müntzer was originally an itinerant preacher in northern and central Germany. Attracted and encouraged by the commotion following Luther's exposure of the ninety-five theses, he became a student of him in Wittenberg 1518–1519.[11] However, he soon continued his vagabonding and became a pastor in Zwickau in 1520 before he fled to Prague, where he published a manifesto combining apocalyptic visions with anti-clericalism and requests for insurrection. In the *Prague Manifesto,* he explicitly refers to Johann Huss, and sees himself as the true heir of the Hussian legacy. From 1523 he was again active as pastor in the town of Allstedt, which belonged to the Electorate of Saxony, and here he wrote the first complete German liturgy, which was then used as the standard liturgy in the church of Allstedt. Because of complications with the town council and the duke, he had to flee to Mühlhausen in Thuringia in August 1524. After being expelled once more, he became pastor in the main church and contributed to a reorganization of the city according to egalitarian ideals, including extensive social work for the poor and the needy. In April and May 1525, he became one of the central leaders in the Thuringian uproar against the nobility.

Müntzer had several confrontations with Luther from 1523 onward, mainly on theological issues but also concerning the political application of theological ideas. Church historian Carl Hinrichs believes that Müntzer tried to establish a new political center of the Reformation, first in Allstedt and then in Mühlhausen.[12] Hence, the conflict between the two may also have been the result of an intensified territorial power struggle between different groups with radically differing ideas concerning the theological emphasis and political consequences of the Reformation. These conflicts became decisive for the lasting legacy of the Reformation as a cultural, political, and religious event in the history of Europe.

The peasants' insurrection contributed to political radicalization, on the one hand, and—as Friedrich Engels has rightly pointed out—a strict counterrevolution on the other.[13] When it comes to political ideals and the question of loyalty to the rulers, different factions of the Reformation movement (understood in the wide sense) are radically opposed to one another. Although Lutherans, Zwinglians, Calvinists, Anabaptists, and radical Spiritualists in various ways appeal to the authority of scripture as opposed to the Catholic Church, they have very different opinions when it comes to the interpretation of Romans 13 and the right to resist the authorities. They are even more split when it comes to apocalyptical perspectives on contemporary historical issues. Luther insisted on a clear distinction between the spiritual and the secular interpretation of God's power, thus renewing Augustine's division between the heavenly and the terrestrial kingdoms, whereas Müntzer argued for immediate political action in order to precipitate the apocalyptical struggle.

A short draft of Müntzer's theologico-political development based on some of his most significant texts from 1521 to 1524 shows that he was actively seeking to exert influence on the course of events, until the course of events achieved its own dynamic and became his destiny. Müntzer did not write academic disputations; most of his texts are short pamphlets, letters, or sermons. Already in the *Prague Manifesto* (1521), three aspects of his theology are worth noticing. First, the spiritual word is given preference over against the written word. Müntzer perceives the written word as dead, whereas he sees the Word of God which is written "in the heart" as a true gift of the spirit. Second, he believes that the church, and primarily the so-called parsons (*die Pfaffen*), have stolen "the key to this book that is locked," and thus use the reference to written texts as pretense for their lack of true, spiritual faith.[14] Although Müntzer also attacks the effort at taking possession of the text, his approach differs from Luther's in rejecting rather than emphasizing the *written* form of the text. And although he refers to scripture as "evidence" in every second sentence, he understands it basically as an oral and spiritual message. Müntzer only acknowledges the spiritual and mystical words that are *hidden* within scripture. Hence, he sees the content of scripture as esoteric rather than exoteric: It is revealed to the "elect," but remains hidden to the others. Third, Müntzer emphasizes the absolute need for *visions* in order to let Christ speak directly to the elect. The simple people should be led to revelations, he claims, with reference to Joel 2:28–29.[15] These visions are seen as authoritative in the sense that laypeople are *empowered* by the spirit—hence they are politically entitled to claim the right to power. These three specific traits characterize Müntzer's spiritual reading of scripture, whereas his interest in apocalypticism follows a broad stream of millennialism that was sweeping across Europe in this period.

Müntzer's *Sermon to the Princes* (1524) is delivered in the church of Allstedt on July 13, 1524. The princes of the Electorate of Saxony have announced their presence, although the preacher has just been accused of spreading dangerous religious and political ideas and risks suspension. The situation into which Müntzer speaks thus contributes to its immediate relevance for the sequence of events. Moreover, the Book of Daniel is the text of the day, namely, the same apocalyptic text that was intensively discussed by Luther and Catharinus some years earlier. Müntzer's approach is different from the other two, though. Setting out from Nebuchadnezzar's dream, he spends some time condemning false dreams that belong to the "kingdom of evil," which deprive people of the truth and the ability to see clearly in order to distinguish between good and evil. Still, he warns the pious people against rejecting "the good along with the evil."[16]

Müntzer therefore proceeds by suggesting some principles for distinguishing between divine dreams and devilish temptations. This is a decisive issue for him, since he has based his theology and authority on the premise that the elect must *experience* God and perceive his continued revelation in their hearts. The vision thus becomes a primary means of God's guidance. This is all the more delicate since the story of Daniel is directly applied to the situation of preaching: Müntzer attributes the authority of interpreting dreams and prophesy to himself, whereas the princes may have dreams but lack the ability to understand and discern the spirits. The implicit conclusion is that, unless they listen to the prophetic voice of Müntzer, they will most probably serve evil rather than good. Hence, in a direct appeal to his noble audience, Müntzer encourages them to follow the example of Nebuchadnezzar; that is, to *kill* the clergy who want to rule the country like the "clever" advisers of the old Babylonian king. At the same time, the following invitation is presented in an apocalyptic tone, from the new prophet to the old princes: "Therefore, a new Daniel must arise and interpret your revelation for you. And this same new Daniel must go forth, as Moses teaches, Deuteronomy 20:2, at the head of the troops. He must reconcile the anger of the princes and that of the enraged people."[17]

On one hand, Müntzer ascribes to himself the role of the great reconciler between the princes and the insurgent peasants. On the other hand, he threatens the princes that if they do not use their sword against the "enemies of Christ," it should be taken away from them or even turned against them. He proclaims in the name of Christ that "godless rulers, especially the priests and the monks, should be killed."[18] Toward the end of the sermon, he comes to the brutal conclusion that the godless have "no right to life," except that which the elect have granted them. These words undoubtedly alarmed the rulers, and Müntzer was fired as preacher only two weeks later. He leaves the town of Allstedt in the beginning of August 1524, but the transition from preaching to actual political intervention, from visions and prophecy to requests for violence, has been fulfilled through his interpretation of the apocalyptic text.

Müntzer's Mysticism and Preference for the Poor

After this confrontation in Allstedt, not only the conflict with the rulers but also the conflict with Martin Luther escalates. In *Highly Provoked Defense*, published in December 1524, Müntzer focuses on the Gospel of Luke, although his interpretation is accompanied by consecutive references to a number of texts from the Old and the New Testaments. Apparently he is eager to prove that he is a *scriptural* theologian after all, although he is sharply critical of all the "scribes" and "Pharisees," be they in Wittenberg or in Rome, who merely relate to the dead letters and not to the living spirit. Luther had published *A Letter to the Princes of Saxony Concerning the Rebellious Spirit* during the summer of 1524 wherein he accuses both Müntzer and Karlstadt of a series of theological mistakes, including misinterpreting the Word of God and despising the baptism of children, enthusiastic fantasies, and calls for violence.[19] Müntzer is insulted by Luther's criticism and calls him Dr. Liar (*Lügner*), Brother Softlife, the pope of Wittenberg, and similar flattering nicknames. Now he counts the theologians in Wittenberg among the godless traitors.

The aggressive response from Müntzer is only understandable in the light of his former admiration for Luther, seeing himself as Luther's protégé and fellow Reformer. In 1523 he still addresses him as his great and admirable teacher and writes that he is convinced about the complete concordance between Luther's position and his own, except for some minor issues. Indeed, he believes his own thought to be a necessary further development of Luther's original approach. When Luther then condemns his theology as heretical, Müntzer immediately accuses him of "false faith." Müntzer's high self-assessment, combined with his marginalized position, presumably contributed to this reaction, and further radicalized his theology.

Luther's criticism makes it necessary for Müntzer to distinguish his own position more clearly in opposition to the other reformers. At the same time, his work as a preacher has confronted him with new challenges in the daily life of the common people, such as farmers, miners, and craftsmen. He finds that they are exploited by the rulers and the monasteries. Hence, he supports civil disobedience and protest actions in Allstedt and Mühlhausen. On Müntzer's advice, the city council of Mühlhausen refused to pay taxes to the local monastery and argued that they needed the money in order to take care of the poor.[20] A chapel for the devotion to Mary nearby was burned down and Müntzer defended the act, claiming that the poor nuns belonged to the "Church of the Devil" rather than the Church of Christ.

Under Müntzer's influence, the city of Mühlhausen was rapidly developing into a socialist experiment, and he soon became a supporter of violent revolution, in case the princes or the monasteries resisted this development. He was perceived as a troublemaker by strong forces in the city and was expelled from Mühlhausen together with his fellow preacher Heinrich Pfeiffer by the end of September 1524.[21] However, he was allowed to return in February 1525 and became pastor in the main church, the *Marienkirche.* From here he organized shelter for homeless people and meals for the poor, contributed to the dissolution of monasteries and abolition of privileges, at the same time mobilizing the people for an uprising. During the same period, from August 1524 to April 1525, scattered groups of resistance were organized all over southern Germany, Switzerland, Austria, and Tyrol.

There is a strong sense of inner consistency between Müntzer's praxis as politician, social worker, and preacher if we look at his reflections on the Gospel of Luke, which is particularly concerned with the poor and with social justice. When he spiritualizes the word of scripture, it is not in order to simplify the interpretation, but rather in order to make it concrete, as a political and theological *program.* He rejects Luther's doctrine that man is justified by faith without works, which he sees as an irresponsible abstraction. On the contrary: He believes that faith is fulfilled and actualized *through* works. Justification, according to Müntzer, unavoidably leads to acts of justice in society and in personal life. The *iustitia Dei* of which Paul writes (Romans 1:16–17) and on which Luther insists, is for Müntzer intrinsically connected to social justice, to a just life, and to the coming of God's justice with the *new* kingdom, already transforming the temporal community. The Gospel of Luke is a paradigmatic example of such reasoning, with its consistent preference for the poor. The suppressed and the marginalized, like Mary, Elizabeth, and Zechariah (compare with Luke 1), have, according to Müntzer, privileged access to the wisdom of God, whereas God despises the powerful and mighty.[22] Hence, Müntzer exclaims: "Oh, if the poor rejected peasants knew this, it would be most useful to them."[23]

For other people, such insight is only achievable through extreme suffering of the heart, Müntzer writes. If not poor in material respects, they ought to be poor in the spirit, he argues, by "walking into the desert"—an idiom the preacher repeatedly returns to. This is an image and a paradigm he picked up from the mystics, by whom he was deeply inspired. Hence, according to the "order" of knowledge which he elaborated already in the *Prague Manifesto,* a true Christian ought to be completely emptied of himself and persist in this empty abyss of the soul *before* God can inhabit the soul and fill it with grace, joy, and goodness. He describes this spiritual rebirth as following after a period of *langweyl* (tediousness) and *gelassenheit* (serenity), expressions well known from the mystical literature of Eckhart, Tauler, and Suso. This rebirth is not to be confused with baptism, he argues, which is merely a "symbolic ritual of water." The spiritual baptism, he claims, ought to *precede* the baptism with water. Hence, he repeatedly refers to the call for a new prophet and preacher like John the Baptist.[24]

When Luther criticizes Müntzer's view of baptism, his spiritualism, and his political rebellion, Thomas Müntzer soon concludes that the first movement of the Reformation has failed. He argues that Luther's Reformation has already fallen into the static passivity of doctrine, which seeks to flatter the rulers in all respects and avoids any topic of potential conflict in order to remain respected by the establishment. If faith remains without consequences in practical life, in society, and in the spirit of the believer, Müntzer sees it as a clear sign of superficial hypocrisy: There have been some minor changes in exterior form, yet at the end of the day, the princes have become even more *powerful*, the scribes even more *learned* and *literal* in their interpretation of the scriptures. The real life is missing, he argues, and the political consequences of the Gospel fail to materialize. The conflict between Müntzer and Luther thus grew increasingly heated and hostile. Müntzer criticized Luther for betraying the basic principles of the Reformation and of letting down the common people who had hoped for his moral assistance in their fight for justice and better life conditions.[25] Hence, he concludes the *Defense* with this last friendly greeting to Dr. Lügner:

> Oh Doctor Liar, you sly fox. Through your lies you have made sad the hearts of the righteous, whom God has not deceived. Thereby you have strengthened the power of the evildoers, so that they remain set in their old ways. Thus your fate will be that of the trapped fox. The people will be free. And God alone will be lord over them.[26]

Müntzer thus explicitly discusses the question of rebellion, about which Luther criticized him. He denies that he has encouraged the peasants to rebel, but he admits that he intends to reorganize society: "I proclaimed before the princes that the entire community has the power of the sword, just as it also has the keys of remitting sin."[27] This is Müntzer's final step in justifying political revolution and redistribution of powers with reference to the Gospel. This is where his theology finds its practical *Sitz im Leben*, whereas his expectations remain firmly based in the Apocalypse and the advent of the Last Judgment.

Luther's Admonition to Peace and Request for Violence

Upheavals were nothing new in southern and central Germany in the sixteenth century, and Luther had already warned against violent protests in the name of the Gospel. When the conflict escalated in 1525, he tried to negotiate between the peasants and the lords. In *Admonition to Peace,* he challenges the nobility to accept some of the peasants' demands which seemed to be reasonable. He responded directly to the Twelve Articles and told the nobility that all the demands should be acceptable and contribute to a better, more peaceful, and more prosperous society for everyone.[28] He also urgently warned the peasants against the misconstruction that they were fighting on God's side in their apocalyptic scenario and threatened them with divine punishment if they resorted to robbery or terror.[29] Since the peasants had taken advantage of Luther's thoughts on scripture and freedom, it looks like he feels obliged to warn against misinterpretations, that is, against political application of texts that originally were written as *spiritual* defense. As we have seen, Luther is often charged with causing turmoil and moral decline. The pamphlet enabled him to correct this image, but it did not contribute substantially to calming down the conflict. On the contrary: He is suspected of betrayal and of playing a double game. Anyway, his efforts are futile, and shortly after, the big revolt breaks out. In this heated situation, Luther publishes another pamphlet, *Against the Robbing and Murdering Hordes of Peasants* (1525), which attacks the peasants for leaving the way of peace and taking recourse to violence, robbery, and terror for their personal benefit. He denies them any right to interpret the Gospel in this direction and accuses them of abusing the Gospel. For these trespasses, Luther insists that the rebellious peasants deserve to die, not only once but ten times.[30] He calls them "devils" and predicts that they will suffer "eternal fire in Hell" for their deeds. In his eyes, this is not only uproar against the princes but against God himself—a violation of God's Law and the words of the New Testament. He explicitly refers to Luke 20:25 ("give the Emperor what belongs to the Emperor") and Romans 13:1 (on obedience to the authorities).[31] Luther insists that the word of freedom and justice in Christ is strictly limited to the spiritual sphere, whereas the fight for earthly goods is regulated by human law and should be defended with the sword. Finally, he crosses the limit between spiritual and political advice, concluding that killing the penetrators is the simple duty of the princes. In doing this, the princes will allegedly fulfill their divine mission and their Christian responsibility. He gives them the following brutal challenge: "Therefore, dear Princes, here you can liberate, here you can save, and here you can help! Have mercy with the poor people! And then—stab, beat, kill, whoever can! If you die thereby, lucky you! You could never get a more blessed death."[32]

The nobility has been hesitant to use violence against the peasants because they are afraid of God's judgment. They share the view that only God can give the power over life and death, and they are afraid that the peasants are fighting on God's side in this apocalyptic showdown. However, when Luther finally defines the insurgent peasants as Sons of the Devil, he gives the nobility the license to kill that they have been waiting for. It can hardly be ruled out that Luther, with his harsh pamphlet, incited the slaughter of thousands of innocents, since the nobility did not stop with the armed rebels. They hunted down all the peasants and punished villages for their support of the insurgence. Up to one hundred thousand people were killed in the revenge acts of the counterrevolution. The disastrous result shows that the Early Reformation remains unsettled on this issue, as it does on the interpretation of Romans 13. Luther's role in the conflict is controversial. He made a rare effort at trying to explain his activity afterward, although he never admitted any failure.[33]

Thomas Müntzer followed the peasants of Mühlhausen to the final confrontation at Schlachtberg, close to Frankenhausen. Although not a military leader, he was the only leader left, and thus he lifted the "sword of Gideon," which he had been waiting for, and led the hordes of peasants like Daniel in his fight against the Midianites.[34] Müntzer is described as a zealous leader, although he had no experience in warfare and hardly knew how to use weapons, not to mention strategically organizing an attack on the trained troops of the lords. He was focused on spiritual encouragement and would not accept that anyone questioned his authority. Just before the battle begins, two of the peasants get cold feet: They are untrained and unprepared, yet they have been persuaded to support the uprising. Now they see how chanceless they are, and they start thinking of their wives and children at home—in short, they want to retire and ask the leader for permission to leave. Müntzer sees them as traitors and commands them to stand at the center of the circle and confess in front of all the others. Then he draws his sword and makes a short shrift of the two men: Their heads are quickly separated from their bodies, and Müntzer commands the rest of the group to get prepared for the final battle.

The peasants had no chance against the superior forces of the princes, and five thousand peasants were slaughtered. The rest were captured, unless they managed to flee. Müntzer fled but was captured on May 15, hiding in a neighboring village. He was imprisoned and interrogated under torture, whereas the city of Mühlhausen was put under siege. The counterrevolution was a done deed. On May 25, the city surrendered to the ruling count, Ernst of Mansfeld, and two days later, Thomas Müntzer was placed before the city wall, facing the masses and the cold iron of *Realpolitik*. This time Müntzer suffered the same destiny he had inflicted on others: He was executed by decapitation.

Apocalypse and Political Ideology

A number of crossing interests and theological convictions are at stake in this conflict, but I will focus on the problematic role of apocalypticism before, during, and after the Peasants' War.[35] The apocalyptical spirit of Müntzer played a vital role in making the war possible in the form it took.[36] The increasing suppression and the difficult economic and political conditions among the peasants were, of course, important material reasons for the insurgence, but the upheavals are hardly imaginable without the inspiration from apocalyptical expectations and imagery. Let me thus point out seven characteristic patterns that made this possible:

1. *A moment of decision.* The temporal perspective of experiencing a *kairos* in history, a decisive moment when the basic conditions of society may actually change and the suppressed will experience freedom. Müntzer interprets this decisive moment Christologically, with strong social implications.

2. *Dystopia and utopia*. The temporality of the Apocalypse is prophetic and directed toward the future rather than the past. Both Müntzer and Luther see the End of Days approaching, and thus expect a total dystopia to destruct and revolt the state of affairs. Yet, *behind* and *after* this dystopia of suffering, tumults, and bloodshed, they see a bright utopia approaching.
3. *Election and sacrifice*. The rebelling peasants believe that they are the few elect; hence, they are willing to risk their lives in order to precipitate the dystopia and pave the way for the fulfillment of God's promise. Their death becomes a minor sacrifice on the way toward a higher purpose, yet at the same time this sacrifice becomes significant in its own terms, as a sacrament of their own bodies.
4. *Community and common destiny*. When Müntzer preaches that they are the few elect, they get a strong sense of community, of sharing everything, including their poverty, destiny, life, and death—like the first apostles are said to have done in Acts 2:44–46. This is the sacred space of their political movement.
5. *Esoteric insight*. The elect are united with a secret and mystical bond, based on esoteric knowledge. Just like the author of the Apocalypse, they believe that the general community is unable to understand their views, but the apocalyptical horizon gives them a firm belief that the world will discover the "real" truth as soon as God reveals it to everyone.
6. *Demonization*. The conflict is universalized and the enemy is defined as evil, thus belonging to the Devil. The enemy thereby loses his human traits and may be killed without hesitation, whereas traitors are despised, tortured, and sometimes even beheaded.
7. *Political myth of revolution*. This eschatological expectation gives the Apocalypse immediate political relevance and creates a political mythology that makes revolution possible, since the world—and indeed the universe—is out of equilibrium and almost anything may happen, every promise may be fulfilled, if only one believes in it.

It is worth noticing that these apocalyptical expectations are not only dominant among the peasants but also among the nobility. They accept the apocalyptical description of the world and expect the End of Days to approach any time. The same applies to Luther's argument against the insurgence: Most of these premises are not contradicted. On the contrary: He takes them for granted but turns the argument the other way around. The *rulers* are thereby understood as God's warriors, and the killing of a poor peasant is justified as a holy act. The sacred space is thus constructed from a different view, but even then violence is justified in order to protect the community in its traditional form, whereas the death of a soldier is seen as martyrdom, as a holy sacrifice of the body.

The princes and their soldiers are told that they conduct a war not only against a group of peasants but also against higher powers, the "Prince of this world." Since both sides share this perspective, the interpretation of apocalyptic texts becomes extremely politicized and ideological. Ideology is there on both sides, and the interpretation of texts is more typically directed by the contradicting power interests than by any effort at understanding the literal or historical sense of scripture. In the case of Müntzer, this is in concordance with his politico-theological ideal; hence, the interpretation is consequent but the consequences disastrous. Luther, conversely, betrays his fragile distinction between the spiritual and the secular power. After some hesitation, he identifies the conflict as an apocalyptical battle between God and the Devil, where the "killing hordes" of the peasants belong to the latter. And the consequences are disastrous. Still, he is unwilling to admit any failure and blames the peasants for the massacre and the excessive suppression during the counterrevolution.

In consequence, however, Luther does not continue questioning the place of the Apocalypse of John in the canon. It plays a significant political role during the religious controversies and wars up to 1648.[37] When he writes the introduction to a Commentary on the Apocalypse in 1530, he leaves the question of authorship and canonicity open but takes recourse to an *allegorical* reading of the text applied to important events in church history.[38] Among the predicted heresies identified in chapters 7–8 of the Book of Revelation, Luther finds both Pelagianism and Montanism. The former is identified with the papal church in his own era and the latter with Thomas Müntzer's spiritualism.[39] Hence, he applies his own interpretation of the text as counterargument against those who condemn the Reformation. In the end, all his enemies are defined as heretics according to John's prophesies at Patmos, whereas the Reformation has allegedly lifted up the true faith once more. This is in Luther's eyes the reason why the Antichrist is so furious and sets the world on fire. He does not speculate much about the future but suggests that the tumults may be the beginning of the Last Millennium.

FIFTEEN

The Hidden God of Revolution and Apocalypse

The decisive role Thomas Müntzer played during the German Peasants' War of 1525 and his prophetic statement about the people being free later did encourage Friedrich Engels to see him as a precursor of all later revolutionaries. Engels's interpretation is deeply influenced by the Left Hegelian historian Wilhelm Zimmermann, himself a politically radical scholar who first identified Thomas Müntzer as a revolutionary figure.[1] Engels sees the incidents during the revolution of 1525 and the following counterrevolution as paradigmatic for the historical dynamic of revolutions in general. Indeed, this also allows him to relocate the historical origin of the communist revolution to the heart of Germany and discuss the relationship between revolution and religion, history and ideology in a context that he finds similar to the events of 1848–1850. Müntzer becomes a revolutionary hero and the first martyr of Marxism. According to Engels, he resisted the temptation to let the Reformation end up with a bourgeois reactionary settlement under the old rulers and instead risked his life for the ideas he believed in: justice for the oppressed, improvement of their material conditions, a total revolution of the established power structures, and eventually the liberation of the entire people. Engels sees in Müntzer, for the first time in modern Europe, a political expression of the *secular* realization of the utopian vision of a "kingdom of God," including freedom, equality, and peace on earth.[2] Hence, before we conclude this analysis of early modern political theology by comparing the thought of Luther, Catharinus, and Müntzer, let us take a short view behind the curtains to the stage prepared for a second volume on the hidden God in modern philosophy, where political theology is analyzed from various perspectives, including the question of Marxism and the utopias of the Apocalypse.

Müntzer and Marxism

Friedrich Engels relates freely to the historical texts, although he relies heavily on Wilhelm Zimmermann's detailed study of the Peasants' War, published in two volumes in 1841–1843. Engels readily admits that he has given no original contribution to the interpretation of the sources. However, that is probably too modest an assessment. His interpretation of Müntzer is at least original, and thus interesting for its own sake. It gives access to an early and archetypical example of Marxist historical reasoning. The two added prefaces and the first chapter reveal the historical method Engels applied, based on historical materialism and his understanding of the development of history through the dialectic of conflict between different classes in society, in particular the class struggle between the rulers and the oppressed people. Consequently, he begins his inquiry with a description of the social classes and their mutual relationships. He gives a detailed account of how such social tensions produced the upheaval and led to the sudden and violent aggravation of the conflict.

This perspective is forceful as a contrast to the traditional church historical tendency to assess Müntzer primarily on the basis of his published texts and Luther's condemnation of him as swarmer (*Schwarmgeist*), political troublemaker, and sectarian.[3] Considering the knowledge available to him, Engels's analysis of the material and social conditions producing the conflict is balanced and convincing. However, the preface also betrays further interests influencing his approach to the historical events.[4] He sees the Peasants' War as an exact parallel to the Revolution of 1848, but the inferences of historical dynamic run from the latter to the former. Hence, the Peasants' War is modeled as an early revolution following the same patterns and interests as the communists and other parties did in 1848, thus also Luther:

> Between 1517 and 1525, Luther had gone through the same transformations as the German constitutionalists between 1846 and 1849. This has been the case with every middle-class party which, having marked for a while the head of the movement, has been overwhelmed by the plebeian-proletarian party pressing from the rear.[5]

Luther is thereby accused of betraying not only the peasant insurrection but even his own protest "against religious and lay authority"—and Engels immediately draws the parallel: "Need we mention other bourgeois who recently gave us examples of repudiating their own past?"[6]

Engels's critique of ideology—itself a critical point in Marxist ideology and historical analysis—takes as a premise that the historian is able to understand historical incidents and their causes more appropriately than the actors did themselves.[7] Hence, when the representatives on both sides refer to the Word of God and divine justice as motive and rationale for their fight, Engels interprets this as a code for something else, namely, a theological rationalization of the class struggle. Thus, Müntzer is portrayed as the archetype of a plebeian revolutionary and his ideas perfectly correspond to those of nineteenth-century communism:

> By the kingdom of God, Müntzer understood nothing else than a state of society without class differences, without private property, and without superimposed state powers opposed to the members of society. All existing authorities, as far as they did not submit and join the revolution, he taught, must be overthrown, all work and all property must be shared in common, and complete equality must be introduced.[8]

The last sentence definitely comes true for Müntzer's position in 1524–1525, but Engels gets so deeply engaged in his presentation of Müntzer that he forgets all references to the historical texts that may eventually correct this idealized image, for example, of what Müntzer may have expected as the "kingdom of God." Moreover, Müntzer becomes the spokesman for all the ideals of the Marxist revolution of 1848, and Engels seems to identify so completely with his hero that he even promotes exactly the same criticism of church and religion as Engels and Marx did: "Faith, he said, was nothing else but reason become alive in man, therefore, he said, pagans could also have faith."[9] For every "he said" the narrative and the notions wander farther away from any historical sources and express precisely Engels's views, including the opinion that there is no Heaven beyond but a heaven to be established here on earth, no Hell, no devils, and, indeed, that Christ was simply "a man like we are." Finally, he admits that these are not exactly the words Müntzer used:

> Müntzer preached these doctrines mostly in a covert fashion, under the cloak of Christian phraseology which the new philosophy was compelled to utilize for some time. The fundamental heretical idea, however, is easily discernible in all his writings and it is obvious that the biblical cloak was for him of much less importance than it was for many a disciple of Hegel in modern times.[10]

This is an interesting turn in Engels's critique of ideology: Müntzer and the biblical cloak! Müntzer, who insisted on being a biblical theologian in all respects, and not merely on the surface. Müntzer, who insisted on the presence of the living Christ and rarely wrote two sentences without referring to the Bible. Engels's explanation of the *real* motivation behind movements in the sixteenth century reveals some typical traits in his understanding of ideology, history, and religion: first, that the ideology critique itself becomes deeply ideological. The reflection of oneself in a historical person indicates not only a lack of source criticism, but also of self-criticism, of the ability to look critically at one's own position. Second, that the understanding of history as a *material condition* for human development seems to be void of sense without the interpretation of its *spirit*—which in this case is the sacred *spirit of the Apocalypse*. Third, Engels identifies with this apocalyptic spirit to such an extent that it dominates even his view of the structure of political revolutions—and their ultimate goal. Hence, whereas he superimposes his own *view* of religion each time he refers to Thomas Müntzer, he implicitly embraces Müntzer's apocalypticism as the ideal of a revolutionary collapse and utopia. Religious ideas and the religious sense of community are thereby translated into an ideal vision of communism.

There is no doubt that Marx early rejected religion as ideology and called it opium for the people, and Engels seems to have accepted this assessment. Still, the religious movement here referred to is the opposite: It is an apocalyptic spirit which inspires the people to class struggle and revolution. Hence, the relationship between politics and religion may be more complex than the young Marx expected it to be. In his critique of Hegel's *Philosophy of Right,* he wrote: "Religious suffering [*Elend*] is at once the expression of real suffering and a protest against real suffering. Religion is the sigh of the oppressed creature, the heart of a heartless world, and the soul of soulless conditions. Religion is the opium of the people."[11] If we take the first part of this quotation and apply it critically for a reconsideration of Marx's and Engels's understanding of religion and politics, religious language seems to be just as realistic and appropriate for describing human reality as the historical-materialistic analysis of social conflict. They are not necessarily mutually exclusive, and it seems like Engels, at least, enthusiastically adopted religious language for describing the expectations and dynamic of revolution when comparing the revolutions of 1525 and 1848.

In *The German Revolutions,* the fervor, the utopia, the high ideals of love, equality, and eternal peace have all been converted to this vision of a communist society. Indeed, Engels is a visionary, and without this vision of a society to come, a society which is already breaking in and transforming the current society from beyond, communism would be a dry sociological theory about the movement of capital and the internal struggle of powers within the modern society. When compared to the seven characteristics of apocalyptical thought we identified in Müntzer, most of them return, in a somewhat altered form, in the revolutionary thought that Engels identifies with the cause of revolution:[12] The revolution is the decisive moment when the basic conditions of society may actually change, hence it represents a *kairos* where the servants may become rulers and vice versa [1]. It conforms to Müntzer's political eschatology and his understanding of justification by faith as political ideal, although not explicitly connected to the person of Christ. The understanding of revolutionary time is directed toward the future and the expectation of a utopian egalitarian community [2], and both Marx and Engels accept destruction and violent resistance as necessary means of achieving the goals of revolution [3]. They describe the suffering and exploitation of the proletariat as the *real* and realistic truth, free from any illusions, but this description is often met with skepticism and repudiated in modern societies; hence, there are uncountable examples of Marxist movements that became sectarian in their structure. They also emphasize the necessity of human sacrifice in order to realize the ideal of the Kingdom of God on earth, that is, a communist society [4]. Engels sees the general "confusion" and "ignorance" of the people as unavoidable, but he expects future generations to accept the view of the few elect as the truth, despite the setback of counterrevolution [5]. The struggle for revolution is understood as a universal struggle on behalf all humanity, and the labor class becomes the elect people who may fulfill this promise in history if they only achieve the right knowledge, if they are *enlightened* in this philosophical but also politico-religious sense [6]. Hence, finally, apocalypticism seems to have played a crucial role in forming the structure of revolutionary thought, although it is transformed into a different political and historical context [7].

Despite the anti-religious rhetoric, it is hardly an exaggeration to label the apocalypticism of the German Revolution of 1525 the *implicit* political theology of Marxism. Given its apocalyptical expectations, its tendency toward sectarianism, its social criticism, and its oscillation between dystopia and utopia, historical materialism is not only a prophetic but even an *apocalyptic* movement in modernity. It relies on a sacred space within society identifying the ultimate ideals of egalitarianism, the existential value of work, and the sacrifice of the individual for the sake of community.[13] These ideals are all worth dying—and killing—for. The apocalyptical formation of Marxism is not identical with the apocalypticism of the first or the sixteenth century, but apocalypticism has never remained identical with itself. It is apocalyptic exactly in terms of its transformative power and its ability to accommodate political, religious, and existential experiences under different circumstances. This brief examination of Engels's book on *The German Revolutions* indicates that apocalypticism may still have massive political consequences, for good or for bad. In the form Engels adopts the spirit of the Apocalypse within Marxism, it may even be called the "mother of all revolutions," both structurally and in terms of historical influence.

The Hidden God and the Power of Interpretation

The three different approaches to the Book of Daniel presented by Ambrosius Catharinus, Martin Luther, and Thomas Müntzer reveal significant differences in their approach to apocalyptical texts, to political conflicts, and to the hiddenness of God, which leaves the interpreters in perplexity and sometimes confusion when it comes to the purpose, causes, and consequences of historical events. For Catharinus, Daniel is a book which indicates that the coming of heresies and heathen kings is inevitable, and they will threaten the power and position of the church. Still, he argues that these threats are bound to fail, because the church has been given divine authority and the pope represents the unbroken tradition back to Peter; indeed, he is the "substitute" of Christ on earth. By mere definition his adversaries therefore represent the opposite power, the Antichrist. Catharinus argues along traditional lines, and thus the unsettling messages of Daniel and the Book of Revelation are not seen as a threat to the power and authority of the church. On the contrary: This allegoric reading implies that the pope, the Curia, and the priests *embody* the church, and hence any reading which questions this power is put on the other side of the narrative and given the role of the betrayers and the deserters. Reformers, political adversaries, and religious preachers who question the magisterial power of interpretation are declared heretic, excommunicated, and/or demonized.

The political and religious consequence is that God's hiddenness is not perceived as an unsettling fact. Rather, God's apparent absence makes it easier to rationalize the meaning and purpose of divine will within an expedient and profitable economy, as the example of indulgences shows. According to Luther, there are no less than twelve signs of such domestication *of* the name of God *in* the name of God within the church. He argues that God's presence is thereby either *temporally* located in the past or *spatially* excluded from the world, whereas the *name* of God is instrumentalized for secular purposes. The exclusion of God "in the name of God" could even be called a linguistic exclusion, thus literally excommunicating the Word of God (as mediated in scripture) in order to give space to a number of other forms of communication, such as, the sermons, the encyclicals, and the letters of indulgences. If Luther's critique of "interpretation" is appropriate, then the critique based on *sola scriptura* announces the return of God, of the *hidden* God, as opposed to the domesticated God of the church.

Luther accuses the Roman theologians who defend the papal title of *Vicarius Christi* not only of blasphemy, but also of nihilism, that is, of rejecting the presence and authority of God.[14] As soon as the *place* of God in theological and political discourse is occupied by some earthly power, it must result from lack of faith in divine power—thus the argument goes. Hence, Luther's argument follows a topological structure which recurs with new force some centuries later, when Nietzsche charges his opponents with nihilism. Like the Madman in Nietzsche's *The Gay Science,* Luther charges Catharinus's God of being "dead" and thus excluded from the life and thought of the church. This is the more profound reason for his offensive language: He feels obliged to make people aware of the disproportion between words of prayer and curses by proving their emptiness. These prayers to a *replaced* God, that is, a mendacious image of God, are rejected as nothing but nihilistic idolatry. The subversive rhetoric we observe in Luther's polemics is therefore the result of, but also the counterstrategy to, such mendacious images: In putting up the mirror of reversal, he intends to show that the opposite allegations may be equally true. By following the reversed logic of Christology, he apparently intends to unveil the logic of Catharinus as abuse of plain or proper language.[15]

This alleged simulacrum is mirrored by the absurd humor of curses that become prayers and prayers that provoke curses and condemnations. Luther thereby does not just confront and destabilize the position of his adversary—he destabilizes his own position, too, and the reader is left in insecurity and indecision. She is forced to take sides, either pro or contra Luther, or, as he argues, pro or contra Christ. Luther challenges the reader by claiming that there is no *indefinite* space in between Christ and Antichrist. No one can serve two masters. If we follow the argument closely, we discover that he reconstructs a shibboleth of double sense in order to provoke a *scriptural* decision, with fateful consequences for the reader or listener, according to her *way of reading.*

Such a strategy is only possible if God's hiddenness is enforced in the rigorous sense, with its linguistic, rhetorical, metaphysical, theological, and even political consequences. Luther thus draws the hiddenness of God into the praxis of reading and interpreting texts, as a condition of understanding. It turns out to be of particular significance when it comes to apocalyptical texts, concerned with revelation. These are surprising, indeed unsettling, texts of hidden messages in dreams and visions; words that seem to be obscure, and thus require some interpreter who can translate them. Translating is in this case a repetition, in political respects an "actualization," but actually more of a *futurization* of the unexpected, of the events to come. This is perhaps the specific contribution of Luther in his sarcastic destabilization of the Apocalypse: It approaches the reader from the future, and hence its message is open and uncertain, yet the uncertainty divides Christ and Antichrist, friends and foes, according to their hearing. It is a word of the hidden God who allows only glimpses of insight to flash up in a moment of disclosure.

Luther's translations and adaptions of the text may thus be open to controversy; in fact, they invite controversy with their ambiguous and divisive style, but if someone rejects the controversy and seeks to take control over the interpretation, this is for Luther the first infallible sign of misinterpretation. And the text, if not its author, will presumably take an awful revenge. The subversive rhetorical strategy is therefore by no means a coincidence, and the humor is not without consequences, as Preston argues.[16] On the contrary: This roaring laughter resounding in the echo of his satire is the whole point and force of the text; its *work,* so to speak, is to undermine the secure and stable sense which substantiates the papal hierarchy, by Luther also called "the *tower* of Babel." The critical force of this work is instituted by the hidden God and transcribed by reference to this hiddenness.

Luther's interpretation of Daniel is thus destructive and destabilizing. It is offensive and seeks to provoke a clarification. The reader has to decide between two readings, and I guess the Reformer hopes, at least, that the hypocrisies of the other side will become apparent. This means that he presents a negation of the other position, but is there even an affirmation, a positive message, as well? I think there is, but not in an overt fashion. The indirect message is directed to the common people rather than to Luther's adversaries. His political stroke of genius is that the text is thus popularized and handed over to an open readership, albeit the readership of Latin texts was limited. The more influential pamphlets were written in German and soon to be translated into other languages. The reader of these writings is questioned and challenged by the text (like a shibboleth) and thus her response and *ability* to respond, her laughter, voice, and political responsibility, are in demand.

When we compare this reading with Thomas Müntzer, the roles are redefined. Müntzer further popularizes the texts, to the extent that each individual is supposed to have visions. The spiritual empowerment of each person is undoubtedly strong, but equally strong is the tendency to produce new myths, including political ones, which imply another instrumentalization of the Apocalypse. Müntzer does not accept Luther's principles of interpretation, namely, *sola scriptura* and the justification by faith alone. On the contrary: Justice is achieved through the works, and the apocalyptic message is achieved by way of a revolutionary movement that acts on God's behalf. The true church is thus identified with the peasants rather than the priests (*Pfaffen*), with visions rather than scripture, and the sword is handed over to the poor in order to let the rulers get killed.

With respect to the hidden God, there is a fine but crucial difference between Müntzer and Luther, a difference with unexpected consequences. Whereas the question of interpretation is ultimately left open within Luther's anti-text, it is defined as revolutionary propaganda in Müntzer's authoritative words of interpretation. In consequence, he leaves the final space of authority for himself as charismatic leader of the violent insurgency. The weapons are supposed to speak when the peasants are silenced. The hidden God is identified with the power of the revolution to overthrow the rulers. When the Apocalypse takes place, here and now, no "remainder" of its fulfillment is left to the future. It is supposed to happen all at once. The hidden God is identified with the eruptive force of history.

All three approaches disclose a broken or direct correlation between notions of the hidden God and political strategy. The *place* of God and of divine hiddenness thereby plays a crucial role. Hence, there is no politics without theology and no theology without political consequences here. From the legal perspective of Ambrosius Catharinus, there is little doubt concerning the divine authority ascribed to the pope. Interpreting the texts and applying the law in this decisive situation is perceived as the duty of the church, thus filling the vacuum of God's absence. In cases of doubt, the decision is left to the pope himself.

In Thomas Müntzer's sermon, the Book of Daniel and even the Gospels are translated into an immediate political situation, although with the opposite message. It is consequently read as a word of disclosure, identifying the poor as soldiers of Christ and the rulers as his enemies. The meaning of God's hiddenness is thus *disclosed* in the apocalyptic events. Hiddenness belongs to the past, but the present is drawn into the events that are described by Daniel and by John in the Apocalypse.

In Luther's case, the relationship between politics and theology is less obvious, exactly due to his emphasis on the absolute hiddenness of God. There is a *rest* in God which is apt to *question* the interpretations performed by humans. For Luther, this hesitation concerning the ultimate sense of the text is a major concern when it comes to the *application* of the text. Hence, more significant than the almost self-evident point, that the absolute will of God remains "no concern of ours," is his emphasis on the very *difference* between hiddenness and revelation, which concerns us in every act of application, interpretation, or protest against the political control of the text. If read accordingly, the Apocalypse may still have secrets in reserve.

The Sense of an Ending

In the early twenty-first century, apocalypticism in various forms is still remarkably present, although five centuries have passed. In the Middle East and on the global political scene, one apocalyptic scenario is followed by the next. Since the terror attacks and the falling towers of September 11, 2001, the images of apocalyptic wars have again filled the social and political imaginary across civilizational borders. Globalization has achieved an apocalyptic dimension, whereby almost every corner of the world experiences the threat of political violence accompanied by some religious horror image.[17] The almost iconic impression from spectacular attacks like the falling towers of the World Trade Center has spread a sense of insecurity all over the world: The war on terror is proclaimed as a global war. Still, most of the terror images seem to be a product of imagination and xenophobia. The terror threat feeds such feelings of anxiety with new and more dramatic images. Academic scholars are hardly an exception from this tendency. Mark Lilla thus warns against the collapse of the religious/secular divide that according to his historical analysis has saved the West from the dystopian destiny of the apocalypse.[18]

The kernel of truth in this analysis is that apocalypses tend to call upon narrative and fantastic imagination as a *mysterium tremendum et fascinans*. Hence, conflicts that are universalized in the apocalyptical sense tend to achieve their own dynamic, enhancing and amplifying the level of violence. At the same time, there are hardly any reasons to believe that the religious/secular division is significant in order to avoid apocalyptical conflicts.[19] If we look at the period of modernity, from the seventeenth century onward, this is when politics are supposed to become independent from religion—that is, secularized. In almost every major crisis in this period, there has been an apocalyptic imagery at work, if we look at the religious wars or the French Revolution, the Marxist revolutions, or the big world wars in the twentieth century. Except for the religious wars in the early seventeenth century, it is hardly plausible to characterize these wars as "religious" or even motivated by religious differences.[20] Still, they are dominated by an apocalyptic imagery, for instance, if we look at the Second World War in Nazi Germany.[21] Hence, the religious/secular divide can be helpful for other reasons, but is not *as such* a protection against apocalyptic war scenarios.

On the contrary: It seems like such apocalyptic narratives, which are flourishing in Hollywood films, Internet games, and science fiction literature, tend to form our world anyway, almost independent of religious confessions. One reason may be the widespread fascination for such images for their own sake. In one way or another, they influence political decisions and actions insofar as the *narratives* we recognize tend to govern our thoughts about ourselves and others, and thus in particular our ways of identifying conflicts. The consequences are huge and sometimes disastrous; for instance, if we look at the contemporary "war on terror." It was once declared as a war against fear (terror), as such. But the dynamic of fear is that it tends to produce more fear and even more monstrous images of the fiend. Hence, this war is by all realistic criteria apt to provoke and produce more of what it is fighting, namely, terror. It falls into the apocalyptic scheme whether this narrative is accepted or rejected. The dynamic of apocalypticism once more indicates a clear tendency of repeating itself, although reproduced in a number of novel formations. The American ambition of surveillance of virtually all citizens around the world (insofar as they communicate electronically) belongs to the same scenario—a scenario which surpasses the wildest imagination of all the George Orwells and St. Johns of this world, but drawing them back to structures discovered in a few visions at Patmos.

This political theology, indicating a theological genealogy of historical narratives, is interesting on its own terms. With its universalizing tendency and its contrasts between light and darkness, good and evil, the dynamic of apocalyptic imagery seems to be almost unavoidable in a globalized world. An investigation of modern political and intellectual history from this perspective that abstains from the almost ritual moral warnings and admonitions typical for Lilla, but also John Gray, is still wanting. Its critical focus would be to identify such historical-apocalyptical narratives in actual discourse, their genealogy, and inherent structure. Giorgio Agamben's analysis of power and glory is an example of how such an analysis could proceed, setting out from a different pair of notions—namely, theology versus economy—but ending with the vision of glory (*doxa*) in Revelation 4:1–11.[22] The key notions of apocalyptic thinking seem to have had a similarly formative effect on the political, literary, philosophical, and historical imagination of the West. This is not a question of fantasy and science fiction; it is a question of the temporality and the spatial formation, indeed also the scripture, the grammar, and the images, that have become formative for buildings, cities, wars, political decisions, and historical events.

From this point of view, the controversy between Luther and his various opponents—such as Catharinus, Erasmus, and Müntzer—achieve a more principal significance. At a point in history when the modern world starts taking shape, there is a fierce controversy on the meaning of apocalyptic texts, in particular their concrete impact on questions of power and political authority. This is a discussion concerning modernity itself, admittedly by authors who would reject the label "modern" for themselves. These opponents compete in being the most "orthodox" and "traditional." Even if they are skeptical about the apocalypse, it is already a part of their Christian tradition and its canonical scriptures. It is a topos within the tradition that eventually will burst the logic and limits of that tradition as previously understood.

Modernity is an era based on the strange idea that society—or the world—is *living from the future* rather than from the past. The apocalypse draws this narrative anticipation of the End of Days into the present, as a scheme for understanding the universal dimension and immediate urgency of a conflict. Hence, a controversy on apocalypticism concerns the *sense* of an ending—an ending which in this case is anticipated and drawn into the present. For Catharinus and Erasmus, these visions need to be subjected to the authority of the church and interpreted accordingly, in order to avoid chaos. They would accept much violence from the authorities in order to prevent such disorder. For Luther, the conflict (and the bloodshed) is necessary and meaningful in the given situation, as a political event transcending the sphere of reason and overturning ecclesial hierarchies. For Müntzer, this revolutionary dynamic becomes a goal in itself, in order to create a new society according to a radically different vision of what the good community entails.[23] The idea of a revolution lives from this dynamic, and by the same dynamic it may easily collapse. But is it also inherent in the accelerating belief in historical progress, in change as a good thing per se, under various modern knowledge regimes?[24]

This book set out from the analysis of Luther's and Heidegger's destruction of metaphysics—one based in scripture and the other in the question for being and existence. Destruction in the philosophical sense means a rejection of a specific metaphysical framework as the basis for truth, for ideas and knowledge, but also a rejection of religious or secular authority and power justified by metaphysical claims (about the almighty, the good, the one, and so forth). The destruction as philosophical operator implies a destructuring of this framework, and thus also a questioning of the ultimate authority and *summum bonum*, in the late-medieval context another name for God. Hence, the highest authority and ultimate power also becomes the most *problematic* and *questionable* topos of thought: the hidden God.

The consequence of destruction is hardly an *elimination* of metaphysical discourse per se, but rather a destabilization, subversion, and recovery of these basic structures of thought, including the structures for reflecting upon God and the distinction between divine hiddenness and revelation. Hence, the disturbing and counterintuitive claims of the *Heidelberg Disputation* express a radical thought, whether we read it philosophically or theologically: In order to think critically about God and the world, about the conditions for human existence, Luther argues that it is necessary to destroy and restructure metaphysics, including the basic antithesis between action and passion, power and weakness, good and evil. It is the logic of the cross, based in passivity, suffering, and sacrifice, which overturns the premises for perception and conceptual structuring of the world.[25]

Our reading of Luther's texts includes an analysis of its linguistic structure and the effort at re-forming or reformatting reality according to the grammar and letter of scripture. The direction of thought is turned elsewhere, from nature and things toward scripture and phenomena. What follows from this turn toward phenomena is a reconsideration of theology, of subjectivity, of morals. A linguistic and philosophical space of thought is opening up, a space of doubt and reconsideration, of subverting and reformulating the basic principles of the economy of life. With his new reading of Paul, Luther insists that there is a false economy at work in the church and a tremendous treachery of ordinary people, epitomized by the letters of indulgences. Another economy is possible, he proclaims, not replacing but destroying and restructuring the barter economy of retribution. Its origin is the unconditional gift of grace, according to the logic of the cross. With this reversal of the premises, not only God is understood otherwise, but also the human being. A new sense of subjectivity emerges in Luther's thought, which becomes crucial for philosophy in the subsequent centuries.

The continuous significance of the notion of a hidden god (*deus absconditus*) lies in Luther's insistence on an original difference within God, within and beyond scripture. Although grace is proclaimed unconditionally, the notion of God is not given unambiguously. On the contrary: The belief in a stable notion of God invites the wish to domesticate and thus control its meaning ("in order to inflate oneself," Luther suspects). Such an option may appear tempting for anyone seeking power or influence, since the notion of God is a powerful notion; either "God" is adored or instrumentalized for specific purposes. The significance of the notion *deus absconditus* is therefore not a particular understanding, definition, or circumscription of God, but adherence to such a *distinction* between seclusion and revelation. The *place* of such difference is thereby identified as a topos of critical reflection.

A similar strategy is perceivable when it comes to the narratives and notions of apocalypse, as structuring narrative of modernity. A basic problem of such an inquiry is its comprehensiveness; it gets difficult to achieve sufficient distance for analyzing it. Rather than approaching the whole narrative at once in its various formations, we have focused on its beginning in the early sixteenth century. Other beginnings could have been chosen, in the first or the fourteenth or fifteenth centuries. Yet when we emphasize the discourses taking place at the time when modernity was in the making, we look for structures of the apocalyptic narratives that may be characterized as generic and formative, insofar as they transcend the horizon of biblical scriptures and become a general script for the construction of history, of specific temporal and spatial formations and re-formations of reality. This general script could be analyzed as the beginning of sense in the modern sense or, alternatively, as the sense of an ending.

NOTES

Introduction

1. Cf. for example Rudolf Malter, *Das reformatorische Denken und die Philosophie* (Bonn, Ger.: Bouvier, 1980), which perhaps comes closest to a contemporary philosophical reading of Luther, although with primary focus on Luther and Kant; Theodor Dieter, *Der junge Luther und Aristoteles: Eine historisch-systematische Untersuchung zum Verhältnis von Theologie und Philosophie* (Berlin: De Gruyter, 2001); and Benjamin D. Crowe, *Heidegger's Religious Origins: Destruction and Authenticity* (Bloomington: Indiana University Press, 2006). I would also like to mention the monumental study by Reiner Schürmann on the history of Western philosophy, where Luther plays a significant role for his understanding of modernity: Reiner Schürmann, *Broken Hegemonies* (Bloomington: Indiana University Press, 2003).

2. See Martin Luther, *Heidelberg Disputation,* LW 31, 53; WA 1, 362. All quotations from Luther's works refer first to the English translations from the standard American edition of *Luther's Works* [LW], edited by Jaroslav Pelikan and Helmut T. Lehmann, and then to the *Weimarer Ausgabe* [WA]: *D. Martin Luthers Werke, Kritische Gesammtausgabe* (Weimar, Ger.: H. Böhlau, 1883–2009), although when the Latin texts are quoted—with reference to WA—the quotation is taken either from the *Lateinisch-Deutsche Studienausgabe,* Vol. 1, ed. W. Härle, et al. (Leipzig, Ger.: Evangelische Verlagsanstalt, 2006), or from the online edition of the *Weimarer Ausgabe* (http://luther.chadwyck.co.uk/). There are minor differences of spelling in the various editions. When the translations are modified, this will be indicated.

3. Cf. Luther, *Heidelberg Disputation,* LW 31, 53; WA 1, 362.

1. History, Hermeneutics, and Political Theology

1. In the second half of the twentieth century, Heiko Oberman made a tremendous effort at understanding the transition from late medieval to early modern thought, where Luther and the other Reformers play a crucial role. He points out that the concept of a forerunner is problematic if applied as a causal category or for the sake of Protestant apologetics, yet indispensable in the sense of an *antecedent* in order to understand the arguments within their historical context: "Thus the use of the Forerunners does not function to establish the *nature of the cause* but the *structure of the change.*" Heiko A. Oberman, *Forerunners of the Reformation: The Shape of Late Medieval Thought* (Philadelphia: Fortress Press, 1981), 39.

2. See James D. Tracy, *Europe's Reformations 1450–1650: Doctrine, Politics, and Community,* 2nd ed. (Oxford, Eng.: Rowman & Littlefield, 2006) and Carter Lindberg, *The European Reformations,* 2nd ed. (Oxford, Eng.: Blackwell, 2011). Cf. also Oberman, *Forerunners,* 35.

3. See Mark U. Edwards, *Printing, Propaganda, and Martin Luther* (Berkeley: University of California Press, 1994).

4. Two of the classical discussions of Biehl, by Oberman and Grane, offer different perspectives on his relation to Luther and the Reformation: Heiko A. Oberman, *Harvest of Medieval Theology: Gabriel Biel and Late Medieval Nominalism* (Cambridge, Mass.: Harvard University Press, 1963). More specifically on Luther's critical reception of Biel: Leif Grane, *Contra Gabrielem: Luthers Auseinandersetzung mit Gabriel Biel in der Disputatio Contra Scholasticam Theologiam 1517* (Copenhagen, Den.: Gyldendal, 1962).

5. Volker Leppin, *Luther* (Darmstadt, Ger.: WBG, 2006). See also the book based on the controversy published four years later: Dietrich Korsch and Volker Leppin (eds.), *Martin Luther—Theologie und Biographie* (Tübingen, Ger.: Mohr Siebeck, 2010).

6. See Philipp Stoellger, *Passivität aus Passion* (Tübingen, Ger.: Mohr Siebeck, 2010), who demonstrates the "Problemgeschichte" of the passivity of perception implied by Luther's "mere passive" from the medieval mystics up to contemporary Continental philosophy; and Martin Wendte, *Die Gabe und das Gestell* (Tübingen, Ger.: Mohr Siebeck, 2013), who reads Heidegger's critique of technics and his phenomenology of the stand (*Gestell*) as analytic approach to Luther's theology of communion in some of his late texts.

7. Cf. Alexandre Koyré, *From the Closed World to the Infinite Universe,* 2nd ed. (Baltimore: The Johns Hopkins University Press, 1968) and Norman Cohn, *The Pursuit of the Millennium,* 3rd ed. (London: Pimlico, 1970).

8. See Lucien Goldmann, *The Hidden God: A Study of Tragic Vision in the Pensées of Pascal and the Tragedies of Racine* (London: Routledge, 1976).

9. Thus Habermas argues that "[. . .] the public consciousness of post-secular society reflects a normative insight that has consequences for how believing and unbelieving citizens interact with one another politically. In post-secular society, the realization that 'the modernization of public consciousness' takes hold of and reflexively alters religious as well as secular mentalities in staggered phases is gaining acceptance." Jürgen Habermas, "On the Relations between the Secular Liberal State and Religion," in: *Political Theologies: Public Religions in a Post-Secular World,* ed. Hent de Vries and Lawrence E. Sullivan (New York: Fordham University Press, 2006), 251–260; here: 258.

10. Cf. Marius Timmann Mjaaland, "Geneatopics," *Studia Theologica,* Vol. 65 (2011), 172–189.

11. Cf. Charles Taylor, *A Secular Age* (Cambridge, Mass.: Harvard University Press, 2007); Talal Asad, *Formations of the Secular: Christianity, Islam, Modernity* (Stanford, Calif.: Stanford University Press, 2003); Hans Joas and Klaus Wiegandt, *Secularization and the World Religions* (Liverpool, Eng.: Liverpool University Press, 2009).

12. Talal Asad, *Genealogies of Religion: Discipline and Reasons of Power in Christianity and Islam* (Baltimore: Johns Hopkins University Press, 1993).

13. See Paul W. Kahn, *Political Theology: Four Chapters on the Concept of Sovereignty* (New York: Colombia University Press, 2011), 17–27.

14. Cf. Mark Lilla, *The Stillborn God,* 2nd ed. (New York: Vintage, 2008), 296–309; and John Gray, *Black Mass: Apocalyptic Religion and the Death of Utopia* (London: Penguin, 2008).

15. See Giorgio Agamben, *The Signature of All Things: On Method* (New York: Zone Books, 2009); Ibid., *The Time That Remains: A Commentary to the Letter of the Romans* (Stanford, Calif.: Stanford University Press, 2005).

16. See Giorgio Agamben, *Homo Sacer: Sovereign Power and Bare Life* (Stanford, Calif.: Stanford University Press, 1998); Ibid., *The Sacrament of Language: An Archaeology of the Oath (*Homo Sacer *II, 3)* (Stanford, Calif.: Stanford University Press, 2010). The most significant publication in our context, which will be more thoroughly discussed in the second volume, is: Agamben, *The Kingdom and the Glory: For a Theological Genealogy of Economy and Government* (Stanford, Calif.: Stanford University Press, 2011).

2. Philosophy

1. See chapter 5.

2. See Martin Luther, *Heidelberg Disputation,* LW 31, 53; WA 1, 362. All quotations from Luther's works refer first to the English translations from the standard American edition of *Luther's Works* [LW], edited by Jaroslav Pelikan and Helmut T. Lehmann, and then to the *Weimarer Ausgabe* [WA]: *D. Martin Luthers Werke, Kritische Gesammtausgabe* (Weimar, Ger.: H. Böhlau, 1883–2009), although when the Latin texts are quoted—with reference to WA—the quotation is taken either from the *Lateinisch-Deutsche Studienausgabe,* Vol. 1, ed. W. Härle, et al. (Leipzig, Ger.: Evangelische Verlagsanstalt, 2006), or from the online edition of the *Weimarer Ausgabe* (http://luther.chadwyck.co.uk/). There are minor differences of spelling in the various editions. When the translations are modified, this will be indicated.

3. For a thorough study of Heidegger's relations to Luther and in particular the concept of destruction, cf. Benjamin D. Crowe, *Heidegger's Religious Origins,* 231–259.

4. Martin Heidegger, *Supplements,* trans. and ed. John van Buren (Albany, N.Y.: SUNY Press, 2002), 124 f.

5. Cf. the intriguing analysis of this historical development in: Joar Haga, *Was There a Lutheran Metaphysics? The Interpretation of* communicatio idiomatum *in Early Modern Lutheranism* (Göttingen, Ger.: Vandenhoeck & Ruprecht, 2012).

6. Cf. Crowe, *Heidegger's Religious Origins,* 134 ff.

7. Herman Philipse, *Heidegger's Philosophy of Being: A Critical Interpretation* (Princeton, N.J.: Princeton University Press, 1998), 194.

8. Cf. Jacques Derrida, *The Gift of Death* (Chicago: University of Chicago Press, 1995), 49.

9. Cf. Gerhard Ebeling, "Existenz zwischen Gott und Gott," in: Ibid., *Wort und Glaube,* Vol. 2. (Tübingen, Ger.: Mohr Siebeck, 1969), 257–286; Eberhard Jüngel, "Quae supra nos, nihil ad nos," in: Ibid., *Entsprechungen: Gott—Wahrheit—Mensch* (München, Ger.: Kaiser, 1980), 202–252.

10. The same applies, curiously enough, to Jüngel's magnum opus with the title *God as the Mystery of the World,* although the subtitle indicates exactly why it becomes so crucial for him to eliminate the questions raised by the *deus absconditus* in the generic sense. The hidden God in Christ serves as an alternative hermeneutic and scriptural *foundation* for his theology. Hence, there is no place left for the hidden God outside scripture. Cf. Eberhard

Jüngel, *God as the Mystery of the World: On the Foundation of the Theology of the Crucified One in the Dispute between Theism and Atheism* (Grand Rapids, Mich.: Eerdmans, 1983).

11. See for example Luther, *De servo arbitrio,* LW 33, 92; WA 18, 654–655.

12. Hence, Luther writes in one of the philosophical theses in the *Heidelberg Disputation:* "He who wishes to philosophize in Aristotle without danger to his soul must first become thoroughly foolish in Christ." LW 31, 41; WA 1, 355. The difference would presuppose sufficient foolishness (*bene stultificetur*) in order to overcome the metaphysical wisdom of the school philosophy. The statement is not without humor, but neither is it alien to the trenchant insights of mysticism.

13. See for example Graham White, *Luther as Nominalist* (Helsinki, Fin.: Luther-Agricola-Society, 1994) and Birgit Stolt, *Martin Luthers Rhetorik des Herzens* (Tübingen, Ger.: Mohr Siebeck, 2000). Cf. also Stolt's dissertation on the topic, which combines the question of rhetoric in Latin and German with an analysis of the structure of the argument: Birgit Stolt, *Studien zu Luthers Freiheitstraktat. Mit besonderer Rücksicht auf das Verhältnis der lateinischen und der deutschen Fassung zu einander und die Stilmittel der Rhetorik* (Stockholm, Swed.: Almqvist & Wiksell, 1969).

14. Thomas Wabel analyzes Luther's linguistic theory based on Wittgenstein's philosophy of language. Wittgenstein's concepts of grammar, clarity, and language games thereby play a constructive role in establishing analytical tools of understanding Luther's theory of language. Still, the *theory* he develops is inherently theological and dominated by the program of *hermeneutic* theology. For the same reason, Luther's notion of the *deus absconditus* is excluded from the inquiry with reference to Jüngel. Cf. Thomas Wabel, *Sprache als Grenze in Luthers theologischer Hermeneutik und Heideggers Sprachphilosophie* (Berlin: De Gruyter, 1998), 221–224.

15. See Günter Bader, *Assertio: Drei fortlaufende Lektüren zu Skepsis, Narrheit und Sünde bei Erasmus und Luther* (Tübingen, Ger.: Mohr Siebeck, 1985).

16. Three centuries of historical-critical approach to the biblical corpus have not changed the canon dramatically, but the general knowledge about the nature of the world, about human beings and their history, about the contingency of language and the philosophical preconditions for understanding texts have undergone enormous changes. It is not self-evident that Luther's approach to the texts is still valid or should have any particular authority. Still, his textual theory, if there is such a thing as a textual theory behind his many commentaries on the issue, may nevertheless be worthy of closer analysis, indeed also an analysis that raises suspicion and critique.

17. See in particular the passage on the originary metaphor and the supplement at the origin in: Jacques Derrida, *Of Grammatology,* trans. Gayatri Chakravorty Spivak (Baltimore: The Johns Hopkins University Press, 1976), 269–316.

18. Cf. Derrida, *Of Grammatology,* 59–65.

19. See Martin Luther, *Operationes in Psalmos 1519/21,* WA 5, 32.

20. Jacques Derrida, *Rogues* (Stanford, Calif.: Stanford University Press, 2005), 174, n. 14.

21. Cf. Jacques Derrida, *Of Grammatology,* 18–21.

22. See Martin Luther, *De servo arbitrio,* LW 33, 264; WA 18, 769.

23. Cf. the introductory sentence of the *Heidelberg Disputation:* "Distrusting completely our own wisdom, [. . .] we humbly present to the judgment of all those who wish to be here these theological paradoxes [. . .]." Luther, *Heidelberg Disputation,* LW 31, 39; WA 1, 353.

24. Both dialectical and hermeneutic theology focus on the question of revelation, and thus the philosophical and textual questions raised by the *deus absconditus* simply appear to be confusing and disturbing, hence "no concern of ours," as Jüngel concludes; Jüngel, "Quae supra nos, nihil ad nos," 649.

3. Topology

1. Cf. Robin Smith, "Aristotle's Logic," in: *The Stanford Encyclopedia of Philosophy,* ed. Edward N. Zalta (Stanford, Calif.: Stanford University: The Metaphysics Research Lab, 2013).

2. Günter Frank, "Wie kam die Topik in die Theologie?" in: *Hermeneutik, Methodenlehre, Exegese,* ed. Günter Frank and Stephan Meier-Oeser (Stuttgart, Ger.: Frommann-Holzboog, 2011), 77.

3. See Frank, "Wie kam die Topik in die Theologie?" 75–76.

4. See Martin Luther, *De servo arbitrio,* LW 33, 16; WA 18, 601. All quotations from Luther's works refer first to the English translations from the standard American edition of *Luther's Works* [LW], edited by Jaroslav Pelikan and Helmut T. Lehmann, and then to the *Weimarer Ausgabe* [WA]: *D. Martin Luthers Werke, Kritische Gesammtausgabe* (Weimar, Ger.: H. Böhlau, 1883–2009), although when the Latin texts are quoted—with reference to WA—the quotation is taken either from the *Lateinisch-Deutsche Studienausgabe,* Vol. 1, ed. W. Härle, et al. (Leipzig, Ger.: Evangelische Verlagsanstalt, 2006), or from the online edition of the *Weimarer Ausgabe* (http://luther.chadwyck.co.uk/). There are minor differences of spelling in the various editions. When the translations are modified, this will be indicated.

5. Luther thus refers to the "supreme mystery brought to light" and asks rhetorically: "Take Christ out of the scriptures and what will you find in them?" Luther, *De servo arbitrio,* LW 33, 26; WA 18, 606.

6. "If the words are obscure in one place, they are plain in another [*Si uno loco obscura sunt verba, et alio sunt clara*]." Luther, *De servo arbitrio,* LW 33, 26; WA 18, 607. Translation modified. See also WL 33, 62; WA 18, 633.

7. Plato, *Timaeus,* 49a.

8. Cf. Donald Zeyl, "Plato's *Timaeus,*" in: *The Stanford Encyclopedia of Philosophy,* ed. Edward N. Zalta (Stanford, Calif.: Stanford University: The Metaphysics Research Lab, 2013).

9. Zeyl, "Plato's *Timaeus.*"

10. Cf. Derrida's essay "Khōra" in: Jacques Derrida, *On the Name* (Stanford, Calif.: Stanford University Press, 1995), 89–130.

11. "Sic habet mea distinction, ut et ergo parum rhetoricer vel Dialecticer, Duae res sunt Deus et Scriptura Dei, non minus quam duae sunt Creatur et creatura Dei. In Deo esse multa abscondita, quae ignoramus, nemo dubitat, sicut ipsemet dicit de die extremo." Luther, *De servo arbitrio,* LW 33, 25; WA 18, 606.

12. Cf. Desiderius Erasmus, *Diatribe de libero arbitrio,* transl. Peter Macardle, in: *Collected Works* [CW], Vol. 76 (Toronto: Toronto University Press, 1998), 11–12; *Erasmus' Werke: Ausgewählte Schriften* [EW] (bilingual ed.), ed. Werner Welzig, Vol. 4 (Darmstadt, Ger.: Wissenschaftliche Buchgesellschaft, 1969), 16.

13. "Diatribe, however, deceives herself in her ignorance by not making any distinction between God preached and God hidden, that is, between the word of God and God himself." Luther, *De servo arbitrio,* LW 33, 140; WA 18, 685.

14. See Luther, *De servo arbitrio,* LW 33, 260–264; WA 18, 767–769.

15. Cf. Carl Schmitt, *Politische Theologie,* 8th ed. (Berlin: Duncker & Humblot, 2004).

4. The Quest for Immorality

1. Chapter 4 is based on a revised and extended version of my article "Immorality" in *Neue Zeitschrift für systematische Theologie und Religionsphilosophie,* Vol. 53 (2011), 450–464. Thanks to De Gruyter for the permission to republish some passages. The original version is accessible online at: http://www.reference-global.com. An early version of the grammatical analysis of *iustitia Dei* is also presented there.

2. See the ninety-five theses published by Luther on October 31, 1517 (later called the Day of the Reformation), in particular the first seven theses, cf. Martin Luther, *Ninety-five Theses,* LW 31, 25–26; WA 1, 233–234. All quotations from Luther's works refer first to the English translations from the standard American edition of *Luther's Works* [LW], Vol. 1–55, ed. Jaroslav Pelikan and Helmut T. Lehmann (Philadelphia: Fortress Press, 1958–1976); and then to the *Weimarer Ausgabe* [WA]: *D. Martin Luthers Werke,* Vol. 1–55 (Weimar, Ger., 1883–2009), although when the Latin texts are quoted—with reference to WA—the quotation is taken either from the *Lateinisch-Deutsche Studienausgabe,* Vol. 1, ed. W. Härle, et al. (Leipzig, Ger.: Evangelische Verlagsanstalt, 2006), or from the online edition of the *Weimarer Ausgabe* (http://luther.chadwyck.co.uk/). There are minor differences of spelling in the various editions. When the translations are modified, this will be indicated.

3. Cf. Luther, *De servo arbitrio,* LW 33, 205; WA 18, 729–730.

4. A point Luther returns to later, for example, in *De servo arbitrio,* LW 33, 207; WA 18, 731.

5. Cf. Luther, *Ninety-five Theses,* LW 31, 25–33; WA 1, 233–238.

6. Cf. the famous first thesis: "When the Lord and Master Jesus Christ said, 'Repent,' he willed the entire life of believers to be one of repentance. [Dominus et magister noster Iesus Christus dicendo. Penitentiam agite. etc. omnem vitam fidelium penitentiam esse voluit.]" Luther, *Ninety-five Theses,* LW 31, 25; WA 1, 233.

7. Cf. Luther's many references to the "Sophists" as name for the Scholastics; for example, in *De servo arbitrio,* LW 33, 67–68; WA 18, 636–637.

8. Cf. Luther, *De servo arbitrio,* LW 33, 35; WA 18, 614 passim.

9. "Verum hic de scripturis non est controversia. [. . .] De sensu scripturae pugna est." Desiderius Erasmus, *Diatribe de libero arbitrio—A Discussion on Free Will,* trans. Peter Macardle, in: *Collected Works* [CW], Vol. 76 (Toronto: Toronto University Press, 1998), 16; and *Diatribe sive collatio de libero arbitrio* [1524] in *Erasmus' Werke: Ausgewählte Schriften* (bilingual ed.) [EW], Vol. 4, ed. Werner Welzig (Darmstadt, Ger.: Wissenschaftliche Buchgesellschaft, 1969), 26. All refererences to and quotations from Erasmus's *Diatribe* are taken from the English translation in *Collected Works* [CW], whereas the Latin text is quoted from the German bilingual edition of selected works [EW].

10. Cf. Luther, *De servo arbitrio,* LW 33, 94–95; WA 18, 656.

11. See Erasmus, *Diatribe,* CW 76, 19–20; EW 4, 32–34.

12. Cf. Luther, *De servo arbitrio,* LW 33, 95; WA 18, 656. Cf. the statement from *Assertio* (WA 7, 97), where Luther concludes that scripture is its own interpreter (*sui ipsius intepres*).

13. See Luther, *Sermons* 1522, WA 10.III, 238.

14. See Erasmus, *Diatribe,* CW 76, 12–13 and 21; EW 4, 18 and 36.

15. "Quantam fenestram haec vulgo prodita vox innumeris mortalibus aperiret ad impietatem, praesertim in tanta mortalium tarditate, socordia, malitia et ad omne impietatis genus irrevocabili pronitate?" Erasmus, *Diatribe,* CW 76, 13; EW 4, 18.

16. See John Cassian, *Conferences,* trans. Colm Luibheid (New York: Paulist Press, 1985), 160. Cf. also Aurelius Augustine, *The Literal Meaning of Genesis,* trans. John Hammond Taylor (New York: Newman Press, 1982), 19.

17. "Constat autem scripturam secum pugnare non posse, cum ab eodem spiritu tota proficiscatur." Erasmus, *Diatribe,* CW 76, 21; EW 4, 36. Luther explicitly argues against all the three forms of spiritual reading and calls it a "miserable escape into the tropes": "Non iuvat itaque Diatriben hoc miserum effugium troporum." Luther, *De servo arbitrio,* LW 33, 164; WA 18, 702.

18. Thus Erasmus's arguments in favor of tropological reading in *Diatribe,* CW 76, 38–39 and 44; EW 4, 70–72 and 84–86.

19. "Porro liberum arbitrium hoc loco sentimus vim humanae voluntatis, qua se possit homo applicare ad ea, quae perducunt ad aeternam salutem, aut ab iisdem avertere." Erasmus, *Diatribe,* CW 76, 21; EW 4, 36.

20. "Si latuisset hominem boni malique discrimen ac voluntas dei, non poterat imputari, si perperam elegisset. Si voluntas non fuisset libera, non potuisset imputari peccatum, quod peccatum esse desinit, si non fuerit voluntarium, nisi cum error aut voluntatis obligatio ex peccato nata est." Erasmus, *Diatribe,* CW 76, 26; EW 4, 46. Translation modified.

21. Cf. Erasmus, *Diatribe,* CW 76, 11–12; EW 4, 16.

22. Cf. Erasmus, *Diatribe,* CW 76, 34; EW 4, 60.

23. For counterarguments, cf. Luther, *De servo arbitrio,* LW 33, 119; WA 18, 673.

24. See LW 33, 21 f.; WA 18,604.

25. Cf. LW 33, 18; WA 18, 602, in particular the words of surprise uttered by Luther: "Esto, sint, qui magistrum spiritum hactenus in meis literis nondum senserunt [. . .]."

26. Cf. Erasmus, *Diatribe,* CW 76, 19–20; EW 4, 32–34.

27. Cf. Graham White, *Luther as Nominalist: A Study of the Logical Methods Used in Martin Luther's Disputations in the Light of Their Medieval Background* (Helsinki, Fin.: Luther-Agricola-Society, 1994).

28. See Luther, *De servo arbitrio,* LW 33, 144; WA 18, 688 passim.

29. Luther, *De servo arbitrio,* LW 33, 190; WA 18, 719.

30. Cf. Luther, *De servo arbitrio,* LW 33, 103–104; WA 18, 662.

31. Cf. Luther, *De servo arbitrio,* LW 33, 121–122; WA 18, 673–674.

32. The critique is comparable to Habermas's and Apel's critique of Gadamer's *Wahrheit und Methode* when they argue in favor of an external critique of tradition and the implicit claim to the power of its language, alternatively requiring a "quasi-transcenden-

tal" critique that functions as a corrective to the concept of tradition as dialectical totality which includes every new interpretation as soon as it is published. Cf. Karl-Otto Apel, "H.-G. Gadamers 'Wahrheit und Methode,'" in: *Hegelstudien* 2 (1963), 314–322, and Jürgen Habermas, "Zu Gadamers 'Wahrheit und Methode'" in *Hermeneutik und Ideologiekritik*, ed. Karl-Otto Apel (Frankfurt am Main, Ger.: Suhrkamp, 1971), 45–56.

33. Over the last decades, a dominant strand of German Protestant theology and philosophy of religion has developed a similar strategy for defining and delimiting the concept of God, thereby rejecting any problematic or disturbing aspect of the divine. The term "orientation" (*Orientierung*) has gained a peculiar prominence in order to harmonize the scriptures and take hermeneutic control over the text, as argued, for example, by Ingolf U. Dalferth in "Self-Sacrifice: From the Act of Violence to the Passion of Love," in *International Journal of Philosophy of Religion*, Vol. 68 (2010), 77–94.

34. Cf. Luther, *De servo arbitrio*, LW 33, 275; WA 18, 775.

35. "The question, however, is what free choice is in itself and as regards its substance; and if that question is to be answered, nothing remains of free choice but the empty name, whether they like it or not." Luther, *De servo arbitrio*, LW 33, 110; WA 18, 666.

36. "Rectius vero Vertibile arbitrium vel mutabile arbitrium diceretur." Luther, *De servo arbitrio*, LW 33, 104; WA 18, 662.

37. "Igitur hic statim in foribus pugnant definitio quid nominis, et definitio quid rei, quod vox aliud significat et aliud reipsa sentitur." Luther, *De servo arbitrio*, LW 33, 104; WA 18, 662. Translation modified.

38. Cf. Wilfried Joest's detailed analysis of the instability of the will, the heart, and thus of the self that depends on God's gift: "Cor bzw. voluntas ist vielmehr je immer schon das in den geistlichen oder fleischlichen Einsatz [. . .] *hineingerissene* Selbst des Menschen. Man kann also tatsächlich den 'Ort' von dem, was sich in ihm 'abspielt,' nicht abheben. Jener Ort ist bereits das Sich-abspielen eines Grund-*Geschehens:* nicht das Selbst, das in sich ruhend die Kraft seiner Selbstbestimmung zu irgendwelchem Einsatz in sich trägt, sondern das Selbst, das 'sich tut' und in einem Einsatz schon begriffen, ja zu ihm ergriffen ist von einer Macht, von der ergriffen und 'engagiert' zu sein zum Wesen eben dieses Selbst gehört." Wilfried Joest, *Ontologie der Person bei Luther* (Göttingen, Ger.: Vandenhoeck & Ruprecht, 1967), 216.

39. "Porro liberum arbitrium hoc loco sentimus vim humanae voluntatis, qua se possit homo applicare ad ea, quae perducunt ad aeternam salutem aut ab iisdem avertere." Erasmus, *Diatribe*, CW 76, 21; EW 4, 36. Translation modified.

40. Cf. Luther, *De servo arbitrio*, LW 33,255–256; WA 18, 761–762.

41. Cf. Reiner Schürmann, *Broken Hegemonies*, 380–407.

42. Moreover, Luther argues that it is necessary to observe the grammatical distinction between that which man is *supposed* to do (imperative), and that which he is *able* to do (nominative). Thus, the logic of a moral reading runs into a dead end.

43. Cf. Risto Saarinen, *Gottes Wirken auf uns* (Stuttgart, Ger.: Franz Steiner Verlag 1989). Saarinen's criticism of German Luther research in the early twentieth century is precise in identifying the moral tenor that dominates the scope of interpretation.

44. See Luther, *De servo arbitrio*, LW 33, 124–125; WA 18, 675–676.

45. Cf. for instance the sixth disputation against the Antinomians during the first controversy (December 18, 1537), where Luther emphasizes that without the law, there is no sin, and without sin, there is no remission of sins—and no grace. Luther, WA 39.1, 358.

46. The Antinomians following Johannes Agricola rejected the validity of the law because the law of the old covenant was fulfilled in Christ and the believers therefore were free to do whatever they pleased, as long as they were guided by love. Cf. for example Volker Leppin, *Luther* (Darmstadt, Ger.: WBG, 2006), 332–334.

47. Luther writes in a letter to Philipp Melanchton in 1521: "Be a sinner and sin boldly, but believe and rejoice in Christ even more boldly." LW 48, 282; BW (=WA, Briefwechsel) 2, 371.

5. The Quest for Destruction

1. See, for example, Martin Luther, *A Response to the Hyperchristian, Hyperspiritual, and Hyperartistic Goat Emser in Leipzig,* WA 7, 621–688. The letter begins with the greeting to Emser, "Dear goat, don't bump me!" and ends with a poem which belongs to the category of *pugna verborum,* but there are also passages of self-irony in Luther's burlesque portrait of the controversy between the two. All quotations from Luther's works refer first to the English translations from the standard American edition of *Luther's Works* [LW], edited by Jaroslav Pelikan and Helmut T. Lehmann, and then to the *Weimarer Ausgabe* [WA]: *D. Martin Luthers Werke, Kritische Gesammtausgabe* (Weimar, Ger.: H. Böhlau, 1883–2009), although when the Latin texts are quoted—with reference to WA—the quotation is taken either from the *Lateinisch-Deutsche Studienausgabe,* Vol. 1, ed. W. Härle, et al. (Leipzig, Ger.: Evangelische Verlagsanstalt, 2006), or from the online edition of the *Weimarer Ausgabe* (http://luther.chadwyck.co.uk/). There are minor differences of spelling in the various editions. When the translations are modified, this will be indicated.

2. Cf. Walther von Loewenich, *Luthers Theologia Crucis,* 5th ed. (Witten, Ger.: Luther-Verlag, 1967). See also Gerhard Ebeling, *Evangelische Evangelienauslegung: Eine Untersuchung zu Luthers Hermeneutik* (Darmstadt, Ger.: WBG, 1962), 326. Ebeling discusses the hermeneutics in *De servo arbitrio* here, but explicitly on the basis of the *theologia crucis* in the *Heidelberg Disputation.* Hence, this pattern is allowed to override other perspectives on the text and the "crucial" truth.

3. Luther, *Heidelberg Disputation,* LW 31, 53; WA 1, 362. Cf. Ex 33:23.

4. See Luther, *Heidelberg Disputation,* LW 31, 44 and 51; WA 1, 357 and 361.

5. See Luther, *Heidelberg Disputation,* LW 31, 53; WA 1, 362; cf. Isaiah 45:15.

6. Cf. Luther, *Heidelberg Disputation,* LW 31, 52 f.; WA 1, 363 and 1 Cor. 1:21–25.

7. See Luther, *Heidelberg Disputation,* LW 31, 53; WA 1, 363.

8. Cf. Jacques Derrida, *Rogues,* trans. P.-A. Braut and M. Naas (Stanford, Calif.: Stanford University Press, 2005), 174.

9. "(XIX) Non ille digna digne Theologus dicitur, qui invisibilia Dei, per ea, quae facta sunt, intellecta conspicit. (XX) Sed qui visibilia et posteriora Dei, per passiones et crucem conspecta intelligit." Luther, *Heidelberg Disputation,* LW 31, 52; WA 1; 361–362 (the Latin

text differs slightly in the standard Weimar Edition and the critical edition of the text in the bilingual *Studienausgabe* [2006]; here I have used the latter).

10. Luther, *Heidelberg Disputation,* LW 31, 53; WA 1; 362. Translation modified.

11. According to thesis 40, the last of the twelve philosophical ones, such an infinite difference is lacking in Aristotelian metaphysics, and thus "being and privation, matter and form, movable and immovable, act and potency, etc., appear to be the same." Luther, *Heidelberg Disputation,* LW 31, 42; WA 1, 355.

12. Cf. Philipp Stoellger, *Passivität aus Passion: Zur Problemgeschichte einer 'categoria non grata'* (Tübingen, Ger.: Mohr Siebeck, 2010), 215–216.

13. "Theologus gloriae dicit, Malum bonum, et bonum malum, Theologus crucis dicit, id quod res est." Luther, *Heidelberg Disputation,* LW 31, 53; WA 1, 362.

14. Cf. the battle on definitions between Luther and Erasmus referred to in *De servo arbitrio,* LW 33, 104; WA 18, 662.

15. Luther, *Heidelberg Disputation,* LW 31, 53; WA 1, 362. Translation modified.

16. "It is namely impossible to avoid being inflated by one's good works, unless one is previously humiliated and destructed through suffering and evil, until he knows that he is nothing in himself and the works are not his but God's." Luther, *Heidelberg Disputation,* LW 31, 53; WA 1, 362.

17. Cf. Chapter 2 for further discussion on the question of metaphysics.

18. Cf. the introduction to the disputation: "Distrusting completely our own wisdom [. . .], we humbly present to the judgment of all those who wish to be here these theological paradoxes [. . .]." Luther, *Heidelberg Disputation,* LW 31, 39; WA 1, 353.

19. Cf. Luther, *The Ninety-five Theses,* LW 31, 25–33; WA 1, 233 ff.

20. Cf. Günther Franz (ed.), *Quellen zur Geschichte des Bauernkrieges* (Darmstadt, Ger.: Wissenschaftliche Buchgesellschaft, 1963), 175.

21. LW 31, 53; WA 1, 362. Translation modified.

22. Cf. Luther, *De servo arbitrio,* LW 33, 52 f.; WA 18, 627 f.

23. One of the interesting questions raised is whether it is possible to isolate interiority, decision, and so forth from political and public life. When Carl Schmitt introduces the term "political theology" in the early twentieth century, it is exactly with reference to a sovereign *decision* in the state of exception.

6. The Quest for Clarity

1. Luther quotes from the bull: "non licet scripturas proprio spiritu intelligere." Martin Luther, *Assertio,* WA 7, 96. Luther's *Assertio* (1520) has not been included in the American edition of Luther's works. Hence, all translations from Latin are my own. All quotations from Luther's works refer first to the English translations from the standard American edition of *Luther's Works* [LW], edited by Jaroslav Pelikan and Helmut T. Lehmann, and then to the *Weimarer Ausgabe* [WA]: *D. Martin Luthers Werke, Kritische Gesammtausgabe* (Weimar, Ger.: H. Böhlau, 1883–2009), although when the Latin texts are quoted—with reference to WA—the quotation is taken either from the *Lateinisch-Deutsche Studienausgabe,* Vol. 1, ed. W. Härle, et al. (Leipzig, Ger.: Evangelische Verlagsanstalt, 2006), or from the online edition

of the *Weimarer Ausgabe* (http://luther.chadwyck.co.uk/). There are minor differences of spelling in the various editions. When the translations are modified, this will be indicated.

2. Luther, *Assertio,* WA 7, 97.

3. "Oportet enim scriptura iudice hic sententiam ferre, quod fieri non potest, nisi scripturae dederimus principem locum, in omnibus quae tribuuntur patribus." Luther, *Assertio,* WA 7, 97.

4. "hoc est, ut sit ipsa per sese certissima, facillima, apertissima, sui ipisius interpres, omnium omnia probans, iudicans et illumans." Luther, *Assertio,* WA 7, 97.

5. Cf. Luther's critique of Erasmus for only emphasizing the first reading, based on his own judgment rather than looking for the judgment of scripture. Luther, *De servo arbitrio,* LW 33, 101–102; WA 18, 660 passim.

6. Nietzsche, *The Gay Science,* trans. Bernhard Williams (Cambridge, Eng.: Cambridge University Press, 2001), 128.

7. For example, through the early modern theologians Flacius and Calov. Cf. Denis Thouard, "Réflexion sur la constitution de l'herméneutique en discipline—Flacius, Hyperius et Augustin," in: *Hermeneutik, Methodenlehre, Exegese,* ed. Günter Frank and Stephan Meier-Oeser (Stuttgart, Ger.: Frommann-Holzboog, 2011), 37–65; and Joar Haga, "Die Biblische Hermeneutik Calovs—Die Klarheit der Schrift innerhalb seiner Metaphysik," in: Ibid., 173–187.

8. Cf. Gerhard Ebeling, *Evangelische Evangelienauslegung: Eine Untersuchung zu Luthers Hermeneutik* (Darmstadt, Ger.: WBG, 1962). The book was first published as early as 1942. Ebeling further developed his hermeneutical approach in *Wort Gottes und Tradition: Studien zu einer Hermeneutik der Konfessionen* (Göttingen, Ger.: Vandenhoeck & Ruprecht, 1964) and *Einführung in theologische Sprachlehre* (Tübingen, Ger.: Mohr Siebeck, 1971).

9. Cf. Gerhard Ebeling, "Die Anfänge von Luther's Hermeneutik," in: *Lutherstudien,* Vol. 1 (Tübingen, Ger.: Mohr Siebeck, 1971), 1–68. See in particular the ambivalence of letter and spirit at pp. 32–38 up to the point where the text is measured according to various "forms of existence" (p. 38).

10. See Volker Leppin, "Der Verlust des Menschen Luther: Zu Ebelings Lutherdeutung," in: *Journal of Early Modern Christianity* 1 (2014), 29–50.

11. See Leppin, "Der Verlust des Menschen Luther," 44–48.

12. Cf. Ebeling, *Lutherstudien,* Vol. 1–3. The work of Ebeling is here not only emphasized for its own sake, but as a characteristic example for three generations of Luther scholars from the last century. Before him we could mention Karl Holl and even Karl Barth, after him Eberhard Jüngel, Gustaf Wingren, Inge Lønning, and Oswald Bayer. Common for these scholars is that Luther's work has basically formed their theological position, although they have emphasized different topics as the most significant and left other parts of his work behind. For Barth, Bultmann, and their contemporaries, it was the Word of God, revelation, and dialectical theology that came to dominate the discourse. For later scholars, it was the word of justification by faith, the word as *speech act,* creation theology, and the scriptural *promise* that became the watchwords for their respective systematic-theological conceptions. For a representative example of the interdependence of Luther studies and (biblical) hermeneutic position, cf. Lønning, *Kanon im Kanon. Zum dogmatischen Grundlagenproblem des*

neutestamentlichen Kanons (Oslo, Nor.: Universitetsforlaget, 1971). Lønning's critique of earlier discussions of the Biblical canon on Luther is, on the one hand, based on a careful reading of Luther's texts; yet, on the other hand, founded in Luther's alleged *intentions* and personal authority. Hence, Luther's opinion is introduced as a *dogmatic* criterion for contemporary discussions of canon in the twentieth century, with the doctrine of justification as the ultimate condition for its truth. As expression of the dilemmas inherent in hermeneutic theology, it is clarifying because of its open ambivalence—yet as a hermeneutic position, it is unsatisfactory. What remains a challenge is the *continuous* work with the "abysmal" questions of canon and interpretation which Lønning suggests toward the end of his study (pp. 271–272). A reformulation of the expression *canon in canon* would then take the form of a shibboleth.

13. See for example Ebeling, "Frei aus Glauben," in: Ibid., *Lutherstudien* Vol. I, 308–329.

14. See Hans-Georg Gadamer, *Wahrheit und Methode,* 6th ed. (Tübingen, Ger.: Mohr Siebeck, 1990), 8–15; 327–328.

15. Gadamer, *Wahrheit und Methode,* 312.

16. Cf. the discussion of Hegel and the *speculative structure of language* in Gadamer, *Wahrheit und Methode,* 460–477.

17. See Graham White, *Luther as Nominalist* (Helsinki, Fin.: Luther-Agricola-Society, 1994) and Risto Saarinen, *Gottes Wirken auf uns* (Stuttgart, Ger.: Franz Steiner Verlag, 1989).

18. Gadamer, *Wahrheit und Methode,* 478.

19. Hence the programmatic doctrinal statements of Jüngel—with explicit reference to Karl Barth's Luther interpretation: "We must therefore say: God's *opus proprium,* his merciful agency, reveals the divine subject, the divine essence, God himself. *God himself* is not hidden, but only his *opus alienum* [. . .], This hidden work of God will only be 'illuminated' in the *lumen gloriae,* in the eschatological light of glory, which will show the harmony of all divine works [. . .]." Eberhard Jüngel, "The Revelation of the Hiddenness of God," in: Ibid., *Theological Essays,* Vol. II (Edinburgh, Scot.: T & T Clark, 1995), 120–144; here: 137.

20. Cf. Luther, *Heidelberg Disputation,* LW 31, 52; WA 1, 362.

21. Cf. Luther, *Assertio,* WA 7, 97.

22. See Luther, *De servo arbitrio,* LW 33, 60; WA 18, 632.

23. See Luther, *De servo arbitrio,* LW 33, 98–99; WA 18, 658.

24. Such a double reading within one and the same text could aptly be called a shibboleth, adopting the Hebrew term which is occasionally seen as the *condition sine qua non* for understanding Luther's *On the Bondage of the Will.* Cf. Klaus Schwarzwäller, *Sibboleth: Die Interpretation von Luthers Schrift* De servo arbitrio *seit Theodosius Harnack* (Munich, Ger.: Kaiser, 1969). The main point in Schwarzwäller's book is that all interpreters since Harnack have misunderstood Luther (thus the misspelling in the title), except for the one and only scholar who has understood him properly in the nineteenth and twentieth centuries, Klaus Schwarzwäller.

25. Luther, *De servo arbitrio,* LW 33, 92; WA 18, 654.

26. Cf. Luther, *Lecture on Romans,* LW 25, 8–9 and 151–153; WA 56, 10–11 and 171–173.

27. Luther, *De servo arbitrio,* LW 33, 265; WA 18, 769.

28. Cf. Luther, *De servo arbitrio,* LW 33, 264–265 ; WA 18, 768–769.

29. "Sic iustitia Dei, latine dicitur, quam Deus habet, sed Ebraeis intelligitur, quae ex Deo et coram Deo habetur." Luther, *De servo arbitrio,* LW 33, 265; WA 18, 769. Translation modified.

30. "Sint ergo Christianorum prima principia, non nisi verba divina, omnium autem hominum verba, conclusiones hinc eductae et rursus illuc reducendae et probandae [. . .] non autem per homines quaeri et disci, sed homines per ipsa iudicari." Luther, *Assertio,* WA 7, 98.

31. "Et ut breviter dicam, Duplex est claritas scriturae, sicut et duplex obscuritas, Una externa in verbi ministerio posita, altera in cordis cognitione sita." Luther, *De servo arbitrio,* LW 33, 28; WA 18, 609. Cf. also *De servo arbitrio,* LW 33, 90–91; WA 18, 653.

32. See Desiderius Erasmus, *Diatribe de libero arbitrio,* transl. Peter Macardle, in: *Collected Works* [CW], Vol. 76 (Toronto: Toronto University Press, 1998), 8–9; and *Erasmus' Werke: Ausgewählte Schriften* [EW] (bilingual ed.), ed. Werner Welzig, Vol. 4 (Darmstadt, Ger.: Wissenschaftliche Buchgesellschaft, 1969), 10. All refererences to and quotations from Erasmus's *Diatribe* are taken from the English translation in *Collected Works* [CW], whereas the Latin text is quoted from the German bilingual edition of selected works [EW].

33. Luther, *De servo arbitrio,* LW 33, 90–95; WA 18, 653–656.

34. With respect to free will, cf. Luther, *De servo arbitrio,* LW 33, 95; WA 18, 656.

35. See Gadamer, *Wahrheit und Methode,* 314–317.

36. "For in Holy Scripture there are some secret places into which God did not intend us to penetrate very far." Erasmus, *Diatribe,* CW 76, 8; EW 4, 10.

37. "[F]or I had this year and am having still, a hard enough fight with those fanatics who subject the Scriptures to the interpretation of their own spirit." Luther, *De servo arbitrio,* LW 33, 90; WA 18, 653. In fact, Erasmus accuses Luther of exactly the same fallacy, that is, for imposing his own opinions on the biblical text. Erasmus, *Diatribe,* CW 76, 7; EW 4, 6.

38. See Luther, *De servo arbitrio,* LW 33, 99; WA 18, 659.

39. Cf. the reference to 1 Corinthians 2:7–10.

40. *De servo arbitrio,* WL 33, 90; WA 18, 653.

41. Cf. Plato, *Politeia,* 518d.

42. "Klar ist die Schrift, so hörten wir oben, sofern Christus sie verkündigt. Klar ist das Wort wohl in sich, aber es liegt an seiner Klarheit, weil es als Gottes rettende Wort klar sein muß. Diese Klarheit ist also nicht zu trennen vom Inhalt des Wortes Gottes. Damit is zugleich auch noch ein Weiteres gesagt. Wenn das so ist, dann ist die Klarheit nicht zu lösen vom Glauben, auf den das Wort zielt." Friedrich Beisser, *Claritas scripturae bei Martin Luther* (Göttingen, Ger.: Vandenhoeck & Ruprecht, 1966), 85.

43. Cf. Beisser's reflections on evidence; Beisser, *Claritas scripturae,* 104 ff.

44. See Luther, *De servo arbitrio,* LW 33, 80; WA 18, 647.

45. "Deum operari bona et mala in nobis." Luther, *De servo arbitrio,* LW 33, 58; WA 18, 630.

46. Erasmus, *Diatribe,* CW 76, 7; EW 4, 6.

47. Cf. Luther, *De servo arbitrio,* WL 33, 98; WA 18, 659.

48. "Verum, quia in contrarium persuasi sumus iam dudum, pestilenti illo Sophistarum verbo, Scripturas esse obscuras et ambiguas, cogimur primum probare illud ipsum primum principium nostrum, quo omnia alia probanda sunt, quod apud philosophos absur-

dum et impossibile factu videretur." Luther, *De servo arbitrio,* LW 33, 91; WA 18, 653. Translation modified.

49. Michel Foucault identifies Descartes as the rationalist who *expels* madness from thought and thus justifies the expulsion of the insane from the civil society in seventeenth-century Europe. He argues that the ultimate decision of the *Meditations* effectively *excludes* the possibility of madness, of dreams, of an evil genius—and thus institutes this typically modern separation of reason from madness, light from darkness, normality from illness. For an extended analysis of Foucault and the subsequent critique from Derrida, cf. my book *Autopsia* (Berlin: De Gruyter, 2008), 54–57.

50. "He who wishes to philosophize by using Aristotle without danger to his soul must first become thoroughly foolish [*stultificetur*] in Christ." Luther, *Heidelberg Disputation,* LW 31, 41; WA 1, 355.

7. The Quest for Sovereignty

1. Cf. Martin Luther, *Lectures on Genesis,* WA 43, 458. All quotations from Luther's works refer first to the English translations from the standard American edition of *Luther's Works* [LW], edited by Jaroslav Pelikan and Helmut T. Lehmann, and then to the *Weimarer Ausgabe* [WA]: *D. Martin Luthers Werke, Kritische Gesammtausgabe* (Weimar, Ger.: H. Böhlau, 1883–2009), although when the Latin texts are quoted—with reference to WA—the quotation is taken either from the *Lateinisch-Deutsche Studienausgabe,* Vol. 1, ed. W. Härle, et al. (Leipzig, Ger.: Evangelische Verlagsanstalt, 2006), or from the online edition of the *Weimarer Ausgabe* (http://luther.chadwyck.co.uk/). There are minor differences of spelling in the various editions. When the translations are modified, this will be indicated.

2. Cf. Luther, *De servo arbitrio,* LW 33, 140; WA 18, 684–685.

3. Cf. Volker Leppin, "Deus absconditus und Deus revelatus. Transformationen mittelalterlicher Theologie in der Gotteslehre von 'De servo arbitrio,'" in: *Berliner Theologische Zeitschrift* 22 (2005), 55–69.

4. Cf. Luther, *De servo arbitrio,* LW 33, 140; WA 18, 684.

5. "Illudit autem sese Diatribe ignorantia sua, dum nihil distinguit inter Deum praedicatum et absconditum [. . .]." Luther, *De servo arbitrio,* LW 33, 140; WA 18, 685. My translation.

6. Immanuel Kant, *Kritik der reinen Vernunft* (Stuttgart, Ger.: Philipp Reclam, 1966), A 254–255.

7. Cf. Kant, *Kritik der reinen Vernunft,* A 268 ff.

8. Cf. Kant, *Kritik der reinen Vernunft,* A 289.

9. Cf. Kant, *Kritik der reinen Vernunft,* A 290.

10. Cf. Luther, *Lectures on Genesis,* WA 43, 458.

11. Cf. Desiderius Erasmus, *Diatribe de libero arbitrio,* transl. Peter Macardle, in: *Collected Works* [CW], Vol. 76 (Toronto: Toronto University Press, 1998), 82; and *Erasmus' Werke: Ausgewählte Schriften* [EW] (bilingual ed.), ed. Werner Welzig, Vol. 4 (Darmstadt, Ger.: Wissenschaftliche Buchgesellschaft, 1969), 178. All refererences to and quotations from Erasmus's *Diatribe* are taken from the English translation in *Collected Works* [CW], whereas the Latin text is quoted from the German bilingual edition of selected works [EW].

12. Luther, *De servo arbitrio,* LW 33, 35; WA 18, 614. Translation modified.

13. Cf. his discussion of Scotus's view of free will and other positions in: Erasmus, *Diatribe,* CW 76, 27–29; EW 4, 48–50.

14. Erasmus, *Diatribe,* CW 76, 21; EW 4, 36.

15. See Erasmus, *Diatribe,* CW 76, 31–32; EW 4, 52–56.

16. Erasmus, *Diatribe,* CW 76, 82; EW 4, 178.

17. See Leif Grane, *Contra Gabrielem: Luthers Auseinandersetzung mit Gabriel Biel in der Disputatio Contra Scholasticam Theologiam 1517* (Copenhagen, Den.: Gyldendal, 1962), 97–148.

18. Cf. Erasmus, *Diatribe,* CW 76, 88; EW 4, 188.

19. "Altera pars summae Christianae est, Nosse, an Deus contingenter aliquid praesciat, et an omnia faciamus necessitate." Luther, *De servo arbitrio,* LW 33, 36; WA 18, 614. Translation modified.

20. Luther, *De servo arbitrio,* LW 33, 37; WA 18, 615. Translation modified.

21. "Hoc fulmine sternitur et conteritur penitus liberum arbitrium ideo qui liberum arbitrium volunt assertum, debent hoc fulmen vel negare vel dissimulare, aut alia ratione a se abigere." Luther, *De servo arbitrio,* LW 33, 37; WA 18, 615.

22. Cf. Simo Knuuttila, *Modalities in Medieval Philosophy* (London: Routledge, 1993), 131–134.

23. "Nonne et rhetores tui docent, De causa aliqua dicturum, oportere dicere, Primum an sit, deinde quid sit, quae eius partes, quae contraria, affinia, similia etc.? Tu vero miserum illud per sese liberum arbitrium his omnibus spolias, et nullam quaestionem de eo definis, nisi unam illam primam, scilicet an sit." Luther, *De servo arbitrio,* LW 33, 36; WA 18, 614–615.

24. Cf. *Disputation against Scholastic Theology,* LW 31, 10; WA 1, 224.

25. "[C]um Deus operetur omnia in omnibus, Ignoratis vero operibus et potentia Dei, Deum ipsum ignoro, Ignorato Deo, colere, laudare, gratias agere, servire Deo non possum, dum nescio, quantum mihi tribuere, quantum Deo debeo." Luther, *De servo arbitrio,* LW 33, 35; WA 18, 614.

26. "An tu credis, quod nolens praesciat, aut ignarus velit? Si volens praescit, aeterna est et immobilis (quia natura) voluntas, si praesciens vult, aeterna est et immobilis (quia natura) scientia." Luther, *De servo arbitrio,* LW 33, 37 ; WA 18, 615.

27. According to Simo Knuuttila, this is the basic question in the debate between nominalists and realists in the fifteenth century. Cf. Knuuttila, *Modalities in Medieval Philosophy,* 43.

28. Cf. the analysis of this problem in K. E. Løgstrup, *Skabelse og tilintetgørelse* (Copenhagen, Den.: Gyldendal 1978); English translation: *Metaphysics,* Vol. I (Milwaukee, Wisc.: Marquette University Press, 1995).

29. Cf. Luther, *De servo arbitrio,* LW 33, 38; WA 18, 616.

30. "Sudaverunt hic sophistae iam multis annis et tandem victi, coacti sunt concedere, Omnia quidem necessario fieri, necessitate consequentiae (ut dicunt), sed non necessitate consequentis, Sic eluserunt violentiam istius quaestionis, verum et seipsos potius illuserunt. Quam sit enim hoc nihil non gravabor ostendere, Necessitatem consequentiae vocant, ut crasse dicam, Si Deus aliquid vult, necesse est ut ipsum fiat, sed non est necesse, ut id sit,

quod fit, Solus Deus enim necessario est, omnia alia possunt non esse, si Deus velit, Ita actionem Dei necessariam dicunt, si volet, sed factum ipsum non esse necessarium." Luther, *De servo arbitrio,* LW 33, 39–40; WA 18, 616–617. Translation modified.

31. See Knuuttila, *Modalities in Medieval Philosophy,* 120 f.

32. Cf. Erasmus, *Diatribe,* CW 76, 82; EW 4, 178.

33. See Luther, *Against the Robbing and Murdering Hordes of Peasants,* LW 46, 54; WA 18, 361.

34. "Imo ut scias, hic est cardo nostrae disputationis, hic versatur status causae huius." Luther, *De servo arbitrio,* WA 18, 614.

35. Erasmus, *Diatribe,* CW 76, 84.

36. Erasmus, *Diatribe,* CW 76, 85.

37. Erasmus, *Diatribe,* CW 76, 86.

38. "Primum an sit, deinde quid sit, quae eius partes, quae contraria, affinia, similia etc.?" Luther, *De servo arbitrio,* LW 33, 37; WA 18, 615. Translation modified.

8. The Quest for Subjectivity

1. Perspectives questioning the value of metaphysical discourse, its limitations, and inherent violence are strangely absent in the otherwise detailed contributions from philosophy and theology to the question of free will in: *Der freie und unfreie Wille: Philosophische und theologische Perspektiven,* ed. Friedrich Hermanni and Peter Koslowski (Munich, Ger.: Fink Verlag, 2004). Cf. in particular the contribution by Friedrich Hermanni: "Luther oder Erasmus? Der Streit um die Freiheit des menschlichen Willens," 165–187.

2. Hence Luther attacks the traditional opinion of free will as a "neutral and unqualified willing" as pure dialectical fiction (*merum figmentum Dialecticum*): Martin Luther, *De servo arbitrio,* LW 33, 115; WA 18, 670. All quotations from Luther's works refer first to the English translations from the standard American edition of *Luther's Works* [LW], edited by Jaroslav Pelikan and Helmut T. Lehmann, and then to the *Weimarer Ausgabe* [WA]: *D. Martin Luthers Werke, Kritische Gesammtausgabe* (Weimar, Ger.: H. Böhlau, 1883–2009), although when the Latin texts are quoted—with reference to WA—the quotation is taken either from the *Lateinisch-Deutsche Studienausgabe,* Vol. 1, ed. W. Härle, et al. (Leipzig, Ger.: Evangelische Verlagsanstalt, 2006), or from the online edition of the *Weimarer Ausgabe* (http://luther.chadwyck.co.uk/). There are minor differences of spelling in the various editions. When the translations are modified, this will be indicated.

3. Cf. thesis 13 in the *Heidelberg Disputation:* "Liberum arbitrium post peccatum, res est de solo titulo [. . .]." LW 31, 40; WA 1, 354.

4. Cf. Desiderius Erasmus, *Diatribe de libero arbitrio,* transl. Peter Macardle, in: *Collected Works* [CW], Vol. 76 (Toronto: Toronto University Press, 1998), 24–26; and *Erasmus' Werke: Ausgewählte Schriften* [EW] (bilingual ed.), ed. Werner Welzig, Vol. 4 (Darmstadt, Ger.: Wissenschaftliche Buchgesellschaft, 1969), 42–46.

5. "Fateor, mi Erasme, non immerito te istis omnibus moveri, Ego ultra decennium istis sic motus sum, ut nullum alium arbitrer esse, qui aeque sit istis permotus, Eratque mihi incredibile ipsi, hanc Troiam nostram, tanto tempore, tot bellis invictam, posse aliquando capi, Et testor Deum in animam meam, perseverassem, adhuc hodie sic moverer,

nisi urgente conscientia, et evidentia rerum me in diversum cogeret. Potes sane cogitare, nec mihi saxeum esse pectus, atque si saxeum esset, tamen tantis fluctibus et aestibus luctatum et collisum potuisse liquescere, dum id auderem, quo facto, videbam omnem illorum authoritatem, quos recensuisti, super caput meum velut diluvium inundaturam." Luther, *De servo arbitrio,* LW 33, 73–74; WA 18, 641. Translation modified.

6. "[W]hy do we hold on to an empty term, deceptive and dangerous at it is [. . .]?" Luther, *De servo arbitrio,* LW 33, 69; WA 18; 637.

7. The ignorance and contempt of God is thus ascribed not only to the inferior but to the superior powers of man, namely, to will and reason. Cf. Luther *De servo arbitrio,* LW 33, 254; WA 18, 761.

8. Cf. Wilfried Joest, *Ontologie der Person bei Luther* (Göttingen, Ger.: Vandenhoeck & Ruprecht, 1967), 212 ff.

9. "Hic homo mere passive (ut dicitur) sese habet, nec facit quippiam, sed fit totus." Luther, *De servo arbitrio,* LW 33, 157; WA 18, 697.

10. "Worauff du nu (sage ich) dein hertz hengest und verlessest, das ist eygentlich dein Gott." Luther, *Großer Katechismus,* WA 30.1, 133. Cf. also Luther's definition of the difference between God and idol, which is based on confidence of the heart: "Also das ein Gott haben nichts anders ist denn yhm von hertzen trawen und gleuben, wie ich offt gesagt habe, das alleine das trawen und gleuben des hertzens machet beide Gott und abeGott. Glaube und trawen machet ein Gott."

11. The redefinition of subjectivity outlined here is elaborated more precisely with reference to the biblical scriptures, in particular Paul and John, toward the end of *De servo arbitrio:* Cf. LW 33, 260–266; WA 18, 765–769.

12. Cf. the fourfold relation (*Geviert*) emphasized by Heidegger in his topology, which corresponds to the temporal Event (*Ereignis*).

13. Cf. the expression *per crucem destruuntur* in the *Heidelberg Disputation* (LW 31, 53; WA 1; 362).

14. Luther, *De servo arbitrio,* LW 33,62; WA 18, 633. Translation modified.

15. Cf. for example Joest, *Ontologie der Person bei Luther,* 280–285.

9. *Deus Absconditus*

1. Paul Celan, *Lightduress,* trans. Pierre Joris (Los Angeles: Green Integer, 2004). German: *Lichtzwang* (Frankfurt am Main, Ger.: Suhrkamp, 1996).

2. Cf. the expression "hoc magis ac magis caligamus" in: Desiderius Erasmus, *Diatribe de libero arbitrio—A Discussion on Free Will,* trans. Peter Macardle, in: *Collected Works* [CW], Vol. 76 (Toronto: Toronto University Press, 1998), 8; and *Diatribe sive collatio de libero arbitrio* [1524], in *Erasmus' Werke: Ausgewählte Schriften* (bilingual ed.) [EW], Vol. 4, ed. Werner Welzig (Darmstadt, Ger.: Wissenschaftliche Buchgesellschaft, 1969), 10. All refererences to and quotations from Erasmus's *Diatribe* are taken from the English translation in *Collected Works* [CW], whereas the Latin text is quoted from the German bilingual edition of selected works [EW].

3. "What is above us, is no concern of ours." Martin Luther, *De servo arbitrio,* LW 33, 23; WA 16, 605. All quotations from Luther's works refer first to the English translations

from the standard American edition of *Luther's Works* [LW], Vol. 1–55, ed. Jaroslav Pelikan and Helmut T. Lehmann (Philadelphia: Fortress Press, 1958–1976); and then to the *Weimarer Ausgabe* [WA]: *D. Martin Luthers Werke,* Vol. 1–55 (Weimar, Ger., 1883–2009), although when the Latin texts are quoted—with reference to WA—the quotation is taken either from the *Lateinisch-Deutsche Studienausgabe,* Vol. 1, ed. W. Härle, et al. (Leipzig, Ger.: Evangelische Verlagsanstalt, 2006), or from the online edition of the *Weimarer Ausgabe* (http://luther.chadwyck.co.uk/). There are minor differences of spelling in the various editions. When the translations are modified, this will be indicated.

4. Luther, *De servo arbitrio,* LW 33, 23; WA 18, 605.

5. Thus, e.g., Eberhard Jüngel in an article carrying this name ("Quae supra nos, nihil ad nos").

6. "Latibulum dei est tenebre: primo quia in fidei enygmate et caligine habitat. Secundo Quia habitat lucem inaccessibilem, ita quod nullus intellectus ad eum pertingere potest, nisi suo lumine omisso, altiore levatus fuerit. Ideo b. Dionysius docet ingredi in tenebras anagogicas et per negationes ascendere. Quia sic est deus absconditus et incomprehensibilis. Tercio potest intelligi mysterium Incarnationis. Quia in humanitate absconditus latet, que est tenebre eius, in quibus videri non potuit sed tantum audiri. Quarto Est Ecclesia vel b. virgo, quia in utraque latuit et latet in Ecclesia adhuc, que est obscura mundo, deo autem manifesta. Quinto Sacramentum Eucharistie, ubi est occultissimus. Unde et illud potest intelligi de incarnatione Christi." Luther, *Ennarationes in Psalmos* (1513/15); WA 3, 124.

7. Dionysius Areopagita, *The Mystical Theology,* in: *The Divine Names and Mystical Theology* (Milwaukee, Wisc.: Marquette University Press, 1980), 211.

8. Dionysius Areopagita, *The Mystical Theology,* 222. Translation modified. Cf. also: Ibid., *The Complete Works* (New York: Paulist Press, 1987), 141.

9. Since Thomas Aquinas and the other school philosophers frequently refer to Dionysius and include his thought in their philosophical systems, this strategy of negative theology, where the hiddenness of God is emphasized more radically, means questioning the conditions of philosophical theology from within.

10. Luther, *Heidelberg Disputation,* LW 31, 52; WA 1, 362.

11. Luther, *Heidelberg Disputation,* LW 31, 54–55; WA 1, 363.

12. "Now it is not sufficient for anyone, and it does him no good to recognize God in his glory and majesty, unless he recognizes him in the humility and shame of the cross." Luther, *Heidelberg Disputation,* LW 31, 52–53; WA 1, 362.

13. Cf. Erasmus, *Diatribe,* CW 76, 8; EW 4, 10.

14. Cf. Erasmus, *Diatribe,* CW 76, 82; EW 4, 182–184.

15. Cf. Erasmus, *Diatribe,* CW 76, 10–11; EW 4, 14–16.

16. Cf. Erasmus, *Diatribe,* CW 76, 5–6; EW 4, 2–4.

17. "Sunt enim in divinis literis adyta quaedam, in quae deus noluit nos altius penetrare, et si penetrare conemur, quo fuerimus altius ingressi, hoc magis ac magis caligamus, quo vel sic agnosceremus et divinae sapientiae maiestatem impervestigabilem et humanae mentis imbecillitatem, quemadmodum de specu quodam Coricio narrat Pomponius Mela, qui primum iucunda quadam amoenitate allectat ac ducit ad se, donec altius atque altius in-

gressos tandem horror quidam ac maiestas numinis illic inhabitantis submoveat." Erasmus, *Diatribe,* CW 76, 8–9; EW 4, 10. Translation modified.

18. Hence, toward the end of this passage he argues for a deferral of secret knowledge until the end of times, when we according to Paul shall no longer look into "mirrors and enigmas" (*speculum et in aenigmate*) but see God's glory revealed, in the face (cf. Erasmus, *Diatribe,* CW 76, 9; EW 4, 10).

19. Plato, *Timaeus,* 48a.

20. Luther, *De servo arbitrio,* LW 33, 23; WA 18, 605. Translation modified.

21. Cf. Erasmus, *Diatribe,* CW 76, 10; EW 4, 14.

22. Luther, *De servo arbitrio,* LW 33, 26; WA 18, 606. Translation modified.

23. "Et ut breviter dicam, Duplex est claritas scripturae, sicut et duplex obscuritas, Una externa in verbo ministerio posita, altera in cordis cognitione sita." Luther, *De servo arbitrio,* LW 33, 28; WA 18, 609; cf. also LW 33, 90–91; WA 18, 653.

24. "Sic habet mea distinctio, ut et ego parum rhetoricer vel Dialecticer, Duae res sunt Deus et Scriptura Dei, non minus quam duae res sunt Creatur et creatura Dei. In Deo esse multa abscondita, quae ignoremus, nemo dubitat, sicut ipsemet dicit de die extremo." Luther, *De servo arbitrio,* LW 33, 25; WA 18, 606.

25. Cf. Luther, *De servo arbitrio,* LW 33, 139; WA 18, 684.

26. Cf. Galatians 6:7.

27. This assessment applies not only to the already mentioned article "Quae supra nos," but also Jüngel's article "The Revelation of the Hiddenness of God" and his book *God as the Mystery of the World: On the Foundation of the Theology of the Crucified One in the Dispute between Theism and Atheism,* trans. Darell L. Guder (Grand Rapids, Mich.: Eerdmans, 1983).

28. Cf. Richard Kearney, *Strangers, Gods and Monsters: Interpreting Otherness* (New York: Routledge, 2003), 194.

29. Luther, *De servo arbitrio,* WL 33, 18; WA 18, 602.

30. "There is nothing to this Corycian cave of yours, then, that is not how things are in the scriptures. Matters of the highest majesty and the profoundest mysteries are no longer hidden away, but have been brought out in front of everybody and made accessible. For Christ has opened our sense, that we may understand the scriptures." Luther, *De servo arbitrio,* LW 33, 26 f.; WA 18, 607. Translation modified.

31. Luther, *De servo arbitrio,* LW 33, 47; WA 18, 622.

32. Luther, *De servo arbitrio,* LW 33, 47; WA 18, 623. Translation modified.

33. Luther, *De servo arbitrio,* LW 33, 52–53; WA 18, 626. Translation modified.

34. Cf. Oswald Bayer's careful elaboration of this topic in: Bayer, *Promissio* (Göttingen, Ger.: Vandenhoeck & Ruprecht, 1971).

35. For a general analysis of this tendency, see Martin Wendte, "Monarchie des Geistes? Gegen den impliziten Hegelianismus in der gegenwartigen Theologie," in *NZSTh* 49 (2007), 86–103. For a more specific discussion of Barthian readings of Luther, cf. Thomas Reinhuber, *Kämpfender Glaube* (Berlin: De Gruyter 2000), 139–140.

36. See Erasmus, *Diatribe,* CW 76, 35–36; EW 4, 60–64 and Luther, *De servo arbitrio,* LW 33, 135; WA 18, 682.

37. Erasmus, *Diatribe,* CW 76, 35–36; EW 4, 64. Translation modified. Cf. Luther, *De servo arbitrio,* LW 33, 136; WA 18, 683.

38. Luther, *De servo arbitrio,* LW33, 139; WA 18, 685. Translation modified.

39. Luther, *De servo arbitrio,* LW33, 139; WA 18, 684. Translation modified.

40. Cf. Althaus, Ebeling, Bayer, Schwarzwäller, et al.

41. Cf. Barth, Jüngel, Roth, et al.

42. Although Luther is not clear in keeping up this distinction, which tends to collapse throughout the text, it is nevertheless there, introduced almost in passing, and emphasized as something other than the divine will and something other than the majesty: "ut secretum longe reverendissimum maiestatis divinae"—the expression could even be analyzed according to a double reading of the genitive, as objective and subjective genitive, but not here and not now. It draws a line of distinction between the majesty and the secret of the majesty, and this *secrecy,* this *abscondity,* is our concern at this point, not the majesty as such.

10. Topology of the Self in Luther

1. See Theodor Mahlmann, "Die Interpretation von Luthers *De servo arbitrio* bei orthodoxen lutherischen Theologen, vor allem Sebastian Schmidt (1617–1696)," in: *Luthers Erben,* ed. Notger Slenczka and Walter Sparn (Tübingen, Ger.: Mohr Siebeck, 2005), 73–136. Cf. also the rather polemical review of twentieth-century theologians by Klaus Schwarzwäller: *Sibboleth: Die Interpretation von Luthers Schrift* De servo arbitrio *seit Theodosius Harnack* (Munich, Ger.: Kaiser, 1969). An early version of my argument presented in this chapter is published under the title "Does Modernity Begin with Luther?" in: *Studia Theologica* 63 (2009), 42–66. Thanks to the publisher for permission to republish.

2. See David Kangas, "Luther and Modernity," *Epoché,* Vol. 14 (2010), 431–452; cf. Reiner Schürmann, *Broken Hegemonies,* trans. Reginald Lilly (Bloomington: Indiana University Press, 2003), 39–40.

3. Cf. Edmund Husserl, *Die Krisis der europäischen Wissenschaften und die transzendentale Phänomenologie,* ed. E. Ströker (Hamburg, Ger.: Meiner, 1996), 22–34 and 80–91.

4. Cf. Husserl, *Krisis,* 3–5.

5. Cf. Husserl, *Krisis,* 104–105.

6. Cf. Schürmann, *Broken Hegemonies,* 353–356.

7. Cf. Martin Luther, *De servo arbitrio,* LW 33, 138–144; WA 18, 684–688. All quotations from Luther's works refer first to the English translations from the standard American edition of *Luther's Works* [LW], Vol. 1–55, ed. Jaroslav Pelikan and Helmut T. Lehmann (Philadelphia: Fortress Press, 1958–1976); and then to the *Weimarer Ausgabe* [WA]: *D. Martin Luthers Werke,* Vol. 1–55 (Weimar, Ger., 1883–2009), although when the Latin texts are quoted—with reference to WA—the quotation is taken either from the *Lateinisch-Deutsche Studienausgabe,* Vol. 1, ed. W. Härle, et al. (Leipzig, Ger.: Evangelische Verlagsanstalt, 2006), or from the online edition of the *Weimarer Ausgabe* (http://luther.chadwyck.co.uk/). There are minor differences of spelling in the various editions. When the translations are modified, this will be indicated.

8. See Schürmann, *Broken Hegemonies,* 367.

9. See Schürmann, *Broken Hegemonies,* 347–348.

10. Cf. Schürmann, *Broken Hegemonies*, 137.

11. Schürmann, *Broken Hegemonies*, 514.

12. Jacques Derrida, who consistently denies being "post-modern," discusses the dilemmas of such skepticism from two different perspectives in *Positions*, trans. Alan Bass (Chicago: The University of Chicago Press, 1981) and "How to Avoid Speaking: Denials," trans. Ken Frieden, in: *Languages of the Unsayable*, ed. S. Budick and W. Iser (New York: Columbia University Press, 1981), 3–70.

13. See Wilfried Joest, *Ontologie der Person bei Luther* (Göttingen, Ger.: Vandenhoeck & Ruprecht, 1967), 79–88; and Rudolf Malter, *Das reformatorische Denken und die Philosophie* (Bonn, Ger.: Bouvier, 1980), 21–46; 90–101.

14. For a more detailed analysis of Luther's *destruction* of metaphysics in the *Heidelberg Disputation*, see chapter 5.

15. Joest, *Ontologie*, 163–193.

16. Joest, *Ontologie*, 212–216.

17. Cf. the discussion of *Topics* by Melanchton and Luther in chapter 3.

18. The German philosopher Erwin Metzke represents an interesting counterpoint to Husserl with his phenomenology of the body based on Luther's understanding of the sacraments. Moreover, he elaborates a history of modern philosophy that includes Luther. Cf. Erwin Metzke, *Sakrament und Metaphysik: Eine Lutherstudie über das Verhältnis des christlichen Denkens zum Leiblich-Materiellen* (Stuttgart, Ger.: Kreuz Verlag, 1948) and *Geschichtliche Wirklichkeit. Gedanken zu einer deutschen Philosophie der Geschichte* (Tübingen, Ger.: Mohr Siebeck, 1935). Both Joest and Malter are indebted to Metzke for their interpretations of Luther.

19. Malter, *Das reformatorische Denken*, 139–146.

20. "Aufhebung des ichhaften Verstehens und Herstellung des spiritualen Verstehens ereignen sich in einem einzigen Vorgang, dem das Wissen passiv gegenübersteht—passiv gemacht gegen seine eigene Intention durch das Gesetz. [. . .] Daß das menschliche Wissen seine metaphysische Bestimmung von außen und gleichwohl als Wissen empfängt, denkt Luther in seiner Lehre von der Rechtfertigung durch den Glauben: sie ist das Zentrum des ganzen reformatorischen Denkens—einfach und zugleich höchst kompliziert wie Descartes' Gedanke vom Cogito oder Kants Idee der transzendentalen Deduktion." Malter, *Das reformatorische Denken*, 140–141.

21. Cf. Malter, *Das reformatorische Denken*, 126–132.

22. Cf. Malter, *Das reformatorische Denken*, 231.

23. See Malter, *Das reformatorische Denken*, 237–240.

24. Cf. Schürmann, *Broken Hegemonies*, 353.

25. Schürmann, *Broken Hegemonies*, 353.

26. Schürmann, *Broken Hegemonies*, 354.

27. Schürmann, *Broken Hegemonies*, 354.

28. Cf. Schürmann, *Broken Hegemonies*, 384–385. This is a point Schürmann has in common with the majority of German Luther research from the 1960's onward, as, for example, elaborated by Gerhard Ebeling in his hermeneutic works on Luther and the word of God: Gerhard Ebeling, *Wort und Glaube* (Tübingen, Ger.: Mohr Siebeck, 1960); *Wort Gottes und*

Tradition (Göttingen, Ger.: Vandenhoeck & Ruprecht, 1964); and *Wort und Glaube II: Beiträge zur Fundamentaltheologie und zur Lehre von Gott* (Tübingen, Ger.: Mohr Siebeck, 1969).

29. Cf. Schürmann, *Broken Hegemonies,* 376.

30. Schürmann, *Broken Hegemonies,* 376.

31. Cf. Schürmann, *Broken Hegemonies,* 347–348.

32. Schürmann, *Broken Hegemonies,* 26–36.

33. Schürmann, *Broken Hegemonies,* 411.

34. Schürmann, *Broken Hegemonies,* 411.

35. Cf. Jacques Derrida, *Of Grammatology,* trans. Gayatri Chakravorty Spivak (Baltimore: The Johns Hopkins University Press, 1976), 69.

36. Schürmann, *Broken Hegemonies,* 373.

37. "Res igitur in scripturis contentae omnes sunt proditae, licet quaedam loca adhuc verbis incognitis obscura sint. Stultum est vero et impium, scire, res scripturae esse omnes in luce positas clarissima, et propter pauca verba obscura, res obscuras dictare, Si uno loco obscura sunt verba, at alio sunt clara, Eadem vero res, manifestissime toti mundo declarata, dicitur in scripturis tum verbis claris, tum adhuc latet verbis obscuris. Iam nihil refert, si res sit in luce, an aliquod eius signum sit in tenebris, cum interim multa alia eiusdem signa sint in luce. Quis dicet fontem publicum non esse in luce, quod hi qui in angiporto sunt, illum non vident, cum omnes qui sunt in foro videant?" Luther, *De servo arbitrio,* LW 33, 26; WA 18, 606. Translation modified.

38. Schürmann, *Broken Hegemonies,* 378.

39. Schürmann, *Broken Hegemonies,* 378.

40. Luther, *Großer Katechismus,* WA 30.1, 133.

41. Schürmann, *Broken Hegemonies,* 396.

42. Schürmann, *Broken Hegemonies,* 410.

43. Cf. Schürmann, *Broken Hegemonies,* 420.

44. Schürmann, *Broken Hegemonies,* 438.

11. Kant versus Luther on Self-Consciousness

1. Cf. David Kangas, "Luther and Modernity," *Epoché,* Vol. 14 (2010), 431–452.

2. Reiner Schürmann, *Broken Hegemonies,* trans. Reginald Lilly (Bloomington: Indiana University Press, 2003), 345.

3. Immanuel Kant, *Critique of Pure Reason,* trans. N. K. Smith (London: Macmillan, 1929), 153. Translation modified. In German, the passage runs as follows: "Also hat alles Mannigfaltige der Anschauung eine notwendige Beziehung auf das: *Ich denke,* in demselben Subjekt, darin diese Mannigfaltigkeit angetroffen wird. Diese Vorstellung aber ist ein Actus der *Spontaneität,* d.i. sie kann nicht als zur Sinnlichkeit gehörig angesehen werden. Ich nenne sie die reine *Apperzeption,* um sie von der *empirischen* zu unterscheiden, oder auch die *ursprüngliche Apperzeption,* weil sie dasjenige Selbstbewußtsein ist, was, indem es die Vorstellung *Ich denke* hervorbringt, die alle andere muß begleiten können, und in allem Bewußtsein ein und dasselbe ist, von keiner weiter begleitet werden kann. Ich nenne auch die Einheit derselben die *transzendentale* Einheit des Selbstbewußtseins, um die Möglichkeit der Erkenntnis a priori aus ihr zu bezeichnen. Denn die mannigfaltigen Vorstellungen,

die in einer gewissen Anschauung gegeben werden, würden nicht insgesamt *meine* Vorstellungen sein, wenn sie nicht insgesamt zu einem Selbstbewußtsein gehöreten [. . .]." Kant, *Kritik der reinen Vernunft* (Stuttgart, Ger.: Philipp Reclam 1966), 175–176 [B 132].

4. Schürmann, *Broken Hegemonies,* 387.

5. Schürmann describes the dependence on the word as follows: "The word that modifies my self-understanding is such that 'no one can grasp it unless they receive it through listening and faith.' (cf. *Romans*) The word works on the new grasp—resumption, representation, reflection, reflexion—in a manner analogous to the work performed by the Kantian categories. In both, the given 'is' only to the extent that I can make it mine. In Kant, being is a category and making mine means to subsume; in Luther, being is the effective word and making mine means to obey." Schürmann, *Broken Hegemonies,* 387.

6. Schürmann, *Broken Hegemonies,* 406.

7. Cf. Martin Luther, *De servo arbitrio,* LW 33, 87; WA 18, 651 passim. All quotations from Luther's works refer first to the English translations from the standard American edition of *Luther's Works* [LW], edited by Jaroslav Pelikan and Helmut T. Lehmann, and then to the *Weimarer Ausgabe* [WA]: *D. Martin Luthers Werke, Kritische Gesammtausgabe* (Weimar, Ger.: H. Böhlau, 1883–2009), although when the Latin texts are quoted—with reference to WA—the quotation is taken either from the *Lateinisch-Deutsche Studienausgabe,* Vol. 1, ed. W. Härle, et al. (Leipzig, Ger.: Evangelische Verlagsanstalt, 2006), or from the online edition of the *Weimarer Ausgabe* (http://luther.chadwyck.co.uk/). There are minor differences of spelling in the various editions. When the translations are modified, this will be indicated.

8. Schürmann, *Broken Hegemonies,* 397.

9. Schürmann, *Broken Hegemonies,* 390.

10. Luther, *De servo arbitrio,* LW 33, 139; WA 18, 685.

11. Schürmann also refers to an Aristotelian causality in *De servo arbitrio,* but gives the impression that this causality is superseded and replaced by a phenomenological causality. Cf. Schürmann, *Broken Hegemonies,* 391–393.

12. Luther, *De servo arbitrio,* LW 33, 175; WA 18, 709.

13. Luther, *De servo arbitrio,* LW 33, 138; WA 18, 684.

12. Spacing the Hidden God

1. Cf. the discussions of time, identity, and difference connected to the One and the Other in Plato's *Parmenides,* and in particular the discussion of the One which is older and younger than itself as well as the Other (151e–152a).

2. See Malpas, *Heidegger's Topology* (Cambridge, Mass.: MIT Press, 2006), 149–155.

3. "A trace is the insertion of space in time, the point at which the world inclines toward a past and a time. This time is a withdrawal of the other [. . .]." Emmanuel Levinas, "The Trace of the Other," trans. Alfonso Lingis, in: *Deconstruction in Context,* ed. Mark C. Taylor (Chicago: The University of Chicago Press, 1986), 345–359, here: 358.

4. In a key passage, Derrida defines the "unheard difference" of the trace as follows: "The unheard difference between the appearing and the appearance (between the 'world' and lived experience) is the condition of all other differences, of all other experiences, and *it is already a trace.* [. . .] *The trace is in fact the absolute origin of sense in general. Which amounts*

to saying once again that there is no absolute origin of sense in general. The trace is the difference which opens appearance and signification." Jacques Derrida, *Of Grammatology,* trans. Gayatri Chakravorty Spivak (Baltimore: The Johns Hopkins University Press, 1976), 65.

5. Derrida, *Of Grammatology,* 65–66.

6. Derrida, *Of Grammatology,* 69.

7. Derrida, *Of Grammatology,* 71.

8. Cf. Luther, *De servo arbitrio,* LW 33, 138–139; WA 18, 684–685 and Jacques Derrida, *On the Name,* ed. Thomas Dutoit (Stanford, Calif.: Stanford University Press, 1995), 64. All quotations from Luther's works refer first to the English translations from the standard American edition of *Luther's Works* [LW], edited by Jaroslav Pelikan and Helmut T. Lehmann, and then to the *Weimarer Ausgabe* [WA]: *D. Martin Luthers Werke, Kritische Gesammtausgabe* (Weimar, Ger.: H. Böhlau, 1883–2009), although when the Latin texts are quoted—with reference to WA—the quotation is taken either from the *Lateinisch-Deutsche Studienausgabe,* Vol. 1, ed. W. Härle, et al. (Leipzig, Ger.: Evangelische Verlagsanstalt, 2006), or from the online edition of the *Weimarer Ausgabe* (http://luther.chadwyck.co.uk/). There are minor differences of spelling in the various editions. When the translations are modified, this will be indicated.

9. Cf. the distinction between God outside and inside scripture in: Luther, *De servo arbitrio,* LW 33, 25; WA 18, 606.

10. In the English translation, it is referred to as a "double will, even a double reality." See Paul Althaus, *The Theology of Martin Luther,* trans. Robert C. Schultz (Philadelphia: Fortress Press, 1975), 276. See also Gerhard Ebeling, "Existenz zwischen Gott und Gott," *Wort und Glaube,* Vol. 2 (Tübingen, Ger.: Mohr Siebeck, 1969), 257–286.

13. The Power of Interpretation

1. See José Casanova, *Public Religions in the Modern World* (Chicago: University of Chicago Press, 1994), 211–233; Jürgen Habermas, *Glauben und Wissen: Rede zum Friedenspreis des deutschen Buchhandels* (Frankfurt am Main, Ger.: Suhrkamp, 2001).

2. Cf. Hans Joas, "Religion post-sekulär? Zu einer Begriffsprägung von Jürgen Habermas," in: *Braucht der Mensch Religion?* (Freiburg, Ger.: Herder, 2004), 122–128.

3. Cf. Charles Taylor, *A Secular Age* (Cambridge, Mass.: Harvard University Press, 2007); Giorgio Agamben, *The Signature of All Things: On Method,* trans. Luca d'Isanto (New York: Zone Books, 2009), 69–75, and *The Kingdom and the Glory: For a Theological Genealogy of Economy and Government,* trans. Lorenzo Chiesa (Stanford, Calif.: Stanford University Press, 2011); Talal Asad, *Formations of the Secular: Christianity, Islam, Modernity* (Stanford, Calif.: Stanford University Press, 2003).

4. Cf. the wide spectrum of contributions in *Political Theologies: Public Religions in a Post-Secular World,* ed. Hent de Vries and Lawrence E. Sullivan (New York: Fordham University Press, 2006). See also the article by Hent de Vries: "Why Still 'Religion'?" in: *Religion: Beyond a Concept,* ed. Hent de Vries (New York: Fordham University Press, 2008), 1–99.

5. See Mark Lilla, *The Stillborn God,* 2nd ed. (New York: Vintage, 2008), 58.

6. Paul W. Kahn, *Political Theology: Four Chapters on the Concept of Sovereignty* (New York: Columbia University Press, 2011), 18.

7. Cf. Irena Backus, *Reformation Readings of the Apocalypse* (Oxford, Eng.: Oxford University Press, 2000), 3.

8. Cf. Norman Cohn, *The Pursuit of the Millennium,* 3rd ed. (London: Pimlico, 1970).

9. Cf. Desiderius Erasmus, *Erasmus' Annotations on the New Testament: Galatians to the Apocalypse,* ed. Anne Reeve (Leiden, Neth.: Brill, 1993), first published 1516.

10. Cf. Backus, *Reformation Readings,* 5–6, for a more detailed presentation of Erasmus's and Luther's positions.

11. See Martin Luther, *Commentarius in Apocalypsin ante centum annos aeditus,* WA 28,123–124. All quotations from Luther's works refer first to the English translations from the standard American edition of *Luther's Works* [LW], Vol. 1–55, ed. Jaroslav Pelikan and Helmut T. Lehmann (Philadelphia: Fortress Press, 1958–1976); and then to the *Weimarer Ausgabe* [WA]: *D. Martin Luthers Werke,* Vol. 1–55 (Weimar, Ger., 1883–2009), although when the Latin texts are quoted—with reference to WA—the quotation is taken either from the *Lateinisch-Deutsche Studienausgabe,* Vol. 1, ed. W. Härle, et al. (Leipzig, Ger.: Evangelische Verlagsanstalt, 2006), or from the online edition of the *Weimarer Ausgabe* (http://luther.chadwyck.co.uk/). There are minor differences of spelling in the various editions. When the translations are modified, this will be indicated.

12. Cf. Luther, *De servo arbitrio,* LW 33, 90; WA 18, 653.

13. See Ambrosius Catharinus, *Apologia pro veritate catholicae et apostolicae fidei ac doctrinae adversus impia ac valde pestifera Martini Lutheri dogmata,* ed. Josef Schweizer (Munich, Ger.: Aschendorffsche Verlagsbuchhandlung, 1956). For the background of this book, see Patrick Preston, "Catharinus versus Luther, 1521," *History,* Vol. 88, 364–378.

14. Cf. Luther, *Ad librum Ambrosii Catharinii responsio,* WA 7, 712–713. There is no translation of this text in *Luther's Works;* hence all translations from Latin are mine and the only references are to the Weimar edition.

15. See Ambrosius Catharinus, *Apologia,* 224.

16. Cf. Psalms 118:22 f.

17. "Nobis autem Paulus dicit. Quae societas lucis et tenebrarum? Que conventio Christi et Belial? Aut ergo Petra solam lucem aut solas tenebras, id est, solum sanctum, aut solum impium significat (. . .)." Luther, *Ad librum,* WA 7, 717; cf. 2 Corinthians 6:14 f.

18. "Ruet enim nunc totum illud abominationis Idolum, meris mendaciis hactenus erectum, fultum atque defensum. Praesidia eorum obtinemus, arma forti abstulimus, in quibus confidebat, Goliath decollavimus gladio proprio, Et Palestinos non alia tortura torquemus quam rapina sua." Luther, *Ad librum,* WA 7, 719.

19. Cf. Luther, *Ad librum,* WA 7, 719.

20. "Nos ergo, qui sub Romana Babylone sumus ea verba tangunt, in nobis impleri oportet, quae Daniel, Christus, Petrus, Paulus, Iudas, Ioannes in Apocalypsi praedixerunt." Luther, *Ad librum,* WA 7, 725.

21. Cf. Luther, *Ad librum,* WA 7, 719.

22. Cf. Luther, *Ad librum,* WA 7, 728–729. Luther quotes the Hebrew text, which he uses in order to correct the Vulgate.

23. "Quibus ergo? faciebus, id est, externa specie, apparentia, pompa, hoc est, ut uno verbo dicam, superstitionibus, ritibus, cerimoniis, quae ad faciem exponuntur, in vestibus,

cibis, personis, domibus, gestibus, et similibus. Inter omnes enim facies seu apparentias, superstitio et hypocrisis, quae est pietatis species, et religionis facies, potentissima, gratissima, ideoque nocentissima est." Luther, *Ad librum* WA 7, 729.

24. Luther, *Ad librum,* WA 7, 740.

25. See Luther, *Ad librum,* WA 7, 736–739.

26. Cf. Luther, *Ad librum,* WA 7, 721.

27. Cf. Luther, *Ad librum,* WA 7, 722.

28. "Stabit rex potens faciebus." Luther, *Ad librum,* WA 7, 728.

29. "ET MIRABILIA VASTABIT." Luther, *Ad librum,* WA 7, 759.

30. "Ambiguus autem est Daniel, ut possint intelligi vel ea mirabilia, quae invadit rex ille ut corrumpat. Vel opera eius, quae perpetrat in corrumpendis illis, ceu res eius gestas appellet mirabiles et incredibiles." Luther, *Ad librum,* WA 7, 759.

31. "Ne deus quidem ipse tanta maiestate et potentia exigit." Luther, *Ad librum,* WA 7, 772.

32. Preston, "Catharinus versus Luther, 1521," 368.

33. Cf. Preston's significant point: "If in the course of this, Luther revealed a remarkable comic gift, his purpose was nevertheless intensely serious." Preston, "Catharinus versus Luther, 1521," 377.

34. See Luther, *Ad librum,* WA 7, 730–736.

35. Cf. Luther, *Ad librum,* WA 7, 736–739.

36. "Meo hic sensu periclitabor." Luther, *Ad librum,* WA 7, 736–737.

37. See the endless accusations of abuses within the church in Luther, *Ad librum,* WA 7, 762–769.

38. Cf. Luther, *Ad librum,* WA 7, 708 passim.

39. Cf. the argument recently presented by literary scholar Terry Eagleton in *Reason, Faith, and Revolution* (New Haven, Conn.: Yale University Press, 2009).

40. Cf. Birgit Stolt, *Martin Luthers Rhetorik des Herzens* (Tübingen, Ger.: Mohr Siebeck, 2000).

41. Antónia Szabari, "The Scandal of Religion: Luther and Public Speech in the Reformation," in: *Political Theologies,* ed. Hent de Vries and Lawrence E. Sullivan (New York: Fordham University Press, 2006), 122–136; here: 122.

42. Cf. Szabari, "The Scandal of Religion," 122.

43. Cf. Mark U. Edwards, *Printing, Propaganda, and Martin Luther* (Berkeley, Calif.: University of California Press, 1994), 165.

44. Luther, *Ad Librum,* WA 7, 742.

45. Szabari, "The Scandal of Religion," 131.

46. Szabari, "The Scandal of Religion," 136.

47. See Taylor, *A Secular Age,* 185–191.

14. Political Theology of the German Revolutions

1. Various versions of the argument presented here, on Luther, Müntzer, and Marxism, have been published previously. Let me mention the following two, with thanks to the edi-

tors and publishers for permissions: "Apocalypse and the Spirit of Revolution: The Political Legacy of the Early Reformation," *Political Theology* 14 (2013), 155–173, and "Der apokalyptische Zwerg der Revolution," in: *Deutungsmacht*, ed. by Philipp Stoellger (Tübingen, Ger.: Mohr Siebeck, 2014), 205–224.

2. Cf. Günter Franz (ed.), *Quellen zur Geschichte des Bauernkriegs* (Darmstadt, Ger.: WBG, 1963), 175.

3. See Martin Luther, *That a Christian Assembly Has the Right and Power to Judge All Teaching and to Call, Appoint, and Dismiss Teachers, Established and Proven by Scripture*, LW 39, 305–314; WA 11, 408–416. All quotations from Luther's works refer first to the English translations from the standard American edition of *Luther's Works* [LW], Vol. 1–55, ed. Jaroslav Pelikan and Helmut T. Lehmann (Philadelphia: Fortress Press, 1958–1976); and then to the *Weimarer Ausgabe* [WA]: *D. Martin Luthers Werke*, Vol. 1–55 (Weimar, Ger., 1883–2009), although when the Latin texts are quoted—with reference to WA—the quotation is taken either from the *Lateinisch-Deutsche Studienausgabe*, Vol. 1, ed. W. Härle, et al. (Leipzig, Ger.: Evangelische Verlagsanstalt, 2006), or from the online edition of the *Weimarer Ausgabe* (http://luther.chadwyck.co.uk/). There are minor differences of spelling in the various editions. When the translations are modified, this will be indicated.

4. Luther, *A Sincere Admonition*, LW 45, 59; WA 8, 678.

5. Luther, *A Sincere Admonition*, LW 45, 61; WA 8, 680.

6. Cf. Luther, *De servo arbitrio*, LW 33, 90; WA 18, 653.

7. Luther, *De servo arbitrio*, LW 33, 90; WA 18, 653. Translation modified.

8. Cf. Luther, *De servo arbitrio*, LW 33, 28 and 90 ff.; WA 18, 609 and 654 ff.

9. Cf. a Marxist perspective on Luther as presented by Gerhard Brendler, *Martin Luther: Theologie und Revolution—eine marxistische Darstellung*, 2nd ed. (Cologne, Ger.: Pahl-Rugenstein, 1983).

10. Cf. Luther, *De servo arbitrio*, LW 33, 90–95; WA 18, 654–657.

11. For Müntzer's biography, cf. Hans-Jürgen Goertz, *Thomas Müntzer: Apocalyptic Mystic and Revolutionary*, trans. J. Jaquiery (Edinburgh, Scot.: T & T Clark, 1993); Walter Elliger, *Thomas Müntzer: Leben und Werk*, 2nd ed. (Göttingen, Ger.: Vandenhoeck & Ruprecht, 1975); Siegfried Bräuer and Helmer Junghans (eds.), *Der Theologe Thomas Müntzer* (Göttingen, Ger.: Vandenhoeck & Ruprecht, 1989); Eike Wolgast, *Thomas Müntzer: Ein Verstörer der Ungläubigen* (Göttingen, Ger.: Muster-Schmitt Verlag, 1981).

12. Carl Hinrichs, *Luther und Müntzer* (Berlin: Walter de Gruyter, 1952), 1–4.

13. Cf. Friedrich Engels, *The German Revolutions*, ed. L. Krieger (Chicago: The University of Chicago Press, 1967), 4.

14. The text normally referred to as the *Prague Manifesto* was translated and published by Baylor under the title "Prague Protest": Thomas Müntzer, "The Prague Protest," in: Ibid., *Revelation and Revolution: Basic Writings of Thomas Müntzer*, trans. and ed. Michael G. Baylor (London: Associated University Press, 1993), 55.

15. Müntzer, *Revelation and Revolution*, 57.

16. Müntzer, *Revelation and Revolution*, 104.

17. Müntzer, *Revelation and Revolution*, 110.

18. Müntzer, *Revelation and Revolution,* 113.

19. See Luther, *Eyn brieff an die Fürsten zu Sachsen von dem auffrurischen geyst,* WA 15, 210–221.

20. Cf. Günter Vogler, *Thomas Müntzer* (Berlin: Dietz, 1989), 184.

21. During some heated days at the end of September 1524, Pfeiffer and Müntzer formulated the so-called Eleven Mühlhausen Articles, which may be seen as a program for revolution in accordance with the Word of God. Cf. Michael G. Baylor, *The Radical Reformation* (Cambridge, Eng.: Cambridge University Press, 1991), 227–230.

22. Cf. Müntzer, *Revelation and Revolution,* 129.

23. Müntzer, *Revelation and Revolution,* 129.

24. Cf. Müntzer, *Revelation and Revolution,* 132–33.

25. Occasionally, this point of view is even adapted as an interpretation of Romans 13, one of the most central but also contested passages in the Bible when it comes to political theology, and the main justification of Luther's doctrine of the two regiments. In his address to the princes, Müntzer tells them how that principle should be applied by faithful rulers: They must cut off the "evildoers who obstruct the gospel" in order to be servants of God, rather than of the devil (see "Sermon" in: *Revelation and Revolution,* 110) The future does not look bright for the courageous preacher, though: "the world is accustomed to beheading good priests." (From "Special Exposure" in: *Revelation and Revolution,* 127).

26. Müntzer, "Highly Provoked Defense," in: *Revelation and Revolution,* 153–154.

27. Cf. Müntzer, *Revelation and Revolution,* 141–142.

28. Cf. Luther, *Admonition to Peace,* LW 46, 22; WA 18, 298.

29. Cf. Luther, *Admonition to Peace,* LW 46, 23–24; WA 18, 300–302.

30. Cf. Luther, *Against the Robbing and Murdering Hordes of Peasants,* LW 46, 49–55; WA 18, 357–61.

31. See Luther, *Against the Robbing and Murdering Hordes of Peasants,* LW 46, 50; WA 18, 357.

32. Luther, *Against the Robbing and Murdering Hordes of Peasants,* LW 46, 54; WA 18, 361. My translation.

33. Cf. *An Open Letter on the Harsh Book Against the Peasants,* LW 46, 63–85; WA 18, 384–401.

34. Cf. Ernst Bloch, *Thomas Müntzer als Theologe der Revolution,* in: *Gesamtausgabe* Vol. 2 (Frankfurt am Main, Ger.: Suhrkamp, 1969), 73.

35. Cf. to this topic: Hinrichs, *Luther und Müntzer,* 146–76; Goertz, *Thomas Müntzer,* 137–57.

36. See Goertz, *Thomas Müntzer,* 152.

37. Cf. Heribert Smolinsky, *Deutungen der Zeit im Streit der Konfessionen: Kontroverstheologie, Apokalyptik und Astrologie im 16. Jahrhundert* (Heidelberg, 2000).

38. See Luther, WA DB 7, 408 ff.

39. Cf. Irena Backus, *Reformation Readings of the Apocalypse* (Oxford, Eng.: Oxford University Press, 2000), 9.

15. The Hidden God of Revolution and Apocalypse

1. Cf. Wilhelm Zimmermann, *Allgemeine Geschichte des deutschen Bauernkriegs* [1841–43], 2nd ed. (Stuttgart, Ger.: Riegers'sche Verlagsbuchhandlung, 1856). For a more detailed discussion of Zimmermann, Marxism, and the Reformation, cf.: Abraham Friesen, *Reformation and Utopia: The Marxist Interpretation of the Reformation and Its Antecedents* (Wiesbaden: Steiner, 1974).

2. Cf. Friedrich Engels, *The German Revolutions,* ed. L. Krieger (Chicago: University of Chicago Press, 1967), 44–48.

3. Cf. Eike Wolgast, *Thomas Müntzer: Ein Verstörer der Ungläubigen* (Göttingen, Ger.: Muster-Schmitt Verlag, 1981), 40–47.

4. Cf. Engels, *The German Revolutions,* 4–9.

5. Engels, *The German Revolutions,* 39.

6. Engels, *The German Revolutions,* 39.

7. Cf. Karl Marx and Friedrich Engels, *The German Ideology,* trans. C. J. Arthur (New York: International Publishers, 1970).

8. Engels, *The German Revolutions,* 47.

9. Engels, *The German Revolutions,* 46.

10. Engels, *The German Revolutions,* 46.

11. Karl Marx, *Critique of Hegel's Philosophy of Right,* ed. Joseph O'Mally (Cambridge, Eng.: Cambridge University Press, 1970), 131. Translation modified.

12. The seven points listed previously are referred to in brackets.

13. Cf. Kahn's discussion of a sacred space in modern political theology: Paul W. Kahn, *Political Theology: Four Chapters on the Concept of Sovereignty* (New York: Columbia University Press, 2011), 17–20.

14. Cf. Martin Luther, *Ad librum,* WA 7, 718–719. All quotations from Luther's works refer first to the English translations from the standard American edition of *Luther's Works* [LW], Vol. 1–55, ed. Jaroslav Pelikan and Helmut T. Lehmann (Philadelphia: Fortress Press, 1958–1976); and then to the *Weimarer Ausgabe* [WA]: *D. Martin Luthers Werke,* Vol. 1–55 (Weimar, Ger., 1883–2009), although when the Latin texts are quoted—with reference to WA—the quotation is taken either from the *Lateinisch-Deutsche Studienausgabe,* Vol. 1, ed. W. Härle, et al. (Leipzig, Ger.: Evangelische Verlagsanstalt, 2006), or from the online edition of the *Weimarer Ausgabe* (http://luther.chadwyck.co.uk/). There are minor differences of spelling in the various editions. When the translations are modified, this will be indicated.

15. Cf. Luther, *Ad librum,* WA 7, 762.

16. Patrick Preston, "Catharinus versus Luther, 1521," *History,* Vol. 88, 377–378.

17. Cf. John Gray, *Black Mass: Apocalyptic Religion and the Death of Utopia* (London: Penguin, 2008), 114–117.

18. Cf. Mark Lilla, *The Stillborn God,* 2nd ed. (New York: Vintage, 2008), 305–306.

19. Thus also Gray, *Black Mass,* 207.

20. Conversely, Philip Jenkins argues that the First World War was fought as a religious war: Jenkins, *The Great and Holy War: How World War I Became a Religious Crusade* (New York: HarperOne, 2014).

21. See Gray, *Black Mass*, 55–69.

22. Giorgio Agamben, *The Kingdom and the Glory: For a Theological Genealogy of Economy and Government* (Stanford, Calif.: Stanford University Press, 2011), 244.

23. Cf. Marius Timman Mjaaland, *Autopsia: Self, Death and God after Kierkegaard and Derrida* (Berlin: De Gruyter, 2008), 78–80.

24. Norman Cohn and John Gray argue that this is the case—and warn against the consequences: See, e.g., Gray, *Black Mass*, 28–35.

25. See Luther, *Heidelberg Disputation*, LW 31, 53; WA 1, 362.

BIBLIOGRAPHY

Agamben, Giorgio. *Homo Sacer: Sovereign Power and Bare Life.* Trans. David Heller-Roazen. Stanford, Calif.: Stanford University Press, 1998.

———. *The Kingdom and the Glory: For a Theological Genealogy of Economy and Government* (Homo Sacer *II, 2).* Trans. Lorenzo Chiesa. Stanford, Calif.: Stanford University Press, 2011.

———. *The Sacrament of Language: An Archaeology of the Oath* (Homo Sacer *II, 3).* Trans. Adam Kotsko. Stanford, Calif.: Stanford University Press, 2010.

———. *The Signature of All Things: On Method.* Trans. Luca D'Isanto. New York: Zone Books, 2009.

———. *The Time That Remains: A Commentary to the Letter of the Romans.* Trans. Patricia Dailey. Stanford, Calif.: Stanford University Press, 2005.

Althaus, Paul. *The Theology of Martin Luther.* Trans. Robert C. Schultz. Philadelphia: Fortress Press, 1975.

Anglin, W. S. *Free Will and Christian Faith.* Oxford, Eng.: Oxford University Press, 1990.

Apel, Karl-Otto, "H.-G. Gadamers 'Wahrheit und Methode.'" In: *Hegelstudien* 2 (1963), 314–322.

Asad, Talal. *Formations of the Secular: Christianity, Islam, Modernity.* Stanford, Calif.: Stanford University Press, 2003.

———. *Genealogies of Religion: Discipline and Reasons of Power in Christianity and Islam.* Baltimore: Johns Hopkins University Press, 1993.

Augustine, Aurelius. *The Literal Meaning of Genesis.* Trans. John Hammond Taylor. New York: Newman Press, 1982.

Backus, Irena. *Reformation Readings of the Apocalypse.* Oxford, Eng.: Oxford University Press, 2000.

Bader, Günter. *Assertio: Drei fortlaufende Lektüren zu Skepsis, Narrheit und Sünde bei Erasmus und Luther.* Tübingen, Ger.: Mohr Siebeck, 1985.

Bak, János (ed.). *The German Peasant War of 1525.* London: Frank Cass, 1976.

Bayer, Oswald. *Promissio.* Göttingen, Ger.: Vandenhoeck & Ruprecht, 1971.

Baylor, Michael G. *The Radical Reformation.* Cambridge, Eng.: Cambridge University Press, 1991.

Beisser, Friedrich. *Claritas scripturae bei Martin Luther.* Göttingen, Ger.: Vandenhoeck & Ruprecht, 1966.

Blickle, Peter (ed.). *Der deutsche Bauernkrieg von 1525.* Darmstadt, Ger.: Wissenschaftliche Buchgesellschaft, 1985.

Bloch, Ernst. *Thomas Münzer als Theologe der Revolution.* In: *Gesamtausgabe,* Vol. 2, Frankfurt am Main, Ger.: Suhrkamp, 1969.

Boyle, Marjorie O'Rourke. *Erasmus on Language and Method in Theology.* Toronto: University of Toronto Press, 1977.

———. *Rhetoric and Reform: Erasmus' Civil Dispute with Luther.* Cambridge, Mass.: Harvard University Press, 1983.

Bräuer, Siegfried and Helmer Junghans (eds.). *Der Theologe Thomas Müntzer.* Göttingen, Ger.: Vandenhoeck & Ruprecht, 1989.

Brecht, Martin. *Martin Luther: Sein Weg zur Reformation.* 2nd ed. Stuttgart, Ger.: Calver, 1981.

Brendler, Gerhard. *Martin Luther: Theologie und Revolution—eine marxistische Darstellung.* 2nd ed. Cologne, Ger.: Pahl-Rugenstein, 1983.

Casanova, José. *Public Religions in the Modern World.* Chicago: University of Chicago Press, 1994.

Cassian, John. *Conferences.* Trans. Colm Luibheid. New York: Paulist Press, 1985.

Catharinus, Ambrosius. *Apologia pro veritate catholicae et apostolicae fidei ac doctrinae adversus impia ac valde pestifera Martini Lutheri dogmata.* Ed. Josef Schweizer. Munich, Ger.: Aschendorffsche Verlagsbuchandlung, 1956.

Celan, Paul *Lightduress.* Transl. Pierre Joris. Los Angeles: Green Integer, 2004. German: *Lichtzwang.* Frankfurt am Main, Ger.: Suhrkamp, 1996.

Cohn, Norman. *The Pursuit of the Millennium.* 3rd ed. London: Pimlico, 1970.

Crowe, Benjamin D. *Heidegger's Religious Origins: Destruction and Authenticity.* Bloomington: Indiana University Press, 2006.

Dalferth, Ingolf U. "Self-Sacrifice: From the Act of Violence to the Passion of Love." *International Journal of Philosophy of Religion,* Vol. 68 (2010), 77–94.

de Vries, Hent. "Why Still 'Religion'?" In: *Religion: Beyond a Concept.* Ed. Hent de Vries. New York: Fordham University Press, 2008, 1–99.

de Vries, Hent and Lawrence E. Sullivan (eds.). *Political Theologies: Public Religions in a Post-Secular World.* New York: Fordham University Press, 2006.

Derrida, Jacques. *The Gift of Death.* Trans. David Wood. Chicago: University of Chicago Press, 1995.

———. *Of Grammatology.* Trans. Gayatri Chakravorty Spivak. Baltimore: The Johns Hopkins University Press, 1976.

———. "How to Avoid Speaking: Denials." Trans. Ken Frieden. In: *Languages of the Unsayable.* Ed. S. Budick and W. Iser. New York: Columbia University Press, 1981, 3–70.

———. *On the Name.* Ed. Thomas Dutoit. Stanford, Calif.: Stanford University Press, 1995.

———. *Positions.* Trans. Alan Bass. Chicago: University of Chicago Press, 1981.

———. *Rogues.* Trans. P.-A. Braut and M. Naas. Stanford, Calif.: Stanford University Press, 2005.

———. *Writing and Difference.* Trans. Alan Bass. Chicago: University of Chicago Press, 1978.

Dieter, Theodor. *Der junge Luther und Aristoteles: Eine historisch-systematische Untersuchung zum Verhältnis von Theologie und Philosophie.* Berlin: De Gruyter, 2001.

Dillenberger, John. *God Hidden and Revealed*. Philadelphia: Muhlenberg Press, 1953.

Dionysius Areopagita. *The Complete Works*. New York: Paulist Press, 1987.

———. *The Mystical Theology*. In: *The Divine Names and Mystical Theology*. Trans. John E. Jones. Milwaukee, Wisc.: Marquette University Press, 1980.

Eagleton, Terry. *Reason, Faith, and Revolution*. New Haven, Conn.: Yale University Press, 2009.

Ebeling, Gerhard. *Einführung in theologische Sprachlehre*. Tübingen, Ger.: Mohr Siebeck, 1971.

———. *Evangelische Evangelienauslegung: eine Untersuchung zu Luthers Hermeneutik*. Darmstadt, Ger.: WBG, 1962.

———. "Existenz zwischen Gott und Gott." In: *Wort und Glaube*, Vol. 2. Tübingen, Ger.: Mohr Siebeck, 1969, 257–286.

———. *Luther: Einführung in sein Denken*. Tübingen, Ger.: Mohr Siebeck, 1965.

———. *Lutherstudien*. 3 Volumes. Tübingen, Ger.: Mohr Siebeck, 1971–1989.

———. *Wort Gottes und Tradition: Studien zu einer Hermeneutik der Konfessionen*. Göttingen, Ger.: Vandenhoeck & Ruprecht, 1964.

Edwards, Mark U. *Printing, Propaganda, and Martin Luther*. Berkeley: University of California Press, 1994.

Elliger, Walter. *Thomas Müntzer: Leben und Werk*. 2nd ed. Göttingen, Ger.: Vandenhoeck & Ruprecht, 1975.

Engels, Friedrich. *Der deutsche Bauernkrieg*, 12th ed. Berlin: Dietz Verlag, 1975.

———. *The German Revolutions*. Ed. L. Krieger. Chicago: University of Chicago Press, 1967.

Erasmus, Desiderius. *De ratione studii ac legendi interpretandique auctores* [1511]. In: *Opera omnia*. Ed. J. H. Waszink, et al., Vol. I.2. Amsterdam, Neth.: North-Holland, 1971, 79–151.

———. *Diatribe de libero arbitrio—A Discussion on Free Will*. Trans. Peter Macardle. In: *Collected Works* [CW], Vol. 76. Toronto: Toronto University Press, 1998.

———. *Diatribe sive collatio de libero arbitrio* [1524] in *Erasmus' Werke: Ausgewählte Schriften* (bilingual ed.) [EW], Vol. 4. Ed. Werner Welzig. Darmstadt, Ger.: Wissenschaftliche Buchgesellschaft, 1969.

———. *Erasmus' Annotations on the New Testament: Galatians to the Apocalypse* [1516]. Ed. Anne Reeve. Leiden, Neth.: Brill, 1993.

Foucault, Michel. *History of Madness*. Trans. Jonathan Murphy and Jean Khalfa. London: Routledge, 2006.

Frank, Günter. "Wie kam die Topik in die Theologie?" In: *Hermeneutik, Methodenlehre, Exegese*. Ed. Günter Frank and Stephan Meier-Oeser. Stuttgart, Ger.: Frommann-Holzboog, 2011, 67–88.

Franz, Günther (ed.). *Quellen zur Geschichte des Bauernkrieges*. Darmstadt, Ger.: Wissenschaftliche Buchgesellschaft, 1963.

Friesen, Abraham. *Reformation and Utopia: The Marxist Interpretation of the Reformation and Its Antecedents*. Wiesbaden, Ger.: Steiner, 1974.

Führer, Werner. *Das Wort Gottes in Luthers Theologie*. Göttingen, Ger.: Vandenhoeck und Ruprecht, 1984.

Gadamer, Hans-Georg. *Wahrheit und Methode.* 6th ed. Tübingen, Ger.: Mohr Siebeck, 1990.

Gillespie, Michael Allen. *The Theological Origins of Modernity.* Chicago: University of Chicago Press, 2008.

Goertz, Hans-Jürgen. *Thomas Müntzer: Apocalyptic Mystic and Revolutionary.* Trans. J. Jaquiery. Edinburgh, Scot.: T & T Clark, 1993.

Goldmann, Lucien. *The Hidden God: A Study of Tragic Vision in the Pensées of Pascal and the Tragedies of Racine.* Trans. Philip Thody. London: Routledge, 1976.

Grane, Leif. *Contra Gabrielem: Luthers Auseinandersetzung mit Gabriel Biel in der Disputatio Contra Scholasticam Theologiam 1517.* Copenhagen, Den.: Gyldendal, 1962.

Gray, John. *Black Mass: Apocalyptic Religion and the Death of Utopia.* London: Penguin, 2008.

Griffiths, Richard. *The Bible in the Renaissance.* Aldershot, Eng.: Ashgate, 2001.

Gritsch, Eric W. *Thomas Müntzer: A Tragedy of Errors.* Minneapolis, Minn.: Fortress Press, 1989.

Habermas, Jürgen. *Glauben und Wissen: Rede zum Friedenspreis des deutschen Buchhandels.* Frankfurt am Main, Ger.: Suhrkamp, 2001.

———. "On the Relations between the Secular Liberal State and Religion." In: *Political Theologies: Public Religions in a Post-Secular World.* Ed. Hent de Vries and Lawrence E. Sullivan. New York: Fordham University Press, 2006, 251–260.

———. "Zu Gadamers 'Wahrheit und Methode.'" In: *Hermeneutik und Ideologiekritik.* Ed. Karl-Otto Apel. Frankfurt am Main, Ger.: Suhrkamp, 1971, 45–56.

———. *Zwischen Naturalismus und Religion: Philosophische Aufsätze.* Frankfurt am Main, Ger.: Suhrkamp, 2005.

Haga, Joar. "Die Biblische Hermeneutik Calovs—Die Klarheit der Schrift innerhalb seiner Metaphysik." In: *Hermeneutik, Methodenlehre, Exegese.* Ed. Günter Frank and Stephan Meier-Oeser. Stuttgart, Ger.: Frommann-Holzboog, 2011, 173–187.

———. *Was There a Lutheran Metaphysics? The Interpretation of* communicatio idiomatum *in Early Modern Lutheranism.* Göttingen, Ger.: Vandenhoeck & Ruprecht, 2012.

Hagen, Kenneth. *Luther's Approach to Scripture as Seen in His "Commentaries" on Galatians 1519–1538.* Tübingen, Ger.: Mohr Siebeck, 1993.

Hamm, Berndt. *Der frühe Luther: Etappen reformatorischer Neuorientierung.* Tübingen, Ger.: Mohr Siebeck, 2010.

Heckel, Martin. *Deutschland im konfessionellen Zeitalter.* Göttingen, Ger.: Vandenhoeck & Ruprecht 1983.

Heidegger, Martin. *Metaphysik und Nihilismus.* In: *Gesamtausgabe,* Vol. 67. Frankfurt am Main, Ger.: Klostermann, 1999.

———. *Pathmarks.* Trans. William McNeill. Cambridge, Eng.: Cambridge University Press, 1998.

———. *Sein und Zeit.* 17th ed. Frankfurt am Main, Ger.: Klostermann, 1993.

———. *Supplements.* Trans. and ed. John van Buren. Albany, N.Y.: SUNY Press, 2002.

———. *Unterwegs zur Sprache.* In: *Gesamtausgabe,* Vol. 12. Frankfurt, Ger.: Klostermann, 1985.

———. *Zur Seinsfrage.* In: *Gesamtausgabe,* Vol. 9. Frankfurt, Ger.: Klostermann, 1976.

Hermanni, Friedrich. "Luther oder Erasmus? Der Streit um die Freiheit des menschlichen Willens." In: *Der freie und unfreie Wille: Philosophische und theologische Perspektiven.* Ed. Friedrich Hermanni and Peter Koslowski. Munich, Ger.: Fink Verlag, 2004, 165–187.

Hinrichs, Carl. *Luther und Müntzer.* Berlin: Walter de Gruyter, 1952.

Husserl, Edmund. *Die Krisis der europäischen Wissenschaften und die transzendentale Phänomenologie.* Ed. E. Ströker. Hamburg, Ger.: Meiner, 1996.

Iwand, Hans Joachim. "Die grundlegende Bedeutung der Lehre vom unfreien Willen für den Glauben." In: Ibid., *Um den rechten Glauben. Gesammelte Aufsätze.* Ed. K. G. Steck. Munich, Ger.: Kaiser, 1959.

Jenkins, Philip. *The Great and Holy War: How World War I Became a Religious Crusade.* New York: HarperOne, 2014.

Joas, Hans. "Religion post-sekulär? Zu einer Begriffsprägung von Jürgen Habermas." In: *Braucht der Mensch Religion?* Freiburg, Ger.: Herder, 2004, 122–128.

Joas, Hans and Klaus Wiegandt (eds.). *Secularization and the World Religions.* Trans. Alex Skinner. Liverpool, Eng.: Liverpool University Press, 2009.

Joest, Wilfried. *Ontologie der Person bei Luther.* Göttingen, Ger.: Vandenhoeck & Ruprecht 1967.

Jüngel, Eberhard. *God as the Mystery of the World: On the Foundation of the Theology of the Crucified One in the Dispute between Theism and Atheism.* Trans. Darell L. Guder. Grand Rapids, Mich.: Eerdmans, 1983.

———. "Quae supra nos, nihil ad nos." In: Ibid., *Entsprechungen: Gott—Wahrheit—Mensch.* Munich, Ger.: Kaiser, 1980, 202–252.

———. "The Revelation of the Hiddenness of God." In: Ibid., *Theological Essays,* Vol. II. Edinburgh, Scot.: T & T Clark, 1995, 120–144.

Juntunen, Sammeli. *Der Begriff des Nichts bei Luther.* Helsinki, Fin.: Luther-Agricola-Gesellschaft, 1996.

Kahn, Paul W. *Political Theology: Four Chapters on the Concept of Sovereignty.* New York: Colombia University Press, 2011.

Kangas, David. "Luther and Modernity." *Epoché,* Vol. 14 (2010), 431–452.

Kant, Immanuel. *Critique of Pure Reason.* Trans. N. K. Smith. London: Macmillan, 1929.

———. *Kritik der reinen Vernunft.* Stuttgart, Ger.: Philipp Reclam, 1966.

Käsemann, Ernst. "Die Anfänge Christlicher Theologie." *ZThK* 57 (1960), 162–185.

Kearney, Richard. *Strangers, Gods and Monsters: Interpreting Otherness.* New York: Routledge, 2003, 194.

Kettel, Joachim and Paul Wietzorek. *Der deutsche Bauernkrieg 1524–26.* Stuttgart, Ger.: Tempora, 1995.

Kierkegaard, Søren. *The Sickness unto Death.* Trans. Howard V. Hong and Edna H. Hong. Princeton, N.J.: Princeton University Press, 1980.

Knuuttila, Simo. *Modalities in Medieval Philosophy.* London: Routledge, 1993.

Korsch, Dietrich and Volker Leppin (eds.). *Martin Luther—Biographie und Theologie.* Tübingen, Ger.: Mohr Siebeck, 2010.

Koyré, Alexandre. *From the Closed World to the Infinite Universe.* 2nd ed. Baltimore: The Johns Hopkins University Press, 1968.

Leppin, Volker. "Der Verlust des Menschen Luther: Zu Ebelings Lutherdeutung." *Journal of Early Modern Christianity* 1 (2014), 29–50.

———. "Deus absconditus und Deus revelatus. Transformationen mittelalterlicher Theologie in der Gotteslehre von 'De servo arbitrio.'" *Berliner Theologische Zeitschrift* 22 (2005), 55–69.

———. *Luther.* Darmstadt, Ger.: WBG, 2006.

Levinas, Emmanuel. "The Trace of the Other." Trans. Alfonso Lingis. In: *Deconstruction in Context.* Ed. Mark C. Taylor. Chicago: University of Chicago Press, 1986, 345–359.

Lexutt, Athina. "Die Rede vom verborgenen Gott. Eine Untersuchung zu Nikolaus von Kues mit einem Blick auf Martin Luther." *Neue Zeitschrift für Systematische Theologie und Religionsphilosophie,* Vol. 47:4 (2007), 372–391.

Lilla, Mark. *The Stillborn God.* 2nd ed. New York: Vintage, 2008.

Lindberg, Carter. *The European Reformations.* 2nd ed. Oxford, Eng.: Blackwell, 2011.

Løgstrup, K. E. *Skabelse og tilintetgørelse.* Copenhagen, Den.: Gyldendal 1978. English translation: *Metaphysics,* Vol. I. Milwaukee, Wisc.: Marquette University Press, 1995.

Lohse, Bernhard. *Thomas Müntzer in neuer Sicht.* Göttingen, Ger.: Vandenhoeck & Ruprecht, 1991.

Lønning, Inge. *Kanon im Kanon. Zum dogmatischen Grundlagenproblem des neutestamentlichen Kanons.* Oslo, Nor.: Universitetsforlaget, 1971.

Luther, Martin. *D. Martin Luthers Werke* [WA]. 120 Volumes. Weimar, Ger., 1883–2009. Online edition of the *Weimarer Ausgabe:* http://luther.chadwyck.co.uk.

———. *Lateinisch-Deutsche Studienausgabe,* Vol. 1. Ed. W. Härle, et al. Leipzig, Ger.: Evangelische Verlagsanstalt, 2006.

———. *Luther's Works* [LW]. English translation, Vols. 1–55. Ed. Jaroslav Pelikan and Helmut T. Lehmann. Philadelphia: Fortress Press, 1958–1976.

Mahlmann, Theodor. "Die Interpretation von Luthers *De servo arbitrio* bei orthodoxen lutherischen Theologen, vor allem Sebastian Schmidt (1617–1696)." In: *Luthers Erben.* Ed. Notger Slenczka and Walter Sparn. Tübingen, Ger.: Mohr Siebeck, 2005, 73–136.

Malpas, Jeff. *Heidegger's Topology.* Cambridge, Mass.: MIT Press, 2006.

Malter, Rudolf. *Das reformatorische Denken und die Philosophie.* Bonn, Ger.: Bouvier, 1980.

Marx, Karl. *Critique of Hegel's Philosophy of Right.* Ed. Joseph O'Mally. Cambridge, Eng.: Cambridge University Press, 1970.

Marx, Karl and Friedrich Engels. *The German Ideology.* Trans. C. J. Arthur. New York: International Publishers, 1970.

Metzke, Erwin. *Geschichtliche Wirklichkeit. Gedanken zu einer deutschen Philosophie der Geschichte.* Tübingen, Ger.: Mohr Siebeck, 1935.

———. *Sakrament und Metaphysik: Eine Lutherstudie über das Verhältnis des christlichen Denkens zum Leiblich-Materiellen.* Stuttgart, Ger.: Kreuz Verlag, 1948.

Mjaaland, Marius Timmann. "Apocalypse and the Spirit of Revolution: The Political Legacy of the Early Reformation," *Political Theology* 14 (2013), 155–173.

———. *Autopsia: Self, Death and God after Kierkegaard and Derrida.* Berlin: De Gruyter, 2008.

———. "Der apokalyptische Zwerg der Revolution." In: *Deutungsmacht*. Ed. Philipp Stoellger. Tübingen, Ger.: Mohr Siebeck, 2014, 205–224.

———. "Does Modernity Begin with Luther?" *Studia Theologica* 63 (2009), 42–66.

———. "Geneatopics," *Studia Theologica*, Vol. 65 (2011), 172–189.

———. "Immorality." *Neue Zeitschrift für systematische Theologie und Religionsphilosophie*, Vol. 53 (2011), 450–464.

Muller, Richard A. and John L. Thompson (eds.). *Biblical Interpretation in the Era of the Reformation*. Grand Rapids, Mich.: Eerdmans, 1996.

Müntzer, Thomas. *Revelation and Revolution: Basic Writings of Thomas Müntzer.* Trans. and ed. Michael G. Baylor. London: Associated University Press, 1993.

Nietzsche, Friedrich. *The Gay Science*. Trans. Bernhard Williams. Cambridge, Eng.: Cambridge University Press, 2001.

———. *Genealogy of Morals*. Trans. Francis Golffing. New York: Doubleday, 1956.

———. *Sämtliche Werke: Kritische Studienausgabe in 15 Bänden* [KSA]. Ed. Giorgio Colli and Mazzino Montinari. Munich, Ger.: Deutscher Taschenbuch Verlag, 1980.

Oberman, Heiko A. *Forerunners of the Reformation: The Shape of Late Medieval Thought*. Trans. Paul L. Nyhus. Philadelphia: Fortress Press, 1981.

———. *Harvest of Medieval Theology: Gabriel Biel and Late Medieval Nominalism*. Cambridge, Mass.: Harvard University Press, 1963.

———. *The Reformation: Roots and Ramifications*. Trans. Andrew Colin Gow. London: T & T Clark, 2004.

Otto, Rudolf. *Das Heilige: Über das Irrationale in der Idee des Göttlichen und sein Verhältnis zum Rationalen*. 13th ed. Gotha, Ger.: Leopold Klotz Verlag, 1925.

Pascal, Blaise. *The Provincial Letters; Pensées; Scientific Treatises*. Great Books of the Western World, 2nd ed. Ed. Mortimer J. Adler, Vol. 30. Chicago: Encyclopaedia Britannica, 1990.

Peters, Albrecht. "Verborgener Gott—Dreieiniger Gott." In: *Der eine Gott und der dreieine Gott*. Ed. Karl Rahner. Munich, Ger.: Schnell & Steiner, 1983, 117–140.

Philipse, Herman. *Heidegger's Philosophy of Being: A Critical Interpretation*. Princeton, N.J.: Princeton University Press, 1998.

Plato, *Complete Works*. Ed. John M. Cooper. Indianapolis: Hacket Publishing, 1997.

Preston, Patrick. "Catharinus versus Luther, 1521." *History*, Vol. 88, 364–378.

Reinhuber, Thomas. *Kämpfender Glaube*. Berlin: De Gruyter, 2000.

Roth, Michael. *Gott im Widerspruch?* Berlin: De Gruyter, 2002.

Saarinen, Risto. *Gottes Wirken auf uns*. Stuttgart, Ger.: Franz Steiner Verlag, 1989.

Schmitt, Carl. *Politische Theologie* [1922]. 8th ed. Berlin: Duncker & Humblot, 2004.

Schürmann, Reiner. *Broken Hegemonies*. Trans. Reginald Lilly. Bloomington: Indiana University Press, 2003.

Schwarzwäller, Klaus. *Sibboleth: Die Interpretation von Luthers Schrift* De servo arbitrio *seit Theodosius Harnack*. Munich, Ger.: Kaiser, 1969.

———. *Theologia Crucis*. Munich, Ger.: Kaiser, 1970.

Smith, Robin. "Aristotle's Logic." In: *The Stanford Encyclopedia of Philosophy*. Ed. Edward N. Zalta. Stanford, Calif.: Stanford University, The Metaphysics Research Lab. Spring 2013 edition: http://plato.stanford.edu/archives/spr2013/entries/aristotle-logic.

Smolinsky, Heribert. *Deutungen der Zeit im Streit der Konfessionen: Kontroverstheologie, Apokalyptik und Astrologie im 16. Jahrhundert*. Heidelberg, Ger.: 2000.

Stoellger, Philipp. *Passivität aus Passion: Zur Problemgeschichte einer 'categoria non grata.'* Tübingen, Ger.: Mohr Siebeck, 2010.

Stolt, Birgit. *Martin Luthers Rhetorik des Herzens*. Tübingen, Ger.: Mohr Siebeck, 2000.

———. *Studien zu Luthers Freiheitstraktat. Mit besonderer Rücksicht auf das Verhältnis der lateinischen und der deutschen Fassung zu einander und die Stilmittel der Rhetorik*. Stockholm, Swed.: Almqvist & Wiksell, 1969.

Szabari, Antónia. "The Scandal of Religion: Luther and Public Speech in the Reformation." In: *Political Theologies*. Ed. Hent de Vries and Lawrence E. Sullivan. New York: Fordham University Press, 2006, 122–136.

Taylor, Charles. *A Secular Age*. Cambridge, Mass.: Harvard University Press, 2007.

Thom, Paul. *Medieval Modal Systems: Problems and Concepts*. Aldershot, Eng.: Ashgate, 2003.

Thompson, Mark D. *A Sure Ground on Which to Stand: The Relation of Authority and Interpretive Method in Luther's Approach to Scripture*. Carlisle, Eng.: Paternoster, 2004.

Thouard, Denis. "Réflexion sur la constitution de l'herméneutique en discipline—Flacius, Hyperius et Augustin." In: *Hermeneutik, Methodenlehre, Exegese*. Ed. Günter Frank and Stephan Meier-Oeser. Stuttgart, Ger.: Frommann-Holzboog, 2011, 37–65.

Tracy, James D. *Europe's Reformations 1450–1650: Doctrine, Politics, and Community*. 2nd ed. Oxford, Eng.: Rowman & Littlefield, 2006.

Vogler, Günter. *Thomas Müntzer*. Berlin: Dietz, 1989.

von Loewenich, Walther. *Luthers Theologia Crucis*. 5th ed. Witten, Ger.: Luther-Verlag, 1967.

Wabel, Thomas. *Sprache als Grenze in Luthers theologischer Hermeneutik und Wittgensteins Sprachphilosophie*. Berlin: De Gruyter 1998.

Wehler, Hans-Ulrich. *Der deutsche Bauernkrieg 1524–26*. Göttingen, Ger.: Vandenhoeck & Ruprecht, 1975.

Wendte, Martin. *Die Gabe und das Gestell*. Tübingen, Ger.: Mohr Siebeck, 2013.

———. "Monarchie des Geistes? Gegen den impliziten Hegelianismus in der gegenwartigen Theologie." *NZSTh* 49 (2007), 86–103.

White, Graham. *Luther as Nominalist: A Study of the Logical Methods Used in Martin Luther's Disputations in the Light of Their Medieval Background*. Helsinki, Fin.: Luther-Agricola-Society, 1994.

Wittgenstein, Ludwig. *Culture and Value*. Transl. P Winch. Oxford, Eng.: Blackwell, 1980.

———. *On Certainty*. Transl. Denis Paul and G. E. M. Anscombe. Oxford, Eng.: Oxford University Press, 1969.

Wohlfeil, Rainer (ed.). *Der Bauernkrieg 1524–26: Bauernkrieg und Reformation*. Munich, Ger.: Nymphenburger, 1975.

Wolff, Jens. *Metapher und Kreuz*. Tübingen, Ger.: Mohr Siebeck, 2005.

Wolgast, Eike. *Thomas Müntzer: Ein Verstörer der Ungläubigen*. Göttingen, Ger.: Muster-Schmitt Verlag, 1981.

Zeyl, Donald. "Plato's *Timaeus*." In: *The Stanford Encyclopedia of Philosophy*. Ed. Edward N. Zalta. Stanford, Calif.: Stanford University, The Metaphysics Research Lab. Spring 2014 edition: http://plato.stanford.edu/archives/spr2014/entries/plato-timaeus.

Zimmermann, Wilhelm. *Allgemeine Geschichte des deutschen Bauernkriegs* [1841–43]. 2nd ed. Stuttgart, Ger.: Riegers'sche Verlagsbuchhandlung, 1856.

INDEX

Marius Timmann Mjaaland is Professor of Theology and Philosophy at the University of Oslo and is the author of *Autopsia: Self, Death, and God after Kierkegaard and Derrida* (2008).

www.ingramcontent.com/pod-product-compliance
Lightning Source LLC
LaVergne TN
LVHW041111090826
844660LV00057B/160
* 9 7 8 0 2 5 3 0 1 8 1 6 8 *